Aristotle

Aristotle

ALEXANDER MOSELEY

Bloomsbury Library of Educational Thought
Series Editor: Richard Bailey

B L O O M S B U R Y
LONDON · NEW DELHI · NEW YORK · SYDNEY

Bloomsbury Academic
An imprint of Bloomsbury Publishing Plc

50 Bedford Square	1385 Broadway
London	New York
WC1B 3DP	NY 10018
UK	USA

www.bloomsbury.com

First published 2010 by Continuum International Publishing Group
Paperback edition first published 2014 by Bloomsbury Academic

British Library Cataloguing-in-Publication Data
A catalogue record for this book is available from the British Library.

ISBN: PB: 978-1-4725-1892-7
ePUB: 978-1-4725-1891-0

Library of Congress Cataloguing-in-Publication Data
Moseley, Alexander, 1943–
Aristotle/Alexander Moseley
p.cm. – (Continum library of educational thought; v. 21)
Includes index.
ISBN 978-1-84706-103-4 (hardcover)
1. Aristotle. 2. Education–Philosophy. I. Title. II. Series.
LB85.A7M67   2010
370.1–DC22

209013714

Typeset by BookEns, Royston, Herts.
Printed and bound in Great Britain

Contents

To my wife Moira and our son Charles

Series Editor's Preface

Education is sometimes presented as an essentially practical activity. It is, it seems, about teaching and learning, curriculum, and what goes on in schools. It is about achieving certain ends, using certain methods, and these ends and methods are often prescribed for teachers, whose duty it is to deliver them with vigor and fidelity. With such a clear purpose, what is the value of theory?

Recent years have seen politicians and policy-makers in different countries explicitly denying *any* value or need for educational theory. A clue to why this might be is offered by a remarkable comment by a British Secretary of State for Education in the 1990s: 'having any ideas about how children learn, or develop, or feel, should be seen as subversive activity.' This pithy phrase captures the problem with theory: it subverts, challenges, and undermines the very assumptions on which the practice of education is based.

Educational theorists, then, are trouble-makers in the realm of ideas. They pose a threat to the status quo and lead us to question the common sense presumptions of educational practices. But this is precisely what they should do because the seemingly simple language of schools and schooling hides numerous contestable concepts that in their different usages reflect fundamental disagreements about the aims, values, and activities of education.

Implicit within the *Bloomsbury Library of Educational Thought* is an assertion that theories and theorizing are vitally important for education. By gathering together the ideas of some of the most influential, important, and interesting educational thinkers, from the Ancient Greeks to contemporary scholars, the series has the ambitious task of providing an accessible yet authoritative resource for a generation of students and practitioners. Volumes within the series are written by acknowledged leaders in the field, who were selected for both their scholarship and their ability to make often complex ideas accessible to a diverse audience.

It will always be possible to question the list of key thinkers that are represented in this series. Some may question the inclusion of certain thinkers; some may disagree with the exclusion of others. That is inevitably going to be the case. There is no suggestion that the list of thinkers represented within the *Bloomsbury Library of Educational Thought* is in any way definitive. What is incontestable is that these thinkers have fascinating ideas about education, and that taken together, the *Library* can act as a powerful source of information and inspiration for those committed to the study of education.

Richard Bailey
University of Birmingham

Foreword

Aristotle was long considered the foremost Western philosopher. For centuries, and in every area of human investigation, he provided the template against which scholars, sages, and philosophers measured themselves. It was only after the rise of modern science challenged his natural teleology that he was to some extent displaced in the Western imagination as 'the master of those who know' (sometimes rendered simply: 'the one who knows').

Today, although he still ranks alongside Plato in the estimation of philosophers generally, Aristotle receives far less attention than the latter in the more specific field of philosophy of education. He is not, generally speaking, to be found listed among the 'Great Educators'; he does not earn a chapter to himself, as Plato and Isocrates both do, in H. I. Marrou's standard *History of Education in Antiquity*. And, unsurprisingly perhaps, there are relatively few monographs on his educational thought. All the more reason, then, to welcome Alexander Moseley's masterly study.

The most obvious reason for the comparative neglect of Aristotle is that he did not leave any sustained treatise on education. Unlike, say, Plato's *Republic*, with its carefully nuanced theory of human development and prescriptions for the education of the rulers of the ideal state, Aristotle nowhere in his voluminous writings presents us with an overall theory of education as such. Instead, his educational views have to be extracted from a variety of places and woven together if we are looking for anything like a lucid account of education. This exacting job of synthesis is further exacerbated by the fact that much of Aristotle's thought has an indirect rather than a direct relevance to education. Hence one is compelled to give careful consideration as to how exactly his various thoughts bear on the educational enterprise. His views concerning moral education, for example, although obviously related to his moral philosophy, can stand quite apart from the latter. That is, one could sensibly and consistently subscribe to an Aristotelian conception of moral education, the essence of which consists in habituating children to act in accordance with virtue ('to do the right thing'), while rejecting his general theory of ethics. This need to extrapolate, integrate, and draw out the implications of his scattered educational thoughts represents a particular challenge to any contemporary author trying to link it all together. It is to Moseley's credit that he has achieved such a synthesis in such a seamless manner.

To stress the fragmented nature of Aristotle's comments and their often abstract nature is not to say that he does not present us with a number of significant educational ideas that have stood the test of time. The fundamental conviction that 'man is a rational animal,' whose ultimate flourishing is, and whose goal should therefore be, to lead the contemplative life for its own sake, is of course of enormous significance. This is especially true in our own era when, even if sometimes for understandable reasons, the emphasis increasingly tends to be on practical necessity, on the immediate, and on (usually economic) utility. And the basic ethical tenet that we should strain to attain *eudaimonia*, abstract though it may be, is of extreme importance too. (I deliberately leave *eudaimonia* untranslated, given that it is misleading to translate it simply as 'happiness.' See Moseley's section on Teleology.) Perhaps the most commonly cited text of Aristotle in respect of education is the *Nicomachean Ethics* (Books 1, 2, and 10 in particular), where he talks about *eudaimonia*.

But no less important are the passages in both the *Ethics* and the *Politics* where he elaborates his thesis that we come to be people of *aretē* (conventionally translated 'virtue') by habitually acting in accordance with *aretē* (thus introducing a quasi-Kantian distinction between acting in accordance with virtue and acting virtuously).

Aristotle's moral theory thus centers on the attainment of virtue. And for most of the history of Western ideas the dominant approach to normative ethics was predicated on his understanding of what constituted virtue and how we might attain it. It was eclipsed only with the onset of the Enlightenment and newly established deontological and utilitarian systems both of which have tended to push Aristotle aside over the past two centuries. But in recent years contemporary strands of 'virtue ethics,' all of which remain inextricably tied to Aristotelian thinking, have garnered increasing interest among moral philosophers, largely as a result of a growing dissatisfaction with liberalism of whatever variety.

Beyond these fundamental points, Aristotle is at least as well known for his account of the so-called Doctrine of the Golden Mean (though I confess that I for one have always found this doctrine in some ways banal and in some ways inadequate, if not obviously wrong), and his evident belief in the state control of education with a view (not un-Platonic) to molding good citizens as a necessary precursor to the final stage of a liberal education. Nor should we forget the importance in educational terms of Aristotle's general emphasis on inductive thinking and the importance of what we now call scientific inquiry. His adage that we 'should seek only that degree of certainty that the subject matter allows' is sage advice for educators at any time. In our own time it is particularly pertinent given the widespread tendency to regard the various types of social inquiry as sciences.

Alexander Moseley has managed to bring all this and more together with elegance and erudition. He has provided a broad and illuminating description of educational practice in Aristotle's time, along with careful consideration of such philosophical themes as the importance of Aristotle's overarching teleological thesis and his work on causation and weakness of will. He has also successfully tackled the extremely difficult but very interesting task of making a reasonable (and readable) tale of the mass of material relating to the reception of Aristotle's educational views over the centuries, and of arguing for their relevance today. My own inclination has hitherto always been to find Plato more rewarding as an educational thinker, and certainly more thought-provoking, than Aristotle. On reading this book, however, I think I may have been (well, slightly) wrong!

Robin Barrow FRSC
Professor of Philosophy of Education
Simon Fraser University

Abbreviations

Aristotle

From *The Complete Works of Aristotle: The Revised Oxford Translation*, ed. Jonathan Barnes, two volumes, Series LXXI.2 (fourth reprint [1984]). Chichester: Princeton University Press, 1991.

An: *De Anima* (On the Soul)
APr: *Prior Analytics*
APst: *Posterior Analytics*
B: Fragment, from Düring's editions, found in Barnes
Cael: *On the Heavens*
Cat: *Categories*
EE: *Eudemian Ethics*
F: Fragment, in Barnes
GA: *Generation of Animals*
GC: *On Generation and Corruption*
HA: *History of Animals*
Met: *Metaphysics*
MA: *Magna Moralia*
NE: *Nichomachean Ethics*
OD: *On Dreams*
On Mem: *On Memory*, trans. J. I. Beare
OS: *On Sleep*
OTU: *On the Universe*
OY: *On Youth, Old Age, Life and Death, and Respiration*
PA: *Parts of Animals*
Phys: *Physics*
Poet: *Poetics*
Pol: *Politics*

Prob: *Problems*
Rhet: *Rhetoric*
Soph: *Sophistical Refutations*
SS: *Sense and Sensibilia*
Top: *Topics*

Plato

From *Plato: Complete Works*, ed. John M. Cooper. Indianapolis, IN: Hackett Publishing Co., 1977.

Leg: *Laws*
Meno: *Meno*
Prot: *Protagoras*
Rep: *Republic*, trans. Jowett – in Open University Reader
Thea: *Theaetetus*

Other translations used or consulted

'On the Soul,' in *A New Aristotle Reader*, ed. J. L. Ackrill, trans. D. W. Hamlyn. Oxford: Clarendon Press, 1986.
The Nicomachean Ethics, rev. J. L. Ackrill and J. O. Urmson, trans. D. Ross. Oxford: Oxford University Press, 1992.
Nicomachean Ethics, trans. C. Rowe. Oxford: Oxford University Press, 2002.
Politics, trans. T. A. Sinclair. Harmondsworth: Penguin, 1986.
On the Soul, trans. J. A. Smith. Kessinger Reprints and ebooks.ade-laide.edu.au/a/aristotle/a8so/.
Ethics, trans. J. A. K. Thomson. London: Penguin, 1976.
Nicomachean Ethics, trans. S. Watt. Ware, Herts: Everyman, 1996.

An indispensable text for researching the Ancient World of Greece and Rome is *Dictionary of Greek and Roman Bibliography*, ed. W. Smith. www.ancientlibrary.com/smith-bio/index.html.

Part 1

Intellectual Biography

Chapter 1

Heritage and Early Influences

Aristotle (384–322 BC) – *il maestro di color che sanno*, 'master of those who know' (Dante, 1995, IV.131) – stands with Plato at the fountainhead of the Western philosophical tradition that flows into early Arabic thought, European Scholastic thinking in the thirteenth century, the Renaissance, and down into the modern era. In all aspects of philosophy, Aristotle is widely studied and debated today and his thoughts on education have prevailed for over two millennia – they stand as an excellent reminder of the importance of the pursuit of virtues and individual flourishing tethered to the responsibilities of citizenship.

Aristotle was indeed one of the greatest minds ever to have been widely intellectually productive, which a cursory glance at the extant number of works reveals (which is only a fraction of what he is said to have written) or which any in-depth analysis only underlines. Even without any explication of pedagogy, Aristotle's thoughts would be important in their own right for any educationalist as the wisdom of one of the most wide-ranging and perceptive thinkers to have lived, and even if we disagree with his conclusions or recognize that elements of his scientific investigations lack the rigor or methods of present science and his sexist and racist attitudes rile the modern mind, his ideas would still require our attention, for the parochial particulars can be jettisoned to leave an immensely erudite philosophy. Moreover, what Aristotle does have to say on education is eminently appropriate and has been highly influential. And while we may disregard particulars, through his extant manuscripts we also get to know an erudite thinker who possessed a sensitive, mature, and realistic view of humanity.

In Part I we reach back into the rivulets and rivers of thought that flow into Aristotle's thinking as well as review some of the known educational programs prior and contemporary to his time. This will take us through the broad milieu of Hellenic education, the Macedonian kingdom to which his career was intimately tied, the medical aesclepiad tradition from which his immediate education was drawn, and the role of Athenian art and theater, which indubitably stirred his mind. In addition, since Aristotle was a philosopher and one of the first we know of to have studied previous philosophers as a historian of ideas, these antecedents are also surveyed relating, where appropriate, how their thoughts can be seen to have affected Aristotle's pedagogical notions.

Aristotle's heritage

When reaching back more than two thousand years, the details of a person's life necessarily become sketchy – yet we do seem to know more about Aristotle than we do Shakespeare; this is due to the scholarship of the classical era, which has also been sustained over much of this period beginning with Roman and Byzantine collectors, Arabic scholars and philosophers, and continuing today with the finds of archaeologists working in Greece and across the routes of the Ancient world from Spain to Afghanistan. Primary biographers from the Ancient world were Diogenes Laertius (dates unknown: third to fourth century AD), and Plutarch (46–120 AD). Diogenes drew upon the Athenian biographer Diocles of Magnesia (fl. second to first centuries BC), Hermippus (c. 250 BC), and Timotheus (dates unknown and whose works no longer exist). Aristotle's work has enjoyed popularity in the Arabian world and, as we shall see in Part 3, his rediscovery in western Europe had a lasting impact on the Roman Catholic Church being entwined with Scholastic teaching, and the early European public school systems spawning in turn influential educational reforms and schemes whose principles remain evident today. Furthermore, studying Aristotle is to engage in a conversation that has lasted over two millennia; careers are made from his work, so there is a specialization abroad with elaborations, discussions, and arguments to which this present work can only hope to contribute without grave distortion or bias.

According to Diogenes Laertius, the Roman biographer via Hermippus, Aristotle had thin legs, small eyes, and dressed in refined clothes, wore his hair fashionably short, and sported rings on his fingers; but this is not reflected in the busts that have survived the centuries, which show a bearded man with a hooked nose and no refinery. According to Laertius, repeating Timotheus the Athenian, Aristotle had a lisp yet was a man of the greatest industry and ingenuity and of ready wit (Laertius, 1853, II.XIII). For Plutarch, he was 'the most celebrated and learned of all the philosophers' (Plutarch, 1878, p. 715). For Thomas Aquinas, he was simply 'The Philosopher.' To Adam Smith, he was 'a man who certainly knew the world' (Smith, 1982, p. 258); to John Stuart Mill, 'the most comprehensive, if not the most sagacious of the ancient philosophers' (Mill, 1884, p. 29). A present Aristotelian, Barnes, summarizes him as 'perhaps, admirable rather than amiable' (Barnes, 2000, p. 1), while Randall perceives him as 'warm and affectionate: he was a kind husband and father, and a true friend, not a mere thinking machine' (Randall, 1960, p. 20), and Ross as 'grateful and affectionate' (Ross, 1977, p. 7).

I find him perennially engaging.

He was born in Stageira, a Greek seaport and colony in between the countries of Thrace, situated to the eastern side of the Chalcidic peninsula, and Macedonia to its west. Stageira, in the Chalcidice peninsula, was founded as an Ionian settlement in 655 BC. The Ionians were Greek colonists who migrated from the Greek mainland following the Dorian invasions of around 1000 BC. They set up trading posts along western Anatolia or modern day Turkey and their towns grew. The Ionians were a relatively advanced people trading between the Greek states and Phrygia and Lydia to the east, and although racially mixed, the Ionian culture insisted on supporting pan-Hellenic culture and attempted to maintain independence against Persian incursions and demands for subservience or tribute, a quasi-nationalist ideal that encouraged many Hellenic thinkers such as Aristotle to see the Hellenic peoples as superior to their neighbors.

The Chalcidice peninsula got its name from the people of Chalcis, who came from the south of the eastern Greek peninsula; Chalcis had been settled by Ionians, and it was to Chalcis that Aristotle went to retire and die in 322 BC in his mother's lands. Chalcidice faced threats from Macedonia, Thrace to the northeast, Thessaly to the southwest; to the east it faced the Aegean Sea and the constant political and military pressure from the vast Persian Empire. Moreover, the Spartans, Athenians, and Corinthians all claimed Chalcidice's cities.

Aristotle was born the son of Phaestias and Nicomachus, who was a court physician to Macedonian King Amyntas III (r. 393–370 BC). Aristotle's father Nicomachus' ancestors may have migrated to the Ionian islands and Stageira from Messenia in the southwest corner of the greater Greek peninsula following the putative Dorian invasions (Howatson, 1989, p. 197). As an aesclepiad, Nicomachus trained as a physician, which probably drew him into the Ionic educational circles where the Ionian philosophers' influence would have been palpable to an educated man. Nicomachus gained employment at the Macedonian court in Pella; it is conjectured that in turn he would have been a dissector of animals and a student of nature (Ellwood, 1938, p. 36), a later pursuit for Aristotle, who effectively founded the science of biology. Aristotle's father and mother both died when he was young, perhaps around the age of 10, after which Aristotle was brought up by his guardian or uncle, Proxenus, also a physician, who sent the youth at the age of 17 or 18 to study at the Academy. Perhaps it had been his father's wishes, for Nicomachus (and/or Proxenus) had probably heard of Plato's Academy through the intellectual grapevines (Dillon, 2005, p. 89). It is an interesting move – the aesclepiad tradition involved mythical-cum-religious elements tied in with a highly practical education of seeking to cure illness and disease, whereas the Academy was intellectual in orientation.

Aristotle's mother, Phaestias, was from neighboring Chalcis in Euboea, another Ionian settlement, and owned lands there to which Aristotle retired in the last years of his life. Euboea was commercially powerful until the Athenians took control – its weights and measures were used as a Hellenic standard down to Solon's time, but invasion and domination by others reduced its standing. Chalcis avoided the depredation that its neighboring city, Eretria, suffered under the Persians, securing a relative independence until Philip II of Macedonia defeated a Greek alliance to impose Macedonian hegemony. Aristotle had an elder sister, Arimneste, and a brother, Arimnestus. Arimneste married Proxenus and had two children by him, a son, Nicanor, and a daughter, Hero. On the death of Proxenus, Aristotle took Nicanor under his wing. Hero's son, Callisthenes – Aristotle's grand-nephew – was fatefully to follow Alexander's campaign into Persia as a biographer. Aristotle himself married Pythias and had a daughter, also Pythias; after his wife's death he had a son, Nicomachus, with Herpyllis, a slave from his home town with whom he passed his last years.

From his parents' connections and culture, Aristotle was well placed for an exceedingly good education, of which he certainly took, or was encouraged to take, advantage.

Macedonia

Macedonia was to play an integral role in Aristotle's life. It rose to political prominence during his lifetime and his own fortunes were directly and indirectly tied to its own. In effect, his teachings and philosophizing rode the Macedonian wave to power and hegemony: his father worked for the court and Aristotle was a contemporary and possible close friend of King Philip, returning to the court to tutor Philip's son, Alexander. As with the life and times of many great thinkers, Aristotle grew up and was surrounded by tumultuous political upheavals and shifts of power: for the most part, he was on the victorious side, which certainly would have made his life easier than otherwise, but when Alexander died and Macedonia looked vulnerable, Aristotle exiled himself from Athens to avoid any anti-Macedonian backlash – such was his dependency on politics.

Despite being hardly known beyond its borders, Macedonia suddenly became important during Aristotle's lifetime. Its rise under Philip and its meteoric expansion into the east under Alexander left, however, a highly visible cultural and genetic imprint on the world. Macedonia's inhabitants were warlike and became famed for their victories because of their tightly disciplined phalanxes, wielding long spears, who would withstand ferocious attacks – their discipline and courage were perfected by Aristotle's contemporary Philip, and enabled his son, Alexander, to subdue people after people in his campaigns.

Philip had taken the opportunity of the political fallout from the Third Sacred War (355–346 BC) and the Athenian Social War (358–355 BC) to expand his kingdom. The Thebans had defeated the Spartans, who had surprisingly allied with the Athenians to check the Thebans, in Aristotle's youth; in turn, Theban temporary hegemony was lost when their brilliant general, Epaminondas, was killed in his moment of victory at the Battle of Mantinea. Philip idolized the Theban, whom he had known and studied under as a youth; when he took the throne he reformed the Macedonian state and military and in 359 BC began a series of campaigns against Macedonia's neighbors. Philip eventually rose to dominate the central Greek Amphictyonic Council by crushing the northern Athenian colonies of Thrace and Chalcidice. Unsurprisingly, given the political conditions, Aristotle's early education could only have given him an acute awareness of faction and shifting allegiances (cf. Laistner, 1947, p. 188). It is a history worth noting, not just because he grew up in the eye of the military hurricane that Macedonia was to become, but also because his philosophy – his wisdom – could not be but reflected in it, hence the noteworthiness of reviewing the relevant part of Macedonian history.

Later Aristotle was to comment in his *Politics* that some are born to rule over others. It is a provocative and simultaneously interesting assertion, which when added to his thoughts on good breeding stand in contrast to the actual dynastic problems of the Macedonian court: Philip's mother was Illyrian, a fact that seems to have caused innuendoes and problems for Philip's reign (O'Brien, 1994, p. 29). Aristotle could boast of good Ionic lineage and may have viewed his employers with some condescension. Weak roots require a powerful compensation and Philip sought this in military power: thoughts of aggrandizement were certainly abroad during his reign: in neighboring Thessaly, Jason of Pherae rose to become a king or *tagus* with ambitions. He had reformed the Thessalian army and created a 20,000 strong *hoplite* force with 8,000 cavalry. He brokered an alliance with Amyntas and later wrote to Philip II, who was to employ Aristotle, perhaps speaking of his ambitions to invade Persia. Jason's ambitions were not unheeded: Philip commenced the plans but Philip's son, Aristotle's pupil, was to enact them.

The Hellenic dream of enacting revenge against persistent Persian attacks and interference had been fired by the spectacular victories earned by the Greeks in the early sixth centuries at the battles of Marathon, Salamis, Himera, Mycale, and Plataea. The power of Persia was phenomenal but the history has been written by the Greeks, who wrapped themselves up in a literary, artistic, and philosophical justification of their victories; not that it was all plain sailing, for Persia sacked Athens in 480 BC and the Persians were not so wooden-headed and myopically imperialistic – they altered their policies according to their subject peoples, but as with any empire, power can only stretch so far before it recoils from dissent and grievances among cultures and peoples far removed from the center. The Hellenic responses to Persia were also mixed, with some *poleis* joining the Persian cause either for protection or to ally against a common enemy.

War between the majority of the Hellenes and Persia originally began in 490 BC. Despite intricate foreign policies and an ostensible pragmatism, the might of Persia was built on an early notion of 'manifest destiny' – in the religious belief that all nations should submit to Persian rule. 'No other religion of antiquity,' writes Burckhardt, 'was so perfectly adapted to foster the arrogance of perpetual self-righteousness and omnipotence as this version of Zoroastrianism' (Burckhardt, 1999, p. 216); nonetheless, the peaceful intercourse between the Asian and south European civilizations was immensely fruitful, for Zorastrian thinking influenced the Greek philosophers, but the Greeks may not have become pragmatically contented subject peoples and the Persians would have had to deal with them brutally. Thus in the wars, the Greeks were fighting for their survival. Arrogance (hubris) in victory was later to spur Aristotle's Alexander into subjugating the Persian Empire: myth wrapped in legend wrapped in history underlay the Hellenic ethos. But victory over the Persians did not produce the pan-Hellenic federation or nation that some wished for – war broke out between the city states across the peninsula and islands. Sparta and Athens formed the main contending parties in the Peloponnesian War that lasted for twenty-seven years, with Sparta eventually defeating Athens, and Sparta then being defeated by the Thebans and all in turn by Philip of Macedonia and his son Alexander.

Politics aside for the moment, let's look at what explicit pedagogical upbringing Aristotle may have enjoyed as the son of aesclepiads.

Archaic educational influences

Aristotle spent much time learning medicine: he was descended through his mother and father from a line of aesclepiads – early physicians. According to the Roman physician and philosopher Galen (131–201 AD), who studied Aristotle and compiled an enormously influential set of treatises on medical works, the aesclepiads taught their children reading, writing, and anatomy. Aesclepiads saw themselves as either descendants or followers of Aesclepius, the Greek god of healing (Magill, 1998, p. 94); they plied their trade around a territory, moving from village to village setting up to cure whoever bought their services (Grayeff, 1974, p. 15), and as with the medical professions today, they formed a guild to protect their economic interests – knowledge was passed from father to son. As a descendant of aesclepiads, Aristotle would have gained a rudimentary medical education; while he did not enter into the profession himself (although he seems to have penned or edited a medical treatise with drawings), his mind was spurred on to learn biology and zoology, and commentators have noted the strong biological underpinning in his theorizing on people. The aesclepiads, however, were divided over the philosophy of medicine, a legacy that remains with us today (Coulter, 1994, Chapter 1). One school emphasized a rationalist approach that extolled apodictic theories of the world, body, and medicine. As such, diagnosis meant fitting the patient into prescribed views. The other preferred an empirical approach in which the patient presented ailments peculiar to him or to her and from which a diagnosis and treatment were to follow. Aristotle was to follow the rationalist view of the elemental humors: disease being an imbalance of a person's humors.

At Cos, Hippocrates (and probably his followers also designated under the same name) practiced and taught medicine – he lived from 460 to 370 BC, within the period of Aristotle's father's time and dying when Aristotle was 14. Hippocrates is known as effectively forming medicine as a science in its own right, although different philosophical strands in his thinking lend evidence to there being more than one author of the Hippocratic writings (Coulter, p. 6ff). Plato, Aristotle's teacher, was a contemporary and mentions him in passing and Aristotle referred to him in the *Politics*; he also mentions Hippocrates' teacher, Herodicus several times (e.g. *EE*, 1243b20; *Rhet*, 1361b5), giving good evidence to suggest that the aesclepiads were aware of each other or their writings across the Greek peninsula and islands. Hippocrates' studies may be seen as a radical progression within the aesclepidian traditions part of which may have been the norm and which Aristotle would have been aware of through his father and uncle, giving him the intellectual means by which to study the animal kingdom.

The children of aesclepiads would have worked with their parents even assisting them in surgery, for it was noted that a woman's or a child's hand was softer than a man's. Accordingly, it would not be surprising to note this influence on Aristotle, who excelled in so many fields: he certainly worked on dissections, producing an illustrated handbook on them and possibly wrote two treatises on medicine; his students were also encouraged to study medicine (Longrigg, 1993. p. 149). However, he did not work on human anatomy and often made glaring errors, for human dissection was impermissible in Hellenic society (Kirk, 1962, p. 122). Often Aristotle makes references to medicine either primarily or through analogies (*Physics*, etc.); he indubitably held that the healthy body is a necessary condition for the good character. In speaking of what produces health in the particular we must refer to the physician, for the language of medicine will be more specific than that of the multitude (*Top*, 110a20).

While the aesclepiad tradition would be the first influence on Aristotle's own thinking, given that his parents and his guardian were of the tradition, other significant tributaries into his intellect can be considered when reviewing explicit and implicit Hellenic educational norms as found in the writings of the history of the schools, the images of childhood commemorated on vases and friezes, and through the words of the poets, playwrights, and politicians. From a murky and prehistoric past, we detect that as the Hellenic peoples enter our historical view, specific and increasing pedagogic thoughts and images emerge.

The first glimmerings of a general Greek pedagogy may be drawn from the early legendary stories and writings in what is known as the archaic period – from Homer and Hesiod. Later, other elements are evinced in political speeches that have survived – from Solon, for instance – as well as through the dramas of Athens in the fifth century as the Athenian *polis* shifted away from military prowess toward a partial democracy. Then the voices of the playwrights and philosophers – the commentators and theoreticians on life and its aims and structures – gain ascendancy, sometimes, we shall note, acting to submerge the cultural forms that much Hellenic education took both in the household and in public.

From Homer, we can discern that early Greek education stressed the importance of doing things, of speaking well – values that we find trickling down to Aristotle's thoughts – and on the importance of character: the good man is bred to speak and to do well. 'Homeric or aristocratic education was designed to produce individual heroes,' writes Barrow (2001, p. 20). The legend of Odysseus presents a man capable of wily connivances, swiftness in thought and in tongue, and being a powerful athlete and warrior to boot. Physical prowess was to be exhibited on the wrestling ground, the race track, and the athletics field, as well as on the battlefield, for which the former were of course the training. The myths speak greatly of the general values permeating through the generations, recited, taught, and learned both for their religious value and for their moral import, reminding audiences of their ancestors' feats but also of the expectations of their lives – perhaps at times with a tinge of regret that the latest generation was not up to the great deeds of the previous. In the Hellenic peoples, we gain a sense of importance and moral supremacy, of a cultural superiority to barbarian peoples within and beyond the Greek peninsula. Part of that stems from the early poets waxing lyrical about how great their own people were, sentiments that became repeated through the oral and, later and more importantly, the literary traditions – it is an attitude that Aristotle readily subsumes in his ethical writings. Thucydides (460–395 BC), the early historian, recognized that the Ancient writers were more interested in pleasing their audiences than referring to historical truths (Thucydides, 1998, I.21.1). The early Greeks informed themselves and their children that they were the original place of humanity, the center of the earth, that they had invented many useful practices such as the sailing ship, the mill, and fire, but they were not averse to accepting the input of foreign ingenuity either – notably geometry, the alphabet, the sundial, and the shield and helmet (Burckhardt, 1999, p. 17). This theme of a racial-cum-cultural supremacy is maintained through the Hellenic period: the Greeks were and are not alone, of course, in describing themselves as superior; it is a common human trait among those who achieve military victories, economic wealth, and/or artistic greatness, but we then have to judge how parochial such views are compared to the possibility of a cosmopolitan vision of moral and intellectual ascendancy proffered for the rest of humanity to enjoy.

In the centuries prior to Aristotle, myth reigned as an explanation of existence and purpose, the Hellenes believing that they were 'the rightful heirs and successors of the heroic age; wrongs suffered in prehistoric times were still being avenged much later' (Burckhardt, p. 25). Legendary heroes – physically powerful, musically adept at singing old ballads but illiterate – were the personifications of entire peoples, with Lycurgus as the father of Sparta and Theseus of Greece: their legendary achievements were hailed by their people, while their faults were also their people's. In turn, the places and landscapes of heroic and mythical endeavor merged into Greek thinking, particularly in the overarching importance of Mount Olympus, home of the gods – it was an education that never diminished, despite the rise of science, for the sense of belonging, of a fragile pan-Hellenic unity, forever stood as a reminder of past greatness and present strengths. Not quite nostalgia and not quite atavism, the Greeks ensured a timelessness to their education and culture; some, such as Aristotle's pupil, Alexander, certainly drew on the myths to form his own apotheosized visions. Moreover, believing that they were all children of the gods would certainly highlight their sense of paramount importance in relation to neighboring peoples, whose denigration has frequently marred later conceptions of them – notably the Persians.

In the golden age of 'Classical Greece' the famous writers and politicians sought to derive their lineage from legendary heroes or even gods of ages past. Plato's parents were said to have descended from Poseidon, and Aristotle followed suit: his parents were said to be descendants of Aesclepius. Neither did the gods disappear from life; they were there, ready to emerge amid their flock as were *daimons*: spirits that aided the great – Socrates was said to possess one.

As the Hellenic economies grew and the division and specialization of labor expanded, education's purposes similarly expanded, to fulfill both the myriad of tasks that broadening economic markets present (i.e. the learning of the technical arts for agriculture, metallurgy, architecture), and the more refined pursuits that political and economic freedom presented especially to the ruling families. The new opportunities afforded by a growing economy tends to raise the value of education especially of literacy and arithmetic. Initially, practicability was a recurrent and lasting theme of Hellenic education, that is education for communal or political purposes; thus formal schooling was biased as it was toward the elite or ruling clans (*phyles*) and their children, who went to school early and left later than poorer counterparts (Plato, *Prot*, 326c). That is also to say that the arts and crafts of the working people was of less concern to the intellectual and political classes; their education was more likely to be hands on, following in the footsteps of the family traditions – a boy working in a shop, a girl learning to weave, for instance. Skilled work was considered beneath the dignity of the upper classes to engage in and was usually the remit of slaves, hence craftsmen could not be citizens. Even the most prominent and spectacular of the Greek craftsmen were derided in comparison to those of noble birth. Philip of Macedon expressed his disdain at Alexander's ability on the lyre: 'Aren't you ashamed to play so well? No youth of good birth ... has ever wished to be Pheidas, Philemon, or Archilochus; even if the work gives pleasure, it does not necessarily follow that the master is worthy of emulation' (quoted in Burckhardt, 1999, p. 194). Good birth, *eugeneia*, good education, *paideia*, and wealth, *ploutos*, formed the necessary conditions for *aretē* or excellence, a theme repeated in Aristotle's ethics.

Earning one's money through skill (*techne*) and through voluntary exchange was held of lower import than living off the work of the slaves: the aristocratic life (reminiscent of the exploits of the gods) filled Hellenic myths and hence its culture. Aristotle was contemptuous of those who earned their living; nonetheless, the lawmaker Solon made it an offense to jeer at certain occupations. Poverty, though, was held to be no disgrace in itself: 'disgrace was failing to escape from it by work' (Burckhardt, p. 187). On the other hand, the early poet Hesiod in his *Works and Days* celebrated the simple nobility of agricultural peasant life ('work is no disgrace, but idleness is') and, like the Romans later, the Greek aristocracy viewed working the land as appropriate to the life of the soldier (Cartledge, 1993, p. 149). The militaristic Romans – in very many respects so similar to the Greeks – maintained the importance of landownership and farming as of value, echoes of which permeate European culture even today.

This aristocratic philosophy attracted many emulators throughout Western history but also attracted many critics who note that the elitist vision of education (sustained by Aristotle) generally failed to acknowledge the economic and moral role of the lower classes and of women. In many respects, this can be explained by the dominance and maintenance of masculine and martial values in the Hellenic world, ameliorated only by the growing interest in science and in medicine predominantly in the aristocratic Ionian subculture. In other words, early Greek education was inherently political and patriarchal – designed to serve the needs of the *polis* and its aims and in terms of the consequences: a man who turned his back on (or was not born into) politics would become, through his huckstering and craftwork, weak and feeble, while the true aristocrat would be strong, well formed physically, and morally good; in contrast, the artists of legend were held up to be of less value, because they were manual workers.

Accordingly, the general pedagogic ends of the aristocracy forged a greater distance from the *banausic* or the mechanical life of artisans, and personal and military excellence (*aretē*) through the gymnasia and hence fighting: much formal education initially centered around the *polis* or the political power of the city state – its intimate relationship only waning with the growth of the *poleis* and the advancement of philosophy, whose proponents, such as Aristotle, enthused about learning for learning's sake.

Literary learning seems to have developed in the eighth century. Children learned their alphabet but mainly by rote learning of the poems taught by the *grammatistes*, music taught by *kitharistes*, and physical training taught by the *paidotribes*. Gradually, fee-paying schools emerged for basic education, which continued to reflect the needs of the *polis* and to which the wealthy sent their boys. The *polis* formed the center of Greek political culture and hence its educational and training curricula. The citizen (male) was very much a citizen of the *polis*, who owed his life to the city state and therefore was responsible for its defense and moral standing; unique in political history with only Renaissance Venice mimicking its form (Burckhardt, 1999, p. 55), the *polis* has attracted philosophical and historical attention as an example of a single-minded, holistic political entity, which Aristotle described as existing logically prior to the individual (*Pol*, 1253a), for the whole is prior to the part. This implies that the *polis* possesses his attention and duty: happiness and sound welfare could only come through the community of the *polis* and, as Aristotle emphasized, the individual without a state is either a bad man or, intriguingly, 'above humanity' (*Pol*); that is, the Hellenic *polis* encouraged individuality but only through the state, unless we are talking of a 'great souled man' (*ho megalopsuchos*), who effectively is unteachable.

In its early histories, the Hellenic peoples attributed success to their *poleis* rather than to individuals who may have, in modern eyes, been heroes; even the heralded playwright Aeschylus preferred on his tomb to remind the visitor that he fought at Marathon. Each man (for their women were deemed second class) would lay down his life for his city – patriotism was a required virtue, but it did not necessarily imply the collectivism that the modern nation state has demanded in recent times. The individual was certainly of great value, but his worth was living through and with his city rather than as an anonymous contributor to its numbers: the *Iliad* of Homer attests to the foundations of this culture of individualism admixed with patriotic fervor in which warriors preparing to fight identify themselves and their ancestors, and as Homer's tongue rolls over many names of those who fell, Greek and Trojan alike are given moral status. Yet while such deeds were commemorated to empower the new generations to rise to the challenges of the present as their ancestors rose to the challenges of the past, the Greeks were not so atavistic as so subdue the living in terms of the dead: the dead, like the abstract of the *polis*, gave the living a foundation. Accordingly, much of Aristotle's political writing begins to fall into place, yet his own pupil Alexander (perhaps

Aristotle's 'great souled man') sought to outdo his ancestors and to impose his own ego on the world in a manner that strikes one as very unbecoming the Hellenic teaching, as found in Homer and the playwrights, not to become hubristic. In traditional Hellenic morals, the individual was ultimately subservient to his city if needs be – hence Socrates chose death over exile from Athens.

Otherwise, a balance between extremes was to be sought, another important virtue emphasized by Aristotle. For the Greeks, seeking a balance or *sōphrosunē* (soundness of mind) was vital – striving for *aretē* (excellence) and kudos or *kleos* (glory) but avoiding hubris (arrogance); similarly, the youth were taught to feel *aidos* or shame. Character was generally assumed to be innate – the good would always be good, their breeding (descent from a god or goddess being assumed) would ensure that their character was incorruptible; yet education was also accepted as forming character, for both the legendary Achilles and Jason were said to be educated by Chiron, the personification of teaching (Burckhardt, 1999, p. 142), and the youth's deeds were to emulate the great legends of the past and thereby gain approbation from his peers.

With growth – economic and imperial – we detect that the morals of the *poleis* shifted away from the strictures of the early small societies upon which they were founded and toward a more complicated, pluralistic, and individualistic morality and culture, hence much of the humor in Aristophanes, whose writings capture the shift away from small-society culture. In economic thinking:

> The inner conflicts of the individual Greek states until the collapse of Greek civilization itself are all variants on the same theme: the fight between the old ruling class and the expanding commercial classes, complicated by the existence of a mass of slaves and impoverished peasants and artisans.
>
> (Roll, 1987, p. 26)

Plato and Aristotle maintained the voice of the earlier people, suspicious of the barbarian (and even presumptive of being his better), derisory toward commerce and its mores. But as the Athenian economy expanded there was necessarily a concomitant rise of individualism as the division and specialization of labor broadened, and so tensions grew between the organized educational forms required for the state and military purposes, and the nascent pull from the diversifying attractions of a broader economy.

For instance, gymnastics formed the principal part of early Greek education – a regime for warriors based on the principle of *agon* or competition, which boys emulated in preparation for the adult games. Gymnastics was such an integral part of the Hellenic education that it did not have to be encouraged formally; it sought to develop the body to perfection both in beauty and in capability, which the extant and copied statues of the Greeks capture and embody so well. In turn, the local gymnasium became the focus of *agon* and the center of much socializing: the instructors were often former Olympic champions and were highly popular – they had the power to dismiss philosophers and rhetoricians who might ply their trade in the midst. Indeed, Plato's Academy and Aristotle's Lyceum were also gymnasia, which indicates the symbiotic pedagogy of physical and mental activity. The sports taught included the pentathlon, boxing-cum-wrestling (*pankration*), discus and javelin throwing. The Athenians, to whom Aristotle was sent, often produced the best athletes at the Olympic games, but the games were dangerous and many lost their lives pursuing victory and honor on the field (Burckhardt, 1999, pp. 161–7).

Music, taught by the *kitharistes*, implied counting, reading, and writing as well as instrumental learning on the lyre and flute. Otherwise specific grammar teachers (*grammatikes*) used the legends and early poets such as Homer to inculcate moral lessons, but not without encouraging the pupil to imbue his readings harmoniously, for the Athenians in particular seemed to have encouraged the development of balance and harmony in their approach to education (Walden, 1909, p. 10). The *polis* was thus an educative force in its own right offering a continual, lifelong education in music and gymnastics but also in the festivities, the plays, the cult rituals, and works of art effecting the virtue of excellence (Burckhardt, 1999, p. 56), which Aristotle was to encourage in his own fashion.

In Athens, this nascent pluralism forming in Greek culture eventually spilled out into the plays and writings of its classical period. Indeed, the early education could be properly construed as 'training' rather than education, the putative difference between the two being that education can be described as learning for its own sake and training for the sake of another purpose – military prowess or carpentry skills, for instance. Festivals and athletic competitions linked learning, training, and religion, initially for patriotic and military purposes, but herein lay the seeds for a broader educational philosophy that became intrinsically Greek, namely the pursuit of personal excellence, beauty, and virtue. It is summed up in the concept of *aretē*, a broad concept including excellence in achievement, reaching the pinnacle of a person's capabilities.

The Athenians were gradually forging a unique democratic political structure in their *polis* – in as much as we know an awful lot about them, relatively speaking to other earlier societies. The Athenian democracy was based on male citizens having a vote on legislation; women, non-citizens, and slaves were excluded, although they, particularly the women (and children), were all expected to have appropriate high standards of behavior and morality. Solon (638–558 BC), the 'lawgiver' of Athens, presided over reforms that were to bring democracy to Athens. Aristotle comments, 'As to Solon, he is thought by some to have been a good legislator ... who established democracy, and harmonized the different elements of the state' (*Pol*, 1273b36). In his youth, he gained a reputation for his poetry, which he used to impress upon his fellow Athenians to reject an oppressive law that forbade them from discussing attacking Salamis; feigning madness, he attracted a crowd and thereupon gave a hundred-line elegiac poem stirring them to overthrow their restrictions and to seize Salamis. Interestingly, he continued to write his policies and thoughts in poetic form, which certainly presents a powerful image of the connections between music (in this case, poetry) and politics. Aristotle notes that Solon's reforms shifted power away from the aristocracy to form a middle-class-based polity (*Pol*, 1296a19), from which we detect the subtle decline of martial virtues and the educational rise of philosophy, science, and the humanities. Arguably, the power of the aristocratic families did not disappear, for, as today in Western democracies, political participation is restricted by poverty, lack of education, and of course confidence, and Aristotle certainly tied his destiny to the powerful Macedonian court.

In Athens in the fifth century, the new directions following Solon's reforms were evident in the advance of theatrical writings and the advance of democratic traditions. The *archon* (leader) Peisistratus (r. 560–527 BC) had the foresight to commit Homer's stories to writing thereby ensuring their eternity; during this period, Aristotle informs in his *Poetics* that tragedy emerged and eventually settled down on its 'proper nature' (1449a15). In their dramas, the Greeks may have drawn upon Egyptian precedents (Roberts, 1962, p. 21) but gradually formed their own style: competitions were held between writers (the annual *Dionysia* and *Lenaia*) and plays were staged in front of thousands of Athenian citizens, in turn encouraging an educational influence both in the content of the plays and in promoting public performance of the city's values and themes. Many writers' works have been lost, but the great tragedies of Aeschylus (525–456 BC), Sophocles (496–406 BC), and Euripides (480–460 BC) give the modern reader insight not only into the morals of fifth century Athens and some of the common themes running throughout human history, but also into the state of education and influence on Aristotle, who refers often to the three giants of Greek theater, Euripides in particular.

Euripides dealt with the Homeric myths and was concerned that impulsive action always produces bad consequences; his chorus in *Iphigenia* notes that people are different but real nobility is obvious. Education is the guide to excellence, and the use of the intellect gives 'exquisite pleasure' to choose the right course (Euripides, 1999, p. 560). He also wrote that 'it is right that Greeks should rule over barbarians, but not barbarians over Greeks; for those are slaves, but these are free men' – aristocratic attitudes Aristotle repeated in his ethical and political writings. Interestingly, Euripides retired to the Macedonian court. On the other hand, Sophocles' *Ajax* hinted at the democratization of aristocratic values, notably *aretē* (Golder, 1999, p. 22), an idea not thoroughly at home in Aristotle's thinking.

Consider Thespis (from whom we get 'thespian,' actor); perhaps a legendary character, he is said to have innovated the individuation of one character from the chorus, who could then engage in a dialogue with the dithyrambic chorus – up to 50 men singing or chanting in unison. This gave a public display to dialogue, and while debate and dialogue is indubitably as ancient as the human voice, a public, literary form of dialogue offered to the crowds of Athens could only have encouraged literary and philosophical presentations to emerge: Plato's writings are in dialogue form as were Aristotle's early writings (no longer extant), with Socrates acting as the antagonist for the 'chorus' of various ideas presented through compatriots.

The playwrights in turn attracted Aristotle's scholarly attention (cf. *Poetics*), which should give us pause for thought. Drama is educational: the fifth-century playwrights were called teachers (Taplin, 1995, p. 18) and can be very powerful and emotive; it can unite a people in reminding them both of the myths of their security and victories, and of the fragility of their freedoms and values in the face of dangers domestic and foreign. In bringing the people of Athens together to enjoy the dramas, a grand public education was subtly effected. As the fifth century advanced, so drama progressed – stages became more elaborate and themes less reverential. Aristophanes (456–386 BC), dying two years before Aristotle's birth, was the master of comedy. He was, in turn, suitably the brunt of Plato's satirical pen in his dialogue on love, the *Symposium*, in which he insisted that true love is the result of God (Zeus) having split people into two in the past and when the two bodies re-encounter, they find true love (p. 189ff). While Plato may have used Aristophanes' argument in jest, Aristotle was later to advance the idea that love was indeed two bodies and one soul (although some have thought that he may have been speaking of Alexander and Hephaestion).

In the *Clouds*, Aristophanes has Superior Argument (or Right Reason) to speak of the Old Education: its focus was on self-control – the child was not expected to complain, despite wearing very little in harsh weather and marching with other pupils to school, where they would sing in unison without any fancy warbling. Etiquette in public and in front of the elders were paramount, and all hedonistic temptations such as running after girls were to be avoided; instead, the virtuous youth was to avoid wasting time in the marketplace and should head to the Academy to race boyishly and healthily with friends. A healthy education, according to this character, would produce a fine physicality, while the alternative paraded on the stage would result in 'pasty skin, round shoulders, concave chest, an enormous tongue, no arse and a very long ... turn of phrase!' (*Clouds*, 1011ff). Inferior Reason rejects the pomposity of Right Reason as hypocritical and archaic, although in so presenting Inferior Reason, Aristophanes is also mocking the sophists (see below) and Socrates, Plato's teacher.

In the fifth century, Athens converged into a democratic form of government, partially so in the sense that only male citizens were permitted to engage in political decisions, but also uniquely so in that the male citizenry were expected to engage in political affairs and to vote. The model became and remains the ideal form of democracy, all permitted and expected to engage in political processes, yet the Greek tragedians toyed with the fate of the individual cast amid powers beyond their control: the Gods, or the decisions of others we can adduce. The Athenian thinker was no collectivist in the Spartan mode – the individual was paramount. Yet as we move through the fifth century, Pericles (495–429 BC) both encouraged educational and cultural expansion to make Athens the center of Hellenic culture and then led Athens into the long Peloponnesian War (431–404 BC), which eventually led to Athens' subjugation, first to the Spartans and later the Macedonians.

Meanwhile, the martial emphasis, and accordingly the anti-commercial attitude, was taken to the extreme in Sparta, which became famous for its restrictive upbringing and regimented life for male children and men. Boys' education in Sparta had, according to tradition, been handed down by Lycurgus, the legendary seventh-century lawgiver (700–630 BC). Training – the *agoge* – was strict and regimental, designed to produce warriors who would stand their ground and die for their country rather than run away, as the famed 300 Spartans against the Persians at Thermopylae testified. In Sparta, the state decided which boy babies would live, exposing the weaker in an early eugenics program designed to produce a strong breed of warriors; the children were state educated from the age of 7 and taught to be cunning and devious, stealing food to supplement their meager diet (Pomeroy *et al.*, 1999, p. 140). They lived collectively and in absolute dependence on traditional codes as enforced by the state.

Aristotle complained of the Spartans that they gave their women too much power, for men had to conform to Lycurgus' totalitarian rules while women were exempt; it is interesting that his sexism, which pervaded and colored his thinking as we read him today, overrode any sense of injustice he could have held of the men's lack of freedom and their brutal conditions. The women were indeed powerful: they could own land, be independently wealthy, trained to fight, and engaged in vigorous competitions – one, an equestrian expert named Kyniska, trained successful Olympic chariot teams (women were not allowed to compete).

Chauvinists believe that the power of Spartan women was the reason for its eventual downfall. However, the Spartan ruling elite, regulated by an ossified code of traditions and conventions, oversaw the foreign and domestic policies and laws of the nation. The education system worked, up to a point: if military success, isolation, and ossification were desired, the totalitarian militarism of Sparta succeeded, but like all ossified systems, eventually it failed to adapt to changing conditions – in 371 BC, the famed Spartans were defeated by the Thebans at Leuktra under the command of Epaminondas, who changed tactics, much to the Spartans' dismay, and for negligible losses smashed the Spartan military (Dupuy and Dupuy, 1995, p. 48).

Nevertheless, the Spartan ideal was taken up by Plato in his idealistic educational program and elements of Sparta persist in modern education circles today: from British public school discipline and collective ethos (admixed with enough Athenian individualism to balance collective tendencies with eccentricities) to National Socialist Germany's own Spartan regiment in World War II. Whenever schools apply regimental orderliness, patriotic and unquestioning obedience, and an indifference to personal suffering, and, it needs to be added against rising romantic notions, a political project to subjugate a population to work the land – in the case of Sparta, a people called the *helots* – we recognize the Spartan model. (The *helots*, incidentally, were Ionian inhabitants who remained in place rather than flee the Dorian invasions that brought the Spartan tribe.)

Along with the Ionians and Dorians, and in contrast to the Spartans, the Aeolian people presented a broader education, permitting music and poetry and some of the early renowned writers including Hesiod (c. 700 BC), Alcaeus (c. 620 BC), and Sappho (c. 630 BC), of whom Aristotle characteristically says that the Mytilenaeans honored her 'despite her being a woman' (*Rhet*, 1389b). The isle of Lesbos, to which Aristotle was to wander in his scientific pursuits,

presented several names of note during this time who contributed to
the literary flows running down to the present day; one can only
conjecture that the Lesbian education leaned more toward the arts
than that on the Greek peninsula.

Hellenic childhood

Within the broad Hellenic culture, images and portrayals of children
and childhood disclose the culture and education of youth in classical
Greece (Neils and Oakley, 2003). The dominating theme across the
Hellenic peoples was the preeminence of males over females: the *polis*
is run by men for men; accordingly, boys are preferred to girls, and
their childhood is molded by explicit and implicit teaching to reflect
the differences in status and expectations due. In the educational
theories of Plato and Aristotle, the purpose of education is to produce
good male citizens and while their explicit theories may extend,
accentuate, or even seek to reform contemporary practices, the
dominance of patriarchy remains evident.

Childhood was generally viewed as something to get through
quickly. Children were compared to adults and thereby failed to meet
the adult standards of morality and physical and mental abilities, yet
that did not mean that the Greeks rejected sympathetic feelings
toward children *qua* children – often their plight was used to invoke a
legal or subtle political message (as the fate of children is still used to
invoke *ad argumentum misericordiam*). However, children were
traditionally grouped as second-class citizens along with women and
slaves and their inability to turn their attention to their futures further
relegates what could otherwise have been seen as the innate potential
of the (male) child to become the proper citizen. For Aristotle, the
child is not yet complete and whole; he is immature. Women, he
noted, possess deliberation but possess no authority, while slaves
possess no deliberation at all (*Pol*, 1260a). Yet children's immaturity
could also be held as an innocence that gave them a better connection
to the divine or to truths – a theory that has not entirely left Western
culture despite John Locke's insistence that children are born with no
innate ideas regarding the nature or content of the good.

Birth was a social affair in the sense that the Greeks permitted first the determination of life and second inclusion in the family home or *oikos*. Exposure was practiced but this was a family decision rather than a state decision as in Sparta; yet even if the neonate was allowed to live, entry into the household was conditional upon a range of factors generally relating to the optimum size of the household (which would include household servants and slaves). To those chosen to live, names were given after ten days (*dekatē*); they were later admitted into the family clan or *phyle*, which apparently had religious or cultic significance, and, in Athens, into the family's *phratries* or brotherhoods. These were loosely ordered filial groupings probably revolving around cousins but which also helped to indicate or define future citizenship into the *polis*. The *phratries* were of political importance but eventually, in Athens, their influence gave way to ideologically based parties as political life became more complicated from the fifth century on, while the connection to clan gradually evolved and diminished into a more benign portrayal of noble descent through gene or direct ancestry rather than through a broad collective.

Until their introduction into full citizenship, young males were held to be incomplete citizens, as Aristotle thought (*Pol*, 1278a). The term *epheboi* captured the status of young adolescent males destined to become full citizens: between the ages of 18 and 20 they shared the harsh discipline of the obligatory military training required for the *polis*, dividing their training according to family status and wealth: *hippeis* (cavalry), *hoplites* (infantry), and *thetes* (light infantry) in order of wealth and capacity to arm themselves.

While the sons of citizens could grow up into free citizenship, daughters remained lifelong minors (Golden, 2003, p. 38). Religious rites acted to bring children into the *polis* through initiations and festivals such as the Aiora fertility festival, the Eleusian mysteries, and the autumnal Oschophoria, which also involved races and cross-dressing. Girls had more opportunities for rituals than boys, whose lives followed the different path of citizenship of the *poleis*; their ceremonies presaged their future domestic lives and to provide a social outlet for them outside of the highly restrictive women's quarters (Golden, p. 49). Communality through schools and festivities helped to cement bonds across families through the *polis*.

Cared for at home by their mothers and other siblings, at the age of 7 boys and girls were differentiated and started their formal education. School activities were strictly supervised by teachers and the tutor-slaves that may accompany the better-off boys – the verb to teach, *paideuō*, also means to correct and discipline in Attic Greek (Golden, p. 64). Attendance was not compulsory and other education was provided by the tutor-slaves in the household. Lessons, as we have noted, divided into *grammata* (reading and writing), *gymnastikē* (physical training), and *musikē* (music and poetry); the format emphasized rote learning over individual creativity and self-expression. Schools integrated rich and poor but the rich tended to attend formal schooling for longer.

Otherwise, children were expected to help out around the house with elder sisters acting as childminders and helping to prepare food. Boys might accompany their fathers in their work as well as run errands and care for animals. Such 'menial duties,' Aristotle wrote, 'are an honor to the free youth [i.e. of future citizens]' (*Pol*, 1333a). Within this framework, children could play: Golden also notes the etymological connection between child, *pais*, and *paizo* 'I play' (Golden, p. 53). They had many games recognizable to the modern reader – chase, tag, monkey-in-the-middle, knucklebones, and ball games, but also 'runaway slave'! As is often the case with thinkers, philosophers musing on the value of education concocted thoughts on the significance, particularly the moral significance, of these games. Plato, for instance, worried that children's lawlessness would evolve into mature anarchic tendencies that would destabilize the *polis* (*Leg*, 797A; *Rep*, 424E). Indeed, that children were the future of the *polis* is an inescapable conclusion governing the purpose of the Hellenic cultural and religious idioms and educational programs: any deviances or potential deviances that could present later problems for the *polis* were frowned upon or chastised. This included the place of sexual relations between citizens and the youngsters.

Sex and gender

'I think I ought to say something of loving boys, as this has a bearing on education,' Xenophon wrote (quoted in Pomeroy *et al*., 1999, p.

146). Indeed, sex education between teachers and pupils, elders and youngsters, was deemed normal and healthy and perhaps a secondary consequence to the competitive spirit firing male achievement in the gymnasia (Burckhardt, 1999, p. 199). Homosexuality and pederasty (with young adolescents, not pre-pubescents) were accepted practice and the Ancient Greeks would look strangely upon modern laws prohibiting relationships between teachers and pupils. The teacher was seen as a guiding, wise role model, who would stretch his teaching for the beautiful youths that he fancied, and so both parties would mutually gain; same-sex relationships also existed between women (e.g. Sappho's lovers) and probably for similar justifications but were thoroughly rejected by orthodox patriarchal, phallocentric culture, which celebrated masculinity and its prowess (Posner, 1992, p. 43). Yet for some, sexual attraction and interaction were not supposed to be lustful, for that would be shameful – the principal motive had to be intellectual, a recognition of beauty and virtue, a line that Socrates and Plato were to explore over the consummation of physical love for the younger male.

Nonetheless, Greek male citizens had a generally free rein over whom they had sex with: young males, women, adolescents; any woman who was not the daughter or wife of another citizen, and they were not responsible for any resulting pregnancies. Class status governed the relationships, such that male citizens could have intercourse with anyone below their class but only engage in mutuality or non-penetrative sex with those of the same class. Yet their mistresses were free to renounce the relationships should they wish to. Abortions and exposure were common, although Aristotle thought that abortion was wrong once the fetus formed a human shape; deformed children were exposed seemingly without remorse (as written by the male philosophers, that is).

With regard to women, the Greeks generally were relatively unenlightened and patriarchal: Hellenic society was misogynist and literally phallocentric, for it deemed women to be intellectually inferior and weaker than men and put their lives in the hands of their fathers and husbands-to-be. (Sparta, interestingly, did not: their women had much more freedom than Athenian women.) Their role in reproduction was passive: male semen provided the seed, while the womb provided the room; model and statuesque phalluses were paraded and exhibited in homes and the theater in celebration of masculinity. Moreover, in securing the domination of the male over the female, the obvious resemblance of children to their mothers was explained by the acquisition of characteristics rather than from any proto-genetic theory. Women – teenagers in Athens – were married off to older men but lived a life mainly separated from their husbands. Marriage was a social duty, so even natural homosexual men had to marry and seek to produce children (Posner, p. 117).

Girls were not to be educated, although some evidence suggests that some girls may have gained some literacy (Neils and Oakley, 2003, plate 46), whereas boys were entrusted to male tutors and to boys-only schools. While the respectable woman was to serve the patriarchal stereotype of chastity and obedience (silence being the cardinal virtue), prostitution was of course not non-existent: in the oldest profession there were women called *hetaerae*, who possessed relatively more freedom than their married sisters or lower-class prostitutes. *Hetaerae* were freer to enjoy men's company and were encouraged to become accomplished; usually of foreign birth (Athenian citizens were not allowed to marry foreign women), they were educated, physically able (probably in dance), and musically talented (Posner, 1992, p. 40). Unhappily married Pericles, for instance, enjoyed the friendship and companionship of Aspasia (c. 470–400 BC), who was noted for her intellectual abilities and who attracted much philosophical and satirical attention with some thinkers wondering who had the more influence in their relationship. In his youth, Plato enjoyed Archaenessa, and Aristotle passed his remaining years with Herpyllis, a household servant, following the death of his wife; and his pupil Alexander took with him the famed Thaïs on his conquering expedition east. Such women were of course rare, yet their presence and intellect were seemingly appreciated – Aspasia held court with men and allegedly their wives, but such women stand out because the norm was otherwise: quiet servitude.

On the other hand, the Hellenic male's social life centered on the symposium, a ritualistic gathering of friends at a house that often involved entertainment, music, games, and conversation. Guests paid a contribution to the cost of the gathering although sometimes the evening may be subsidized by one man. After a washing of the hands, food was brought in, then a flute girl (or woman) would play to invoke a libation which would be sung by the guests. There followed much song and drinking of wine and good talk freed from constraint and loosened by alcohol. The Greeks prided themselves on their conversations; moreover, intellectual conversation, rather than gossip or chitchat, is thoroughly educational; while it may not invoke a purpose or follow a prescribed format with set texts, it is indubitably one of humanity's greatest vehicles for the dissemination and exchange of ideas. The symposium is idealized in Plato's dialogue of that name, providing a stage for his own philosophical ideas, but it also gives an insight, complemented by Xenophon's *Symposium*, of the nature and breadth of the ideal symposium conversation (2006). In public, friends would meet in the *agora* (marketplace), which formed a looser, more informal version of the symposium, permitting conversation and exchanges and cementing social bonds. Here intellectuals may have gathered to ply their education of rhetoric, knowledge, and philosophy.

At this point it is appropriate to survey the philosophy of those whom Aristotle drew upon.

Chapter 2

Antecedents and Contemporaries

The pre-Socratics

'Greek philosophy begins with childishly simple questions and ends with complex and subtle theories' (Ackrill, 1981, p. 5). It begins in earnest with the Ionians.

Of the early philosophers, the Ionians produced several critical thinkers whom Aristotle read and discussed. The Ionians were a very interesting people making up one-third of the Hellenic peoples, the others being the somewhat militant Dorians and the relatively quieter Aeolians. The Ionian people, who play an important part in Aristotle's upbringing, had been displaced by Dorian invasions in the twelfth or ninth centuries. (Although controversy exists on whether there were invasions or merely a evolution of culture, either way, the Spartans were of Dorian descent, the Athenians of Ionian heritage.) Those Ionians who became refugees headed east and took with them their political system of 12 *poleis* – city states controlling a specified area and which tolerated no other political competition within its jurisdiction; each was the political and cultural center as well as refuge for its people in times of danger. Alliances between city states were only briefly successful, but a proud jealousy of its own origins and strength sustained an attitude of self-reliance and cultural identity centered on sufficiency and power. The *polis* was to play an important role both in Aristotle's own education and in his fortuitous rise to fame and fortune.

Ionian culture produced a group of philosophers now known as the pre-Socratics; only fragments of varying sizes remain of their work and quotations by later philosophers such as Aristotle who studied them. The Ionians formed a league to defend and pursue their interests (which included defeating the original inhabitants) and the area flourished despite attempts by outsiders to control it. In the face of looming hegemony from Persia, Ionians lived on the edge of Hellenic civilization. Their city states were agrarian trading centers, highly parochial, geographically isolated, and overshadowed by the 70 million Persians who were gradually moving army camps into their northern backyard; as with Macedonia, unwise political inaction or action could prove crucial to Ephesus and ultimately to all within the Hellenic circle.

The people remained relatively independent until the sixteenth century AD. Their culture produced a group of thinkers (as well as outstanding artists) that were to change thought, for they sought above all to employ reason and rationality. That is not to say that their pursuit was necessarily cumulative, for they pursued different topics; nonetheless, they were all connected by attempts to raise thinking above the typical irrationalism that pervades vulgar thought (Barnes, 1989, p. 4).

From the Ionian town of Miletus, Thales (624–546 BC) was considered by Aristotle to be the first scientifically minded thinker, for he predicted an eclipse and posited that everything was water (*Met*, 983b20–2) and that magnets had souls (*psychē*) for they attracted other objects. In proposing that everything is water, Thales asserted a reductionist theory that everything we perceive can be reduced to a single, underlying elemental nature. It was a rudimentary beginning, we may think, but one that separated thought (*logos*) from myth (*mythos*), a critical step in presenting a vision of what education could also be about: learning to think critically and deploying observational as well as reasoning skills. Mythical education, in contrast, demands uncritical acceptance and dogmatic exhortation – the world was created by Cronus because that is what I have been told, and who I am to question the mysteries? Thales also noted that a healthy body indicates a readily teachable mind: the idea no doubt captured a well-known or commonsensical view that the body and mind are intimately connected – we meet the same idea explicated in the Roman Juvenal in his *Satires* and repeated by John Locke in his *Some Thoughts Concerning Education*.

Like Aristotle later, Thales apparently was nationalistic, asserting that the Greeks were better than their barbaric neighbors (Herodotus,

1998, I.75): this was apparently a common trait for the culturally connected Ionic people's thinkers, who had been pushed into migration by the Dorians and whose existence on the west coast of modern day Turkey was precarious. Arguably, this is a common trait of any people who are threatened by neighboring powers to assert a cultural dichotomy, but in the case of the Greeks, the notion of a superior culture amid inferior cultures pervades not only political but also educational thinking from that time down to its intellectual descendants today. Western political thought has been predicated on the assumption of its greatness vis-à-vis the rest of the world and it has drawn heroic allegories from the Greeks, notably of their defeat of the Persians at Marathon (490 BC), Salamis (480 BC), and Plataea (479 BC).

With these meager insights into the past, we nonetheless have the beginnings of a scientific outlook – Aristotle considered him as such and modern studies thus far justify his claim (Barnes, 2000, p. 11ff). There are other philosophical precursors of course; indeed, it would seem strange for there not to be: Solon has been noted as a statesman who sought impartiality in some of his thinking; and Homer and Hesiod (c. 700 BC) continued to influence thinkers and Hellenic culture.

After Thales, Anaximander (610–546 BC), probably his student or even a colleague, certainly followed Thales' scientific bent: he wrote on a variety of subjects in his *Concerning Nature* with a breadth that we later find in Aristotle, drew possibly the first map of the world, asserted that the universe was infinite and that the earth was a cylinder suspended in the infinite, and gauged the size of the sun. Most importantly, in a description that was to become very familiar to philosophers and astronomers down to the seventeenth century, Anaximander described the world as surrounded by concentric spheres that represent the orbits of the stars, the moon, and the sun – Aristotle was to accept this basic mechanistic vision. He did not, however, accept Anaximander's conjecture that life on earth was mutable: the animals that lived in the past would have been different, Anaximander conjectured, but it was the immutability of life asserted by Aristotle that was to retain a grip on thinking for the next two millennia.

Critically, Anaximander argued that the universe was characterized by understandable laws: this is known as the natural law thesis, which permeates human thought from thereon down to today. Directly and indirectly, such a thesis could only shift educational thinking away from traditional or atavistic patterns toward a more scientific conception and, indeed, the following centuries were to bear this out: philosophers gradually turned their attention to the laws of society and of people and hence to programs of education designed to support both the formation of the just or good society and the application of education to academic and social topics. It can be retorted that educational programs would tend to produce curricula befitting the relevant social norms, which is no doubt a defensible thesis, but it is another theory that education should be rationally concocted, and this is the thesis that begins to germinate in the Ionian thinkers' writings – here we detect its implicit beginnings in Anaximander's assertion that the world is knowable.

A colleague of Thales and Anaximander was Anaximenes (fl. 546 BC), who followed his older colleagues in seeking a fundamental material to the universe, which he believed to be *aer* or mist. As Barnes points out, this can be seen as considering the chemical nature of the universe (Barnes, 2000, p. 44), which again underlines the scientific direction philosophy was beginning to take and implicatively the contemporaneous educational remit to think about the nature of the universe, albeit in a reductive manner but one certainly and increasingly removed from *mythos*.

Heraclitus, who died around 475 BC, was one of the most enigmatic of the early thinkers, a character by all accounts, who gave up family wealth and prestige to pursue his thought; apparently, he was enamored with oppositional relations: from hot and cold comes warmth, a thesis which Hegel was to extol in the early nineteenth century. Heraclitus grew up in the Ionian town of Ephesus, yet despite the buzz of this trading town, he was a strange, unsociable, morose, anchorite who sought to distance himself from the world and its affairs, moaning and weeping when others were enjoying themselves. In later life he went the way of pure cantankerousness and tried to live as the beasts do by eating grass in the mountains. This made him ill, so he tried living on a dung heap to soak up its moistures and warmth (after all, 'it is a pleasure for souls to become moist' he had declared).

But that proved medicinally ineffectual and, unsurprisingly, he died not long after aged 65.

Foremost, Heraclitus was interested in science and he approached the subject with respect: 'Let us not make aimless conjecture about the most important things,' he stipulated (quoted in Barnes, 1987, p. 112). A very recommendable start indeed for a philosopher and one that resounds in Aristotle's thinking. Heraclitus observed that 'the things that can be seen, heard, and learned are what I prize the most' (quoted in Barnes, 1987, p. 103), thus emphasizing the importance of the physical world and the senses in learning about it, a strand we read in Aristotle. The entire world is in a constant flux ('you cannot step twice into the same rivers'; 'the sun is new everyday') and because of this, the world changes through the clash of elements toward a unity. Heraclitus is considered the first philosopher to postulate the existence of change (or natural processes that do not terminate) as a philosophical hypothesis, *panta rhei*: all things are in flux. The intellectual breakthrough for scientific thinking should not be underestimated. The unity to which all is subject, the 'one' is reason or *logos*. Don't listen to me as Heraclitus, he intoned, but to the arguments I give, which is a nod to what we now call the ad hominem fallacy: 'It is wise to hearken, not to me, but to my Word, and to confess that all things are one ... Wisdom is one thing. It is to know the thought by which all things are steered through all things' (Graham, 2006; Barnes, 1987, p. 102).

Initially, the Ionians took tentative and speculative steps, based on observing the flows in the world, with commentators differing on the extent to which these early philosophers remained embedded in religious thinking; nevertheless, the Ionians, living in a precarious political hinterland, were impressed by change and sought to explain it (which became a significant part of Aristotle's thinking). More importantly, they conceived of an all-encompassing law to which life and nature were subject – some seeing it as a material unity and others as an abstract unity that could explain the laws of the universe in which anarchy, the Ionians were wont to note (physical or social), could not exist.

Across the Mediterranean, a new school of thought was emerging that would impact upon Aristotle through its influence on Plato. The famous Pythagoras (sixth century BC) founded a school of mathematics in Croton in southern Italy. It possessed the characteristics of a sect; students had to agree to some stringent and strange terms such as not eating beans or divulging mathematical secrets to outsiders. One hapless student, who worked out that $\sqrt{2}$ is irrational, was allegedly put to death. Pythagoras had worked out a proof of what is now known as Pythagoras' theorem ($a^2=b^2+c^2$) relating to right-angled triangles, which in itself was a critical step in both mathematical thinking and logic: no matter the size of the triangle, the proof explained that the theorem held true – the mathematician therefore did not have to measure and prove observationally the theorem each time a new orthogonal triangle was encountered. That a valid argument could be produced to describe a set of relations, in this case mathematical, fired Plato's mind and in turn Aristotle's. It was a revolutionary development in intellectual history. Deductive reasoning could thus provide a way to understand truths, and while Aristotle was not a mathematician, the appeal of deductive reasoning is patent in his exploration of the principles of logic. Pythagoras also explored the role of mathematics as applied to music and described how the basic differences in pitch that our voices tend toward and which do not jar the ears as it were – thirds, fourths, fifths, and octaves – were simple fractions. This led him to assert that the nature of the universe is fundamentally numerical: everything can be reduced to number, and this helps to clarify the religious explication of his teachings. We still encounter examples of Pythagorean number mysticism today: certain numbers are held 'lucky' or 'unlucky' and present-day intellectual descendants 'discover' meanings in dates and other numbers (cf. Nostradamus, Kabbalism, and even Galileo and Descartes, who held that the book of nature is written in the language of mathematics); indeed, modern physics in many respects still unravels the implications of Pythagoras' teachings. His followers split between those who furthered the mystical elements of his thinking and those who furthered the scientific elements, the 'mathematicians.'

The Ionians dismissed Pythagorean mysticism while tackling the philosophy's cosmology; Parmenides (b. 510 BC) rejected Pythagorean thought that space and geometry are mutually binding and presented what is held as the first non-mythic metaphysical vision of philosophy that all is One; in his poem, *The Way of Truth*, Parmenides discussed the nature of being, which became an important part of Platonic and hence Aristotelian thinking. He rejected plurality, time, and motion and was seemingly delighted in securing conclusions that none could accept yet the logic remained secure; similarly Zeno of Elea (b. 490 BC), Parmenides' pupil, presented paradoxes (such as Achilles and the Tortoise) that still attract our attention, both for the internal twist on logic and for their modern day solutions.

Anaxagoras (500–428 BC) worked in Athens. Like Socrates and Aristotle, he was charged with impiety, a useful ploy to rid the town of an awkward or influential thinker whose political thoughts may have made him suspicious to those of different leanings. He rejected the monism of his older contemporary Parmenides and believed that matter is infinitely divisible, a thesis that Aristotle rejected, declaring the mind to be corporeal, whereas to Plato mind becomes distinguishable from body. Anaxagoras also taught the great Athenian statesman Pericles, along with Damon and Pythocleides, famous musicians who taught Pericles the importance of music ethically and politically. He is said to have taught Pericles bearing, dignity, and a capable rhetoric that gave him the reputation of speaking like thunder and lightning, values passed down from the early Hellenic period and which never disappear – in Aristotle, we find a similar ethic in training the youth to be virtuous and accomplished.

Among the Thracians was Protagoras of Abdera (485–420 BC), continuing the scientific revolution of the Ionians with his assertion that 'man is the measure of all things.' This remains a powerful reminder of the limits and anthropomorphism of human thinking: all science is effectively human based, and this presents intimate issues and problems for both observation and reason, implying that knowledge, all knowledge to extreme skeptics, is relative and stands on shaky grounds. He also wondered whether virtue could be taught and the thought became an integral element of Plato's dialogues (*Prot*, *Thea*), and thereby of Aristotle's thinking on virtue.

Democritus, a younger colleague and townsman of Protagoras, expounded the notion that tends to sit well with modern ears that all matter is atomic: it is finitely divisible into the uncuttable (which is what the Greek *atomos* means). He and his older friend Leucippus are renowned as the first atomists, but we must recall that as Ancient thinkers, their description is pure conjecture; no experimentation could back up their thesis, which was merely one conjecture competing among many, and later attracting Aristotle's critical attention. Democritus presented a naturalist theory of ethics, removed from supernatural justifications as to why we should pursue the good.

All these thinkers' ideas were percolating across the Hellenic intellectual world, which we can imagine as highly interconnected through trade, ideational discussions, and rumors. From the Ionian frontier, intellectual centers grew up in Greek colonies in southern Italy and then in Athens itself – at Plato's Academy.

Sophists

From the fifth century on, traveling intellectuals sold higher educational services to the Greeks; they converged on Athens as the center of philosophy and learning and gained the ire of Socrates and Plato as charlatans: philosophers, it was held by their critics, should not charge for their services as such, and the sophists' services were deemed to be superficial. Of the famous sophists were Gorgias, Protagoras, Hippias, Prodicis, and Thrasymachus.

Sophists were criticized by Socrates and Plato, but somewhat unfairly; we now call something sophisticated to imply complicated or of high (affected) quality. Then, the sophists were educators; they charged for their services, which riled aristocratically minded critics, who believed that any form of payment for a service demeans that service (preferring instead to live off the labor of slaves). Charges against the sophists are not quite fair: they taught rhetoric to the elite but also strove to delve deeper into issues such as the nature of conventions and status of women and foreigners (Blondell *et al.*, 1999, p. 14). The sophists supplied a service to meet the growing demand for higher education beyond the basics of reading, arithmetic, music, and gymnastics – they taught languages, rhetoric, mathematics, science, and geography, generally with an emphasis on producing politically capable young citizens. They became very popular and earned fortunes from their teaching of wisdom (hence 'sophist' – *sophia* = wisdom) and in doing so brought about and reflected an educational revolution in the Hellenic *poleis*, notably Athens. Their teachings were symptomatic of a cultural-intellectual shift away from the rote learning of traditional aristocratic or Homeric education of the archaic period toward an inquisitive, self-questioning, scientific, skeptical method, yet retaining that notion of supremacy drawn from the early legends.

The sophists also produced the first textbooks, hence at this time a book trade developed, copied out by slave scribes onto papyrus and later in the first century BC into a primitive but easier to handle book form: the codex (Howatson, 1989, p. 92). The proliferation of books gave formal education a boost and it was not long before collections were being formed, notably by Aristotle, whose Lyceum became a research library.

The sophists, who traveled from town to town, generally taught to consider different sides of an argument – this would have been part of a lawyer's or politician's training, for example, and salespeople in modern times have been taught to argue from different perspectives to encourage an ability to turn their minds to sell anything. Defending the weaker position was renowned sophistic exercise, which still entertains lawyers and philosophers today; indeed, the sophists trained some of Greece's greatest (most powerful) politicians. Fluency in speech was encouraged, and Gorgias boasted that he could answer any question on the spur of the moment. While this was construed by Plato as Gorgias believing that he was better than experts, it can also be understood as a mental exercise in fleshing out the logic and nuances of a topic. It was not long before Gorgias and other sophists were committing their teachings to writing, producing stock phrases for students to imitate and textbooks on eloquence (Burckhardt, 1999, pp. 266–7). Aristotle in his *Topics* echoes the sophist's ability to discuss: 'Our treatise proposes to find a line of inquiry whereby we shall be able to reason from reputable opinions about any subject presented to us' (*Top*, 100a), nor was he averse to considering how to play rhetoric, noting that one should use deductive reasoning against dialecticians (from the Academy) but induction against the crowd, and other tips on arguing (*Top*, 157a–164b).

Aristotle took issue primarily with their arguments, although the well-patronized philosopher could not help swinging at their profession: 'the art of the sophist is the semblance of wisdom without the reality, and the sophist is one who makes money from an apparent but unreal wisdom' (*Soph*, 165a). Their logic failed, they produced fallacies, and paraded conclusions unconnected to logical precision: their aim was the 'appearance of wisdom without the reality' (*Soph*, 171a). The sophists necessarily deal with philosophical issues, Aristotle remarked, but only deal with the appearances of philosophical thought (*Met*, 1004b).

Socrates – Plato's mentor – had also chastised the sophists for not knowing properly, that is philosophically or logically speaking. Their knowledge, Socrates insisted (as we read of his conversations through his pupils Plato and Xenophon), was shallow and inconsistent and the fact that they charged for their services he seems to have thought was immoral. While Socrates did not deploy logic in the sense that Aristotle was to later, he nonetheless used a basic form of argument – dialectic – to dissolve his opponents' arguments into contradictions or into baseless presumptions. Eventually, he annoyed a sufficient number of people to be prosecuted for 'introducing new gods' and for 'impiety,' both of which were hardly tenable claims but were commonly used to help remove nuisances from Athens through ostracizing them. However, as Gandhi was to say many centuries later, perhaps in imitation of Socrates, he accepted the literal meaning of the law of his *polis*, in this case that he should be put to death rather than outlawed; that is, he chose the death sentence of drinking hemlock. Partly this was in acceptance of the rule of law but also because he did not believe that this world was all that important relative to the other world – the Elysium of his philosophizing, as far as we can reach his thinking through Plato.

Plato

Plato had been taught by Socrates and proposed in his *Republic* and *Laws* a rationalist vision of education and politics; indeed, the purpose of education was to ensure a rationally ordered political society, one run by philosophers according to reasoned-out principles. Platonic education embraced the function and purpose of citizenship: citizens were to be brought up like Spartans – removed from their mothers early on, brought up in single-sex camps, trained (or indoctrinated if you will) to serve the state, and, as each individual's talents emerged, separated accordingly into three broad classes of people: the producers, the police, and the philosopher-kings. Of course, there is much more subtlety to Plato's thinking on education concerning the nature and development of pedagogy and children as well as its breadth and other purposes (cf. Barrow volume on *Plato*). Yet the rationalist vision of educating citizens to reason often precludes competing models of thought – the youth are to be taught to follow in their leaders' footsteps to ensure continuity, and what a rational education implies is often much narrower than what reason can unfurl in the human world politically, culturally, economically, and legally. Since Plato's *Republic* many writers have produced visions of what they think the perfect, reasoned-out world should be like; this is tantamount to the influence of the early Academicians' optimism and Plato's political blueprint, yet such visions tend to collapse into an individual's own rationalizations and peculiar visions of how people should behave and act – they also tend to demand a high degree of hierarchical control in which rational leaders engineer their society according to these visions (cf. More, *Utopia*, etc.). In other words, one person's idealized 'rational polity' is not another's, which, logically speaking, is not what we would expect if all thinkers adhered to the principles of reason as universal principles. Whereas logically we can accept that if A>B>C then A>C, validity is not so forthcoming with political (and hence educational) programs. Each rationalist philosopher presents a series of premises upon which a political edifice is logically deduced – all aspects and functions of society are to be outlined, often in seemingly relative minutiae. If a premise (such as the description of human nature or the ends to which a society should be organized) is changed, then the conclusions concerning how that society is formed will also change. Hence, a different philosopher, preferring a different stance, will offer an alternative program – and so debate begins.

Plato's optimism attracted political attention: if philosophy could offer so much hope for humanity, if it could offer the way to resolve political disputes both within polities and internationally, then philosophers should become the new leaders, or at least the advisers to the politicians. And herein lies another problem, for the actuality of politics – which essentially concerns power – divides in a multiplicity of ways that individual thinkers often cannot surmise: the existence of factions reduces the justification of universal philosophy and the individual philosopher is likely to fall prey to such interests. In response, rationalist philosophers would thus prefer to remove factions and competing power blocs (a requirement that Thomas Hobbes was to insist upon in his own version of the ideal state), which naturally means that the philosopher is thus subject to criticisms of favoring one party over another. So, while Plato's philosophy sought to further the impartial analysis of problems through reason, when philosophy sought involvement in political affairs the results were not as fruitful or as intellectually clean as the philosophers wished. Power tends to attract those who are willing to use it; the Greeks were fully conversant with the role of ambition and the interplay of political interests as a reading of Thucydides will

Plato's Academy

Athens, the 'veritable hall of wisdom' as Plato termed it (*Prot*, 337d), itself was, although predominantly Ionian, an amalgamation of the Hellenic cultures; its history brilliant yet checkered, forthright yet compromised; freedom of speech was encouraged (unless it invoked impiety), innovation permitted, and literature flourished. From such a military, cultural, artistic, and intellectual cauldron, a heady realist education was to be learned for those who were to survive, elements of which did not go amiss with Aristotle, who was later to ably expound on political machinations.

Philosophically, the Athenian world was in ascendancy, a trend that would have not gone unnoticed in Macedonian circles. It was an incredibly fertile time for intellectual pursuit: victory against the Persian Empire had also encouraged Greeks to consider themselves culturally superior to their neighbors and even to dream of taking on the Persian Empire in the name of true civilization. Athenian culture was particularly de rigueur, and the Macedonian court had attracted Euripides the playwright and other artistic luminaries; Greek rhetoricians were employed by the Macedonians, perhaps seeking to give themselves an aura of civility in contrast to their growing bellicosity and designs for the rest of Greece and Persia.

In this context, Aristotle's birthplace, the Ionian outpost of Stageira, probably felt itself to be socially and culturally superior in the minds of its Ionian inhabitants relative to the barbaric Thracians, who lived in open villages in the barren hinterland, and perhaps relative to the growing Macedonian power too. But Stageira's strategic position was of paramount importance to both the Athenians and the Macedonians. It was effectively a frontier town, and thus in an easier position to revolt from Athens, which it did in the eighth year of the Peloponnesian War; the famous Athenian general Cleon failed to retake the town, and the peace of Nicias recognized its independence (although it had to continue paying an old tribute to Athens [Thucydides, 1998, IV.88; V.6.8]). Perhaps because of Stageira's relative vulnerability, Aristotle's father sought work in Macedonia – a propitious move for his family, for it tied the future career of his young son to the ascendant power of the age, giving him, serendipitously, somewhat precarious but certainly obvious benefits and access to critical patronage. Nicomachus died without knowing what his son grew up to become, and his guardian, Proxenus, after ensuring Aristotle was educated in the aesclepiad tradition *and* Greek poetry and rhetoric, sent him to the Academy in Athens.

He could have raised Aristotle to pursue the medical traditions of his family or sent him to learn under the Athenian Isocrates (436–338 BC), who had another school. Isocrates, a contemporary of Socrates, was a rhetorician who, after his family lost its wealth in the Peloponnesian War, set up a popular school to educate citizens in the art of rhetoric, not just for its own sake but as a means for understanding. Politically, although critics complain that he would argue for any cause, Isocrates was certainly a pan-Hellenist, and it would have made sense to send a competent youth such as Aristotle to a school devoted to unifying the Greeks. Indeed, Theopompus (c. 380 BC), one of his pupils and a contemporary of Aristotle, became a famous rhetorician and wrote Philip of Macedonia's history.

Isocrates was highly influential in his own right and apparently acknowledged so by Aristotle as 'the old man eloquent.' Isocrates recognized that he did not have the power in his voice to be a good rhetorician, so became a teacher of rhetoric, which then entered the educational mainstream (Freeman, 1999, p. 228). Isocrates' style impressed the Greeks and the Romans, although Plato held that his was empty of philosophy. As a member of the Academy, Aristotle followed suit and criticized Isocrates, which did not go down too well with the Isocrateans (Ross, 1977, p. 2). Although Isocrates could offer a curriculum of rhetoric and some excellent students and in turn had an influence on Aristotle's thought, Plato's Academy was, however, the rising intellectual center. The Academy was founded in 385 BC just prior to Aristotle's birth, and had run studies for almost two decades on philosophy, dialectic, mathematics, and the sciences. It sought to cultivate the examination of thought itself, a thoroughly philosophical enterprise, and its growing fame gave it an appealing quality to those interested in furthering education. Grayeff's thesis is worth considering at this point: 'One must appreciate what great enthusiasm, even euphoria, filled the Academy in its early period, and that, as is only natural with a new discovery, excessive hopes for the future were pinned on it' (Grayeff, 1974, p. 17). Indeed, Plato and his students believed that philosophy had the power to right the world, so long as people were educated in philosophy – or rather, those capable of becoming philosophers should take the reins of power.

Plato was absent when the young Aristotle arrived; he had been called upon to help resolve a political dispute in Syracuse. Perhaps his philosophical acumen had been heard of, but Plato's presumed optimism of effecting a philosophical revolution of politics was to be dashed. The Academy, given its position, was, in the eyes of critics in Syracuse, necessarily pro-Athenian in its inclinations or at least in its roots, so Plato was entering a dangerous game. He soon fell into political games and traps – his patron, Dionysius II of Syracuse, suffered a *coup d'état* and Plato was taken prisoner, which ironically acted to spread his fame across Greece. He was freed following intervention by a southern Italian statesman, Archytas. Other philosophers from the Academy were also active in political affairs, but such meddling acted to politicize the Academy, making it the target of political ambitions in turn – a warning that has rarely been heeded in the history of universities since.

Once ensconced in the Academy, Aristotle learned the traditional curriculum of mathematics, poetry, rhetoric, dialectic, and of course the philosophy of Plato. He was to remain in Athens for the first time for twenty years, and as he rose through the ranks, he penned propaganda pamphlets for the Academy and supported Athenian interests – immersed in the political games of the time, it is hardly surprising to find the philosopher taking up the pen in support of his patrons. He became a teacher and an author in his own right – Plato called him *nous* (reason or mind). In return, he wrote of Plato, 'he, alone or the first of mortals, showed clearly by his own life and by the courses of his arguments that a man becomes good and happy at the same time' (*Poet*, 2463). Initially, he seems to have echoed his master's voice: in the lost *Eudemus* dialogue, he explored Plato's conception of the soul as a Form (F46R) and that it is better to be dead than alive – a highly Platonic–Socratic viewpoint (F44R); in the lost *Protrepticus*, he considers the soul's union with the body as a punishment for an evil committed in an earlier life (B107). Yet in Plato's *Parmenides* dialogue, we find an Aristotle replying to Parmenides' expansion of the logic of being (137c) and in various fragments from his days at the Academy, we sense an interest in the philosophy of the good life.

Since Jaeger's work in the 1920s (Randall, 1960, p. 11) commentators have noted that Aristotle began to distance himself from Plato's thought, rejecting eventually the existence of a higher realm of Ideas or Forms, from which every particular entity that we perceive is supposed to be drawn. Observation, he later argued, was more important than dialectic deduction, yet throughout his works, the Platonic vision is always present, always close – he may have rejected Plato's metaphysics of an ulterior realm of Ideas, but the possibility of perfection remained real.

Plato's death

In 348/347 BC, Plato died and his nephew Speusippus took over the Academy, continuing Plato's ideal of furthering ethics, dialectics, and physics. Although it is thought that Aristotle would have been upset at not getting the post, commentators also point out that it is likely that as a foreigner (*metic*) in Athens, Aristotle would not have been eligible to take over the post. So he went traveling. It's worth noting that anti-Macedonian feeling may have also prompted the philosopher's travels – Philip had sacked the Greek city of Olynthus in 348 BC, which caused consternation in Athens, a city that had been roused to be suspicious by Demosthenes' famous speeches against Macedonian aggrandizement.

In this tumultuous atmosphere (347 BC), our intrepid philosopher was invited by Hermias to Assos in northwestern Asia Minor to set up a small school to assist the spread of Greek ideas, something, apparently, Philip also wanted to do via Macedonian power. Assos, an Aegean coastal town on what is now the Turkish coast, was of great strategic interest for Philip and his ambitions to invade Persia. Assos was ruled by upper-class Ionians, Aristotle's people. Hermias was a freed slave of the banker Eubulus, and had been a student of Plato and hence a colleague of Aristotle at the Academy until he inherited the town of Artaneus from his old master; Hermias extended his rule to Assos and attempted to be a Platonic philosopher-king. Aristotle's guardian, Proxenus, heralded from Artaneus, so the social circles through which Aristotle walked were highly connected indeed. He traveled to Assos with his Academy friend Xenocrates (396–314 BC), who was later to take over the Academy. Xenocrates was benevolent and industrious according to Laertius' sources – he acted as Philip's diplomat at times after Plato had taken him to Syracuse on his failed mission to advance politics by philosophical means.

So perhaps we can detect good evidence of some continuity between the Macedonian court and Aristotle's career: Hermias negotiated with Philip (Copleston, 1985, p. 267) and Aristotle was lavishly honored by Hermias for his work – he offered him the hand of his daughter (or niece), Pythias. From all accounts, Aristotle loved Pythias – they had a daughter together, also Pythias; on his wife's death, ten years later, he erected a shrine in her memory.

Aristotle's work on Assos was phenomenal: here he effectively founded biology as a science in its own right, and organized a research crew to gather in materials for his biological studies written up in extant texts; in effect, this was his first university. Assos already boasted a couple of Academy teachers – Erastus and Coriscus, both disciples of Plato, whom we can imagine Aristotle working with. Incidentally, Aristotle's writings corroborate well with the current fauna of the area as explored in modern times.

Unfortunately, the political winds changed again: Demosthenes in Athens let the Persians know of Philip's plans for Assos and Artaneus; the Persian king, Artaxerxes III (425–338 BC), sent a military force around 342 BC to besiege Artaneus. Hermias was eventually captured and executed after being tricked into a conference with the enemy. Aristotle had already left the island by then, probably in 345 BC, although some authors have it that he fled Assos with his family on a ship to Lesbos, where he later erected a statue and cenotaph to his late friend Hermias.

At Mytilene, the capital of Lesbos, Aristotle continued his interest in biology. The Macedonian court plied him with 800 talents for his research (although possibly also for new or previous diplomatic work) and it is here that the native Theophrastus (371–287 BC) joins his entourage: Theophrastus would in time become his intellectual heir; he had also studied under Plato, and later was the beneficiary of Aristotle's will, becoming a notable writer and philosopher in his own right.

During his year in Lesbos and against a backdrop of further political turmoil, Aristotle advanced his theory that all species exist for a purpose – this teleological principle (Aristotle's 'final cause' for which things are intended) influenced scientific thinking until the nineteenth century. His observations of the animal life of Lesbos and its inlets still stir biologists' hearts (Singer, 1959, p. 22); seemingly he had the energy and leisure to collect and observe without political interference or worries. That Aristotle was able to study biology between 347 and 343 BC and possibly continuing as late as 335 BC suggests also that his thinking on biology should hold a greater weight than his purely philosophical writings, as several Aristotelians began to argue in the early twentieth century (Burnet, 1903, p. 2; Randall, 1960, p. 224), and that perhaps we should see his ethical and political writings as emanating from the biological (which makes a good deal of sense) and his thinking on logic as complementing his scientific work. Berlin commented in passing that for Aristotle perhaps the path to truth was biology whereas for Plato it had been mathematics (Berlin, 2000, p. 6).

Meanwhile, Philip was subduing rebellions in Epirus and took Thrace (straddling modern Bulgaria, Greece, and Turkey) from the Persians for the first time in 343 BC, at which point he invited Aristotle back to the Macedonian court at Pella to teach his son Alexander.

Aristotle at the Macedonian court

Aristotle left Lesbos and returned now with his library and collections to Macedonia. He seems to have passed through his home town of Stageira on his way back. The town had been destroyed by Philip and Aristotle may have been encouraged by the citizens to intercede on their behalf at the court, for soon afterward, perhaps in recompense for tutoring Alexander or for his earlier diplomatic intercessions with Hermias, Philip commanded that the town be restored. Aristotle may have also spoken on behalf of the Athenians, for they are supposed to have inscribed publicly that he had served the people of Athens well, 'especially by intervening with King Philip for the purpose of promoting their interests' (Barnes, 2000, p. 11).

There may have been other overlapping political reasons for being invited back: Philip enjoyed playing the patron and cultivated Hellenic culture (while remaining at heart a Macedonian outsider), and Aristotle had written well-received tracts supporting the Academy, the *Edemus*, and *Protrepticus*, to give him sufficient credence with those who were already employed by the Macedonian court. Contrary to simple legend, Aristotle would not have been the only tutor at court – already there were Leonidas, his maternal uncle, and the orator Lysimachus from Acarnania (Grayeff, 1974, p. 32; Plutarch, 1878, p. 714). Philip had also enticed Anaximenes the rhetorician, who later accompanied Alexander; Theopompus the historian, who wrote Philip's history; Apelles, one of the greatest painters of Antiquity; and Lysippus, one of the greatest sculptors (Brunt, 1997, p. 295). Nonetheless, these characters can be viewed as Philip buying in culture for his court – it is quite common for martial minds to employ or patronize the arts for purposes of aggrandizement, and since Aristotle may have been acting as a diplomat for Philip, his choice as a tutor for

Alexander would thus appear more natural. Philip had Aristotle remove to Mieza (near modern day Nouasa) to teach Alexander, a move resonant with political undertones, perhaps gauged to appease possible court factions.

There has been much romance created around these two characters: one of the ablest minds of all times and one of the world's greatest military leaders. Common to many legends drawn from even Roman times, it has been thought that Aristotle educated Alexander in the path of higher thought as well as to be like an Achilles or Ajax, the archetypal Homeric warrior but also one immersed in philosophy and medicine (according to Plutarch, 1878, p. 716). Modern academics tend to reject the fanciful in favor of a more restrained understanding of the tutor–pupil relationship, with Laistner reasonably conjecturing that Aristotle would have taught the youth science, philosophy, and a love of Hellenic culture (Laistner, 1947, p. 292). Indubitably, Alexander was taught and enjoyed the Greek poets and rhetorical flourishes, but his unbridled lust for domination was far removed from the prudential political and ethical outlook of his master. Although a letter to Alexander by Aristotle is rejected as a later forgery, it is known that Aristotle kept up a correspondence with his former pupil – Aristotle wrote *On Monarchy* and *On Colonies* for Alexander (Ross, 1977, p. 4) – and that he gave him his copy of Homer, which Alexander apparently kept under his pillow (Kenny, 2004, p. 73).

It is of course difficult to assess the impact of any teacher on a student, but other differences are certainly apparent: against Aristotle's teachings that the Greeks should dominate the barbarian Persians and not marry into them, Alexander took a more cosmopolitan view of the lands he conquered, dismissing Aristotle's firm distinction between the civilized Hellenic world and the barbaric rest of the world. After all, Alexander traveled further afield; and to cement his cosmopolitan outlook, he took a Persian princess as his wife and forced his generals to do the same. On the other hand, Aristotle constantly warns against factions in his *Politics,* and it is not stretching imagination too much to consider Alexander as actually following his master's thinking in this regard. While encouraging the Hellenization of the East, Alexander also took up some aspects of its culture, namely the obeisance of others in his presence and the expectation that they prostrate themselves, an exaggeration of his authoritarianism that created dissent and eventually mutiny on the campaign east.

Whatever Alexander learned from this famous meeting of minds, it only lasted for three years, before Aristotle retired to his home town in 339 BC. Philip had begun to lose interest in the Academy and Aristotle, favoring the rhetoricians over the philosophers, particularly Theopompus, who opposed both Plato and Aristotle.

Philosophically, though, it was a fruitful time for Aristotle: while he apparently did not engage in the biological researches that he had enjoyed in Assos and Lesbos, readers have suggested that while never shedding his master's concepts fully, it was during this sojourn that he began to shift away from Plato's philosophy.

In 340/339 BC Speusippus died and the headship of the Academy passed to Xenocrates (396–314 BC) – this time foreign status was no bar, for Xenocrates hailed from the Chalcedonian province of Bithynia; however, his pro-Athenian political credentials were sufficient. He turned out to be a good administrator for the Academy and was also active in Macedonian–Athenian diplomacy. Yet in his criticism of Xenocrates' philosophy, we perhaps detect the subtle shift away from Plato's theories in Aristotle's maturing mind that modern commentators note: he is 44 and the biologist was just beginning to find his philosophical strength.

The following year saw the beginning of Macedonian hegemony over the Hellenic peoples. In 339 BC Demosthenes (384–322 BC), a contemporary of both Aristotle and Plato, rallied the citizens of Athens and its allies to fight the Macedonians and their growing influence and power, but at the decisive and bloody battle of Chaeronea (338 BC), Philip utilized what he had learned while being held as a captive as a youth by the Theban Epaminondas to defeat a powerful Hellenic alliance of Athenians and Thebans. It was at this battle that Aristotle's former pupil, Alexander, made his first mark in military history in commanding one of the cavalry ranks. According to the Roman Plutarch's sources, Alexander allegedly led the charge that led to the destruction of the famed Theban Sacred Band. But victory was not followed by punitive policies against the Theban confederation that had faced Philip: he offered peace on the condition that the Greeks provide him with an army to invade Persia – which they readily agreed to. Philip spared Athens from having a Macedonian garrison, for he reasoned that the lessons of history required Athens to be a cooperative member of any pan-Hellenic alliance in order for a hegemonic power to control Persian sea forces in the Aegean. Nonetheless, although Demosthenes lost power in favor of the pan-Hellenist Damades, the Athenians were uncomfortable with Macedonian supremacy and, consequently, Aristotle's standing in the city fluctuated.

After repressing the Thebans, Philip confederated the Greek city states and became its chairman, but wisely left Athens unmolested in order to better secure its allegiance; some have conjectured that in these matters he may have relied on Aristotle's advice, which may or may not be true, for we must not forget that Aristotle had been away from Athens for several years by now and Philip's interest in his old friend had been waning. This was emphasized in the allegiances that were now forming around the Macedonian court: Alexander and his mother formed an opposing faction to Philip, which Aristotle supported. Situated politically in Alexander's faction would have been a vulnerable situation: on the one side was Philip, now master of Greece, and on the other Athens, which, while relieved that Philip had not punished them as he had the Thebans, would not have been unsuspicious of Macedonian-employed philosophers in their city. However, three years later in 336 BC, Philip was assassinated. He had divorced Olympias in favor of a Macedonian noblewoman who, he hoped, would give him another heir. Olympias' home province rebelled against Philip but murder came from another root, albeit not wholly unconnected.

Only Aristotle has left any reasons for the assassination – Philip was killed by his bodyguard Pausanias because the latter had been offended by Philip's father-in-law Attalus (*Pol*, 1311a). Details between the lines were fleshed out by later writers: Philip and Pausanias had been lovers, but Pausanias had been jilted for another young man, Attalus' nephew; the latter was killed in battle in a fit of romantic pique saving his king, and Attalus had Pausanias gang-raped in a strange twist of revenge, hence Pausanias' motive to kill Philip. He may have been encouraged to do so by interested Persians, though. It's a wonder Shakespeare did not work on this plot!

Alexander quelled Macedonian rebellions and secured the throne – Aristotle was on the right side of politics. Alexander offered a non-interventionist policy toward the Academy and in 335/334 BC, aged 50, Aristotle returned to Athens with Theophrastus. According to some sources, he wore very refined clothing and dined like a prince waited on by slaves. The chancellor of Athens, Lycurgus, secured land northeast of the city for Aristotle, who, as a foreigner, could not purchase land directly; here, Aristotle opened up a new university by leasing the Lyceum and its Walk – the Peripatos. Aristotle's students and followers through many centuries were termed peripatetics, and even today it is a term used in English schools to designate a visiting teacher. The new university flourished and its teachers migrated around the Hellenic world, which expanded enormously thanks to Alexander's exploits.

The Lyceum

Under his directorship, the Lyceum's curriculum was broad: whereas the Academy was interested in mathematics and Isocrates in rhetoric for the court, the students at the Lyceum were charged with finding out about the world delving into a range of philosophical and scientific issues, covering biology, theology, metaphysics, botany, meteorology, ethics, astronomy, mathematics, and the history of philosophy. The university possessed a library and its fellows pursued their own research into scientific matters (Copleston, 1985, p. 268). While not dismissing Plato's philosophy completely, there was a palpable shift toward empiricism with contemplation.

Aristotle did not pursue science using the methods of experimentation and replication that we use today, for they emerged much later in the sixteenth and seventeenth centuries, but he stressed the importance of observation over contemplation, which is the beginning of any scientific endeavor. Details were held to be more important than sweeping statements and contemplation was to be impartial; the unfolding method pointed to what became the strictures of scientific method, but politics unfortunately got in the way of what may have been an earlier arrival at the scientific revolution that characterizes the modern world. Timon criticized thus: 'Nor the sad chattering of the empty Aristotle. Such was the life of the philosopher' (Laertius, 1853, VIII).

According to Laertius, Aristotle preferred to do much of his teaching walking up and down the Peripatos, the colonnade, discussing philosophy, but when numbers grew, he encouraged them to take seats: 'It would be a shame for me to hold my peace, and for Isocrates [his competitor] to keep on talking' (quoted in Laertius, 1853, IV). He seems to have first taught his students philosophy or logic in the daytime and the general public in the evening, probably following his commitment to teaching and research, for he believed that the two went hand in hand.

He collected hundreds of manuscripts and his library formed the basis on which the libraries at Alexandria and Pergamon were founded; he also brought in maps and relics with which to explain his lectures. Students were elected on a rolling basis of ten days to lead discussions and to defend theses against opponents; a symposium was held monthly (Ross, 1977, p. 5).

In the late nineteenth century, a new Aristotelian document was found in Egypt: the *Constitution of Athens*, a major discovery that also indicates the breadth of his researches. Similarly, a more recent archaeological discovery at Delphi found that Aristotle and his grand-nephew, Callisthenes, researched a history of the Pythian games for which they were honored and crowned. In so doing, he would have had to sift through masses of historical documents and to impose some sort of chronology upon the scheme – although he did not make the leap to providing a standard time frame, his was a certain contribution in that direction (Barnes, 2000, p. 12).

Philosophically, this period was the most productive of his life; it also coincided with Alexander's defeat of the Persian Empire and his victories against far-flung tribes right up to the Indus river and the Afghan mountains, yet, interestingly, Alexander's campaigns do not make an impression on Aristotle's political thinking. Perhaps they had been written earlier or he was seeking to assert an impartiality in his writing: he looked at the sophists impartially and his pupils refrained from engaging in political activities, or perhaps he had learned from the dilemmas and frustrations that Plato had brought upon himself. Indeed, instead of philosophers becoming kings, Aristotle tempered the principle to kings employing philosophers as advisers. The Lyceum was beginning to have effects on politics and culture.

Athens did well under Macedonian suzerainty: trade flourished and many of its citizens left to colonize Alexander's conquered areas. The elite had their sons educated at the Lyceum, many of whom left to help rule the empire – a policy reflected in the training of diplomats in the public schools in the heyday of the British Empire in the late nineteenth and first half of the twentieth century. Aristotle kept in contact with Alexander and probably enjoyed close relations with his viceroy for Greece, Antipater, a friend from when he tutored the boy (Ross, 1977, p. 4). His grand-nephew Callisthenes followed Alexander's entourage east, but he fell foul of the king, criticizing him for his ways; he was thrown into prison and possibly executed.

Alexander's campaigns were highly successful from the military perspective, but the further east he went, the more his troops wanted to return home, and finally, to avoid a mutiny, Alexander agreed. He brought his army back to Persepolis in 323 BC. Not long after arriving there, Alexander died, possibly of a viral or parasitical infection picked up from his travels, although having been wounded a few times we cannot rule out a septicemia. Some have read political machinations into his death – he certainly had made enough enemies close to him to warrant a motive for poison. Moreover, news of his death altered the political situation right across his fragile and temporary empire: newly conquered lands were split between his generals while the more independently minded peoples sought revolution. Anti-Macedonian feelings resurfaced in Athens, and they rejected honors they had once plied Aristotle with, as did the Delphians; Demosthenes returned to popular applause, and it was not long before Aristotle, tutor to the late king and good friend of the Macedonian regent of Greece, Antipater, was charged with *asebeia* or sacrilege. Prudentially and to character, Aristotle made his exit again, not wishing, as he put it, to let the Athenians make the mistake of sinning against philosophy a second time. He retired to his mother's estates at Chalcis with his mistress Herpyllis and their child Nicomachus, where he died a year later at the age of 62 or 63 of a chronic stomach ailment and perhaps after drinking a draft of aconite (Laertius, 1853, VII). His will testifies as to his character and generosity as an Ionian of high status.

Part 2

Critical Exposition of Aristotle's Work

Chapter 3

Fundamentals of Philosophy

Introduction

> Learning is the greatest of all pleasures
>
> (*Poet*, 1448b13)

Aristotle's theory of education is explicated in his political and ethical works, but it is also embedded in his thoughts on biology, politics, and ethics as well as his grander philosophical visions of metaphysics and epistemology and the overarching teleological thesis that practically everything that exists does so for a purpose. In other words, his thoughts on education are broad as well as deep, entwined with analyses of the mind, the body, psychology, and the nature of reality, and because of that we can only approach his educational thinking with an eye to his other expositions. However, we must bear in mind that the driving thrust of Aristotle's educational thinking is to deal with the maturing adult mind, not the mind of the child. He is concerned with forming wise citizens, though, so in his political writings we learn of his plans for youth (male, high class) as they are expected to become political men, which somewhat mimics Plato's utopian writings; however, his words on children do not yield the intricate analysis that he affords the mature mind, which in many respects is a shame for Aristotle was perspicuous and possessed a sharp eye for detail.

In Part 1, we reviewed the general cultural and historical milieu into which Aristotle's life and thought fell; in this Part we shall initially review the philosophical threads leading into Aristotle's thinking on education. We begin with an overview of Aristotle's theory of the world, for there is much in his metaphysics, physics, and epistemology that have direct relevance for his thoughts on education as well as having an enormous impact on following thinkers. We move through his theory of teleology and causation before looking at what he had to say about experience and the mind; from there we are in a better position to understand Aristotle's theory of action and hence of morality and politics and the highest pursuit we are capable of – the *eudaimonic* life. It must be noted, though, that energetic debate flourishes on all aspects of his descriptions and theories as critics try to elucidate what he meant, what his theories implied, whether he or they were consistent, as well as applying Aristotle's philosophy anew in the modern world.

Metaphysics

In many respects, we cannot better begin Aristotle's thoughts on education than with his opening comments to the *Metaphysics* and the wonderfully optimistic premise that 'all men desire to know' (*pantes anthropoi tou eidenai oregontai phusei*) (*Met*, 979b22). Here in a nutshell is the natural law doctrine that he expanded (usually quite consistently) through his works on practical education (*phronēsis*) and which will permeate philosophy down to the present: man is a curious animal, whose very nature – indeed basal appetite – predisposes him to want to know. But more needs to be unraveled at this point to garner the flavor of Aristotle's educational outlook. One would immediately imagine that he could have adjusted this to 'all children desire to know,' for we are accustomed to the persistent and unquenchable questions of infants, but in Aristotle's mind the child is an immature being, not ready for adult thought or control of emotions and desires; only adults and particularly men are capable of learning in the sense that Aristotle explains – of using their mind to its fullest. Then within the human collective some are better at learning and hence of attaining the highest that human nature has to offer better than others, whose lack of ability or poor habits scupper their achievements rendering them dependent on others (masters) or lashed to their lower emotional and appetitive drives. Children fall into this group – temporarily if they are bred and educated properly, for right breeding and education helps to bring out the potential latent in the best children – but we have to understand that such a process will be a long one.

Children, as implied in other writings, do not learn as such, for learning is a matter of using the mind (see 'Thinking' below); instead, Aristotle believes that they take on information and behavioral habits from their tutors, but do not comprehend that they are learning in the sense that an adult can by thinking about thought (asking questions such as what is thought composed of, how is it oriented to the extramental world, what is the imagination, etc.). They are too immersed in an irrational world of self-indulgent desires and powerful appetites, too close, that is, to the lower world of animals. No one, Aristotle opined, would want to live with the intellect of a child for the rest of his life (*NE*, 1119a35–b14; 1174a1), for that would be to live as an undeveloped person, which for Aristotle would be a very unnatural regression or a cessation of the natural flow of things to find their higher functions. For a human the highest function is to know and to understand – a pleasurable activity in itself for it exerts our highest available faculty – the mind (*nous*).

The second significant and relevant premise to his metaphysical philosophy is that the world is – for the most part – knowable. Understanding first principles of philosophy is the subject of the *Metaphysics* and the *Categories*, whose aim is to explore the nature of wisdom and hence of our knowledge through exploring the nature of the world. To Aristotle, we do not reside in a chaotic universe in which our mind is incapable of grasping relations between things and causes or of defining the things we encounter; besides, no understanding through demonstration can come from chance things (*APst*, 87b19): our mind can learn about the world for it is replete with principles of nature and necessary connections that we can deduce. The mind is able to divide what is knowable into ten categories or predicates of knowledge: substance (man), quantity (5ft 7), quality (pale), relation (single), place (in the library), date (yesterday), posture (sitting), possession (clothed), action (reading), passivity (is annoyed by the fly). The 'ten categories' become highly influential, sparking debate down to the present; the great metaphysician Kant remarked that 'this rhapsody must be considered (and commended) as a mere hint for future inquirers, not as a regularly worked out idea, and hence it has, in the present more advanced state of philosophy, been rejected as quite useless' (Kant, 1977, §323), but that did not stop the quarreling about what actually enables us to understand the world and how we proceed in forming categories or abstracts of what we perceive.

Aristotle admits that perhaps the ultimate reason for the universe or the ultimate substratum upon which everything exists is beyond our mind's ability to comprehend (and so it remains today), but the rest is knowable. For an educator, that is an important original premise – often assumed in teaching, no doubt – that what is to be taught can be taught because the content is knowable and hence teachable. Education would surely otherwise be a ridiculous task, yet even if we agree with Aristotle's premise, we may not agree with the means or the extent to which our mind can know the world well – in effect that becomes the argument among philosophers of metaphysics and epistemology after Aristotle.

Since the *Metaphysics* deals with the initial principles of human thought and of the reality of the world, it thereby deals indirectly with education as the opening salvo on man's innate curiosity indicates: all men desire to know and since our knowledge comes primarily from the senses so we delight in the use of the senses. They then provide us with memories and with experience; from experience we gain skills that rise to the level of craftsmanship or art, and when we turn our attention to the nature of learning, skills, entities, and purposes, we deal with science or philosophy – the realm of wisdom (*Met*, Book I [A]).

Learning and the philosophy of change

For Aristotle, learning effects a change from something that possesses a potential to become something else and from a something that possesses the capacity to impart that potential, from the teacher who knows to the student who does not know. There is also an element in the description that does not change: the boy was ignorant, now the boy is learned. Therein lies an awful logical and metaphysical thicket, which we shall skirt around rather than getting stuck on the briars and brambles that have fired Aristotelian disputes. The problem invokes the theory of causation, which must be intricately related to a philosopher's metaphysics: if the world is unknowable, then whatever causal factors generate the apparent changes that we observe must be hidden from view and there would be no use in searching for them; if it is knowable, then change must be similarly understandable.

Why things happen, as Aristotle explained, relates either to chance or to causes; that is, things happen of their own accord without prior causal factors being involved, or that event E has happened is due to cause C, or because of a single or plurality of causes. But his theory of causation is broader than our present orthodoxy. Aristotle posited four kinds of causes (*aitia*, from which we get etiology): material cause – that from which a thing is made, for example a statue from a bronze block; formal cause – that blueprint from which a design for the statue is made; efficient cause – the agent bringing about the change; final cause – that for the sake of which the change is brought about (*Phys*, II.3). Aristotle's four causes underpinned scientific and logical analysis for over two millennia and they still retain an intellectual attractiveness for critics.

Evidently, chance events and spontaneous events do happen (*Phys*, 196a12): some animals, Aristotle believed, are generated spontaneously, such as some plants or testacea – shelled invertebrates (*GA*, 759a6; *HA*, 539a23; 547b18). He noted, however, that some spontaneous generation of animals comes from decaying earth matter and whose generation is seasonally dependent (*GA*, 715b26; 743a34), which implies a division between those things that are generated obviously by themselves, by a mother and father, or by the matter of the earth. And we should note that spontaneous generation has not disappeared from scientific thinking, for those who are keen to explain the whence of life seemingly face two possibilities: life emerged out of the primordial soup of the early earth (analogous to Aristotle's decaying matter) or it came from outer space on a meteorite, which implies that it was generated somewhere else, possibly spontaneously or with the birth of the universe. Science, despite some insights into the spontaneous formation of amino acids, has yet to offer a cogent explanation of life's generation (cf. Aristotle's own musings, *GA*, 762b29–763a3).

Given that chance and spontaneous events are observed, Aristotle sought to explain their logic. In education we should be intrigued by how learning occurs – we may sometimes say I learned of X accidentally (by chance), but to say I learned it spontaneously does not seem as cogent; of course, Aristotle's curiosity is broader for he may be said, in many respects, to be laying out the foundation stones of philosophy. Events, he writes, may be due to necessity – they either always or often occur given a set of causal circumstances (*Phys*, 196b10), not far removed from modern science, which elaborates in terms of statements of necessity or of probability. But, Aristotle noted, some things also happen by chance or spontaneously. Things that happen by chance he defines as being the result of unexpected *human* interaction: 'I was not expecting a brief encounter on the bridge or to cut my finger while slicing avocado.' Such instances are nevertheless explicable as a concatenation of actions that can in turn be examined and noted, although some such events become increasingly trivial or background conditions. Chance results, he defines, are thus accidental to what was intended but emanate from within myself (*Phys*, 197a6–9; 197b36): 'I wanted to cross the bridge to go to the museum on the other side as I had heard of a new exhibition of Greek artifacts; I was hungry and wanted to satisfy my appetite, not cut my finger.'

A favorite phrase of Aristotle in this context is doing something 'for the sake of which'; that is, there is a purpose or goal intended in action (and as we shall see in 'Teleology' for nature as well). In the case of chance events, the purpose was something other than what was intended. Educationally, while we explain a subject to a pupil, her interest may be sparked by something completely incidental to the main goal and we would describe her new interest as arising accidentally: 'I became interested in Aristotle's *Poetics* after hearing the lecturer mention the work in passing in my Shakespeare class; now I'm planning to do an MA in Ancient Literature.' The outcome of chance can either be fortuitous (a pleasant friendship develops from the chance encounter on the bridge) or evil (slicing one's skin from cutting an avocado), but such events are distinguishable from spontaneous events in which there is no human involvement (*Phys*, 197a25).

Spontaneous events thus involve inanimate objects or non-human animals; he gives the example of a horse trotting over and though that saved him, it was not for the purpose of saving himself that he trotted over. Or another example: the tripod fell by itself (*Phys*, 197b14–18). Such things are spontaneous for they are not the product of thought, thus one cannot be said to learn spontaneously. But Aristotle baulks at renouncing the possibility of some cause and returns to the thesis that every event has a cause. This cause he terms 'from spontaneity' (*Phys*, 197b20); they become events of 'chance' when they affect people, who are capable of choosing what to do in the circumstances such as when I do something 'in vain' and the result intended is not forthcoming, but purely spontaneous events involve an inanimate or non-human animal doing something, such as a tile falling from a roof and killing a man – it was not the intention of the tile to kill the man (*Phys*, 197b30), i.e. not causeless but perhaps presently inexplicable or unexpected. Things that happen which are contrary to nature are also termed spontaneous, and their causal nexus is external to the objects rather than internal to them in contrast to people's actions which emanate from thought, in other words that I cause the book to be read is because of the purpose I have in wanting to read the book, which in turn may resolve into a higher value of seeking to expand knowledge. Thought permits a new matrix of causality.

Aristotle submitted that what is meant by change is to ask what indeed can change in an entity. These he called a thing's substance, its quality, its quantity, or its location. We expect to change when learning something new, but what is going on with us – is it evident or observable in any meaningful manner, or is too subtle for even ourselves to indicate? While going on a weight-losing diet presents a highly observable set of behavior guided by explicit purposes, going on a course to learn of Alexander's exploits in Persia, apart from the time spent listening, has less publicly obvious implications.

A substantial change can mean either coming into being as in generation – the birth of a child, for instance, or going out of being – as the death of a person, or the drawing of a picture and its being ripped up. In other words, the physicality of the object or person undergoes an observable alteration in that before it did not exist and now it does but tomorrow it may cease to exist. A qualitative change involves remaining the same substance but undergoing a descriptive change, such as a boy tanning in the sun. A quantitative change implies an alteration in size, such as a plant growing more leaves or a boy's physical maturation. A change with respect to location simply occurs when there is movement from one place to another.

Summarizing, he relates that spontaneous and chance events are the product of unintended causes, although still effected by causes either intelligent or natural, but because the effects are unintended or accidental, they cannot be held to be contributory to final causes: unlike when I study Greek for the purpose of learning Greek, I do not slice my finger in order to eat avocado. Thus the spontaneous and chance happenings follow intelligence and nature rather than are prior to them (*Phys*, 198a5–12).

The theory of causation quickly becomes complicated for it impinges upon a variety of philosophical concerns such as the nature of reality, time, mental actions, and events, and upon how we know things are happening or not. To sustain the connection with education, consider the process of teaching: in a standard example of imparting information (the conjugation of the French verb *être*, for example), what is the process involved? Mere exposure to the information can invoke sufficient interest or it can produce a memorization of the forms; usually, the teacher insists that the information is rehearsed perhaps formally and in applied examples to help the pupil learn. Implicitly or explicitly, we can refer to the need or desire to gain competency in French or a wider, more liberal goal of gaining an understanding of how other languages work so as to enjoy or appreciate better one's own language. In the process, we can check whether learning is taking place ('How do you say "she is" in French?'), and do so periodically until it is internalized. But behind these familiar scenes are a wide range of philosophical and psychological complexities, so it may help to have a simple touchstone to unravel both our own thoughts and Aristotle's.

Let's step back a bit. In studying, Aristotle asserted that we aim to understand and to contemplate the universality of things rather than mere accidentals, such as man rather than Socrates, although grasping that certain things are accidentals are part of the journey required by the mind. To learn something implies, as we have seen, that it is learnable, which appears tautological, but it also implies that spontaneous or chance happenings and the incidental or accidental properties of things are rendered less important than the universalities or principles of nature, although they require some explanation too. What is learnable for Aristotle in the bedrock of the physical world is the matter and form that things take. Matter is made up of the four elements that the Greeks believed constituted the world and combinations thereof (we now [2008] recognize 117 elements); natural objects, involving matter and form, are subject to change, growth, alteration, and decay – of the two, matter is less susceptible to change relative to form (the bronze block becomes a statue and then is melted back down into a block) and there is also an essential element – *ousia* – which also remains throughout alteration (see below).

When matter fails to actualize itself or to be actualized into a form or the form for which it is intended, then there is deformity – deviations from the natural mean: a baby may be born deformed because it failed to achieve its proper form, or the statue fails as artwork because of a mistake in proportions, or the exam was failed. Why such things may happen is due to something, a primary cause, or set of causes, by which the statue becomes misshapen: the artist drank too much wine during his lunch and used a blunt chisel, or the fetus was malformed because of an underlying and unnoticed disease its mother was harboring, and the exam was failed because of a lack of sleep the night before and a lack of revision notes. Into this Aristotle takes us, and although we need only skim the surface as it relates to education, the gist is critical for seeing how his philosophy fits together.

The pre-Socratics got stuck on explaining change, Aristotle believed, for they reasoned that nothing comes to be or passes away, because whatever comes to be must either emanate from what is not or from what is, and they concluded that these were not possible options: what is, cannot be said to come to be, since it already is; and nothing can come from what is not (*Phys*, 191a25–34). So, the implication went for Aristotle, change was considered to be either illusory or illogical to the human mind; this created a logical impasse which Aristotle sought to remove. Plato's metaphysics, he noted, had sidestepped the entire problem in describing eternal and changeless Forms or Ideas, of which the phenomena of the world that we inhabit are poor echoes or representatives. In the eternal world which the soul inhabits between lives, eternal Forms exist and as souls we know them; however, when the soul returns to a body, we descend to the world and have to rely on our senses, which become confused amid the anarchy of change – only when the mind becomes free of the senses can it think upon the eternal and proper nature of things and their relationships. For an empirically minded philosopher whose own educational upbringing and philosophical disposition was earth oriented, something was obviously amiss.

Is change an epistemic anarchy that confounds the senses and leaves the agent confused and befuddled? That would certainly leave learning in the lurch. Yet Socrates' dialogues often show how his interlocutors really did not know what they were talking about, which, whatever the real Socrates believed, Plato took to indicate that the senses and mundane beliefs and opinions could not be trusted, and that the world of changing appearances which meets our senses could not provide any epistemic certainty. Nonetheless, Socrates still teaches us, there, amid the superficiality of the disputant's beliefs, is a perennial desire to know more and to push the questions further, so Plato did not conclude that the world is unteachable as such, but that what knowledge leads us to is the realization that the world is a reflection of higher Forms or Ideas from which all else is derived and such things as the Idea of Beauty exist independently in their own realm. Aristotle rejected his master's metaphysical flight, while retaining the driving curiosity to know more and an adjusted account of the Forms as universal concepts rather than angelic or divine entities in their own ontological right.

Another aspect of his master's thinking on change that Aristotle challenged was that Plato's thinking implied that when a person learns something he or she is merely recollecting that which the soul really knows, which has been imparted between lives, so in effect the person does not change as such, for what he or she gains in knowledge was already there in the first place, just masked by the body. In the *Meno* dialogue, Socrates famously guides a boy slave (presumably someone chosen who was deemed to be lacking any formal education and perhaps of assumed lower intelligence) through a complex mathematical process, which eventually the slave grasps: for Plato's Socrates, this constituted evidence of unraveling the bodily confusions which he does through 'numbing the body' and stirring the mind into a 'dreamlike state' (*Meno*, 82–6). Socrates insists to Meno that he is not teaching the boy anything, but at each stage he does feed him an awful lot of information, permitting the boy to make logical or intuitive leaps to fill the gaps. Aristotle was not enamored with the theory either, so he sought to establish what is meant by change more carefully and thereby to have a better grasp of what it is to learn something compared to falling into a recollection of the knowledge from the insubstantial world of Forms.

Consider potentiality: when teaching, we presume that the pupil possesses a potential for change, regardless of how we envisage how that change actually takes place. We will see that Aristotle offers in many respects what we would accept as hinting toward the modern view of neurological alteration, for much of what he relates regarding how we learn involves the senses and so the body and its functions. So, anything that exists has a potential to be something else, although as a potentiality, it may never reach its goal: the fetus fails to develop a heart, the statue a good representation of its subject, or the student fails to get into the university of her choice. In this Aristotle draws our philosophical focus to the logical possibility of change that is implicit in any discussion on the analysis of 'becoming' and hence of attaining potential, and a discussion that earlier thinkers, he believed, including Plato, had not produced anything coherent. Thus in seeking to educate we presume that a change can be effected, otherwise what would be the point? I cannot teach a brick Pythagoras' theorem, although I may demonstrate the formula on its surface and so alter its form in a trivial way, analogous to exposing you to a new experience that should alter your form somewhat – getting a tattoo or showing you around a morgue. Indeed, in teaching or conversing with some children or adults we similarly feel that we may as well be talking to a brick, for their minds are not receptive to alteration – a choice that they have made to be disengaged or which may be due to some other failing (Aristotle hints at the ultra-plasticity of young minds and the hardness of old). Yet in education we presume that we are seeking to effect a change and for the most part we may change perceptions or impart knowledge.

In claiming that we seek a change we can assess to what end and by what means, and of the early philosophers Aristotle certainly laid much of the groundwork regarding the logic and analysis of change. As Ryle comments, 'It was because Aristotle found himself and others reasoning now intelligently and now stupidly ... that [he was] able to give to their pupils the maxims and prescriptions of [his] art' (Ryle, 1970, p. 30). Consider: if change is admitted, what is it from and into what will it become, can it be measured or even acknowledged, and if change does exist, what does that say about the ultimate nature of the universe? Such questions provoked the early philosophers, and still retain their grip: 'Am I the same as I was yesterday? And am I what I am now because of necessity, art (human creation), spontaneity, or chance?' All relate to how things change, and, incidentally, are usually of increasing interest to the maturing mind, for our natural need to know develops (unless limited by a range of factors) into struggling to explain not just how things are but also how they came to be. Heraclitus is accorded the principal philosopher to have written about change in a philosophical manner ('everything is in ceaseless flux'; 'you cannot step into the same river twice'); others developed his thoughts, with some arguing that you cannot step into the same river once – things are in such flux as to be devoid of discrete elements. Others, following Plato, rejected change as a mere appearance, for the real stuff of the Forms does not change. Aristotle's insightful studies sought to provide the logic of change with some rigor and to distinguish between those things that must of necessity be, those things that come about because of a variety of causes, and those things that come about spontaneously.

In many respects, Aristotle's explanations seem rather obvious to us, that is because we are in so many respects his intellectual descendants (even if we disagree with elements of his analysis), but also he taught that in order to grasp a subject its definitions and logical structure need to be described, otherwise words hang loosely and we remain ignorant of that which we speak. So he again delved deeper.

Ousia – or what does not change

To clarify what we are talking about when discussing change, Aristotle noted in the *Physics* that given the four elements things can be either simple or compound. Individuals (and logical statements) can also be simple and compound; that is, X is X, which is its identity, or X can also be a Y in the sense of accidentally possessing it. If a thing is a simple entity, it is what it is: Colin is Colin. But if it is a compound entity then another description is added: Colin is a gardener. The identity of Colin *qua* Colin refers to what is necessarily him: male, adult, 5ft 8; the reference that he is a gardener is accidental, for being a gardener does not constitute his identity as such – if we were to ask a boy, 'Where is the gardener?' he may or may not know whom is referred, especially if there are several gardeners in view or he knows of several. On the other hand, if we were to ask, 'Where is Colin?' he would generally understand whom is referred. Colin possesses one identity (he is numerically one, as Aristotle would put it) but he can possess many characteristics – there he is as a rugby player, there a father, there as an artist, etc. Accordingly, there is an actuality involved in Colin (i.e. what he is) and potentiality too (i.e. what he can be). The man can thus change from being unmusical into being musical after having some lessons and learning some musical habits, but Colin remains an underlying substance or presence, not just a label identifying his name, or what Aristotle called *ousia*. This implies in turn, for Aristotle, that there is Colin before he became musical, Colin after he became musical, so there is Colin. Musical is a simple characteristic, as is Colin: together they are compounded when Colin becomes musical.

By examining the differences between simple and compound things, the philosopher can now grasp causational direction; for instance, 'Colin can become musical' makes sense, but 'musical can become Colin' does not. Then we can consider some things that do change in the sense of coming into being as well as coming into existence from something else. For instance, a statue is said to come into being from bronze; the bronze does not become a statue by itself. Things can be said to come into being, whereas most of what we think about as undergoing change comes to be from something else requiring an efficient cause (an agent) and sometimes a formal cause (blueprint).

The underlying 'thing' – the *ousia* – is usually translated as the substance, but Sachs makes an interesting argument that *ousia*, which literally means 'fortune' or 'monetary capital,' is better translated as thinghood, for 'substance' was a word effected by Latin translators, who were not too taken with Aristotle's philosophy, Sachs argues. Socrates, he notes, had been playing with the term *ousia* in referring to the unchanging thinghood and Aristotle, who learned his philosophy from Plato, followed suit. Greek does not possess a word for 'thing,' Sachs observes, so many problems ensue in trying to get a reasonable definition (Sachs, 2006). *Ousia* can either imply *to on*, which means whatever is – blue, 2ft length, walking; or it can imply *to chrema*, which means a thing used up or consumed. Such controversies are not merely academic: Christianity split at the Niceaen synod in 325 AD over the word as found in *homoousian* and *homoiousian*, implying 'same thinghood' and 'similar thinghood': are God, the Son, and the Holy Spirit the 'same' or 'similar'? Therein lay the enormous Trinitarian controversy, with the Roman and Greek churches assuming 'sameness' and detractors, notably the Arians, 'similarity.' Perhaps there is the origin of the phrase 'I don't give an iota'! An analogy from economics may be useful for clarity: money, like grain, is fungible: when 20 pound coins are put into a pot then five are removed, it does not matter which five coins are taken out – they are interchangeable, and this fungibility is analogous to the *ousia* of an entity undergoing change. The capital or its *ousia* remains, albeit diminished until replenished, and so it may be said to undergo changes in quantity but not in its *ousia*, for it exists to change.

So if something changes, as Aristotle claimed, there must be a something in it that does not alter – an underlying substratum that retains the thinghood that makes Colin Colin throughout his life even though physically he is in constant flux and that his qualities alter. But is Aristotle right in this?

In learning something new, we may be said to undergo a change, but is it 'substantial' (*qua ousia*), qualitative, or quantitative? The immediate retort is that learning constitutes a qualitative change in as much we are altered by the new impressions that we make or by the new insights that are gained, yet Aristotle is (to large extent) a materialist believing the senses impress upon the soul (or brain) and are thereby deposited there substantially. In an age of analogies with computers, his claim cannot be dismissed: neurology and artificial intelligence studies maintain that the brain and self with all of its knowledge are the same and that incoming data from the senses is indeed stored through a physical alteration (electrical-chemical stimuli). There remains something that does not change, though –

that would be the boy's neurons, say. Apparently, central nervous system neurons last for life, although when pushed, neurologists may accept that their molecular constituents are forever being swapped (or potentially so), returning us to the world of Aristotle's concerns of what remains if something is constantly changing! If the form is said to remain the same, then like a football team or corporation, we may allow that its members alternate while the functioning form continues. So the boy may learn something new, his body may be adjusted by new impressions or new connections between old impressions stored in his memory, but it remains the case that it is the boy who is the one learning while his learning is said not to survive (*Phys*, 189b32–190a21): this implies that his form has changed. The boy's form is broader than the shape he exhibits, for it involves what he is and what he is doing – if he is learning, his form alters from that when he is playing or sleeping (Robinson, 1995, p. 17). The boy's *ousia* thus remains the subject that undergoes the change in form, or in Ackrill's description, '*he is a reidentifiable subject of change*' (orig. italics; Ackrill, 1981, p. 120).

Returning to the initial thoughts on change, recall that Aristotle believed that there existed in anything that could change a potentiality for change (otherwise it could not change). The theory is also known by its Greek word, *entelechy*, which merges *telos* and *echein*, 'end' and 'have' implying that an object has its end within it. That is, the potential has the capacity to become its actuality, so a fetus may become a neonate, a neonate an infant, an infant a child, and so on. Behind every potential, logically speaking, is this actuality; the actual is always produced from the potential, as man is produced by man, Aristotle noted. What is actual – the learned pupil, for instance – is temporally and logically prior to the potential, for actuality is the end, the sake of which potency is acquired or exists. This is true for a pupil as well as a tree; the man is the actuality of the boy, so the boy's actuality is driven by his maturation of what he will become, but Aristotle was quick to note the differences in meanings and to accept that the boy is temporally prior to the man in the usual sense that is meant, but what is actual can only (logically) be produced by another actual – a musician by a musician, and so a man by a man (*Met*, 1049b5–29). In turn, actuality drives the process in which the potential becomes the actuality through, in the human sphere, action. We learn to become a musician by playing an instrument, and gradually what was not becomes what is (unmusical becomes musical), but only by doing and fulfilling the end to which we aim, which in turn has acted as the cause of our action. Acting and choosing to act is of course necessary even to begin fulfilling one's potential and thereby actualizing the self. Ultimate fulfillment is beyond us, though, for otherwise, actualization would logically make the processes and purposes of life redundant.

A person thus has to be involved, to be active (*energeia*) in learning as a logical necessity. To what extent he or she is capable of learning, or of choosing the right course of action according to morality, is a separable issue (see '*Akrasia* – moral weakness' below), one that Aristotle connects to his thinking on human nature and particularly his theory that people differ in capabilities, that some are well born and deserve to rule those who are not, that men are naturally more intelligent than women, that some men possess better physiques for learning than others. In all, Aristotle presents a hierarchical view of human nature that links inextricably with the end or goals, which need to be examined as the philosophy that he produced is still influential, but emphatically nature and thereby humanity (or sometimes, in his view, humanity and therefore nature) does nothing in vain (*GA*, 744a36). All is for a purpose and it is to that which we now turn.

Teleology

Whatever exists is, as we have seen, subject to causes – even chance events (the unintended product of human action) and spontaneous events (unintended product of natural events) are causal. And these causes produce a result or what can also be considered to be a finality that all things tend toward. This final cause may be said in turn to cause things to happen: that I aim to write a book is a causal factor in my researching and writing. The theory that actions are determined in part by the ends that they eventually tend toward is called teleology. The Greek *telos* means 'completion' or 'end' and Aristotle used it to imply the end to which things aim. Aristotle's metaphysics is teleological; that is, it is end oriented: things happen because of the end to which they tend or which they are chosen, or in general, actions and events exist in order to serve a higher end. This, he accepted, is not always so given that men do things without consideration of what may be in their best interests and similarly, nature does things that we often wonder, wherefore? But generally, the world's events and humanity's actions are governed by the ends to which they aim.

This is an interesting philosophical stance and while seemingly the province of metaphysical disputation, it has enormous implications for educational thinking. Education, we often assume, involves aims that in turn prompt us to consider the nature of institutions, curricula, pedagogical methods, and assessments, and these aims may be implicit or explicit, and the resulting education instrumental – serving specific or intrinsic ends (Winch and Gingell, 1999, pp. 10–13). Broadly speaking, Aristotle viewed education as an instrument to form men of good character whose lives would help secure the good of the *polis*, as they are in turn formed well by a properly formed *polis*, but he also explored some key values that we can claim to be intrinsic or worthwhile in themselves. He was not a strict utilitarian or deontologist believing that acts may be judged solely on their consequences or solely on intrinsic moral rectitude: there must be ultimate ends to which most things are predisposed, for the universe is so well ordered such that everything tends toward the best state.

This last is an important addition – that things change, we can accept, and that they change because of a variety of causes seems reasonable; that things may be said to possess functions or be used for human purposes (such as tools), we may too accept; but that they tend toward 'their best state' is something that is highly controversial, for that would mean a host of dubious results would have to be considered to be the best outcome. For instance, does a failure to learn imply a move toward the best state? That would seem ironic, unless we redefine failure as not being a failure at all but an event that surreptitiously does bring about an improvement (the 'every cloud has a silver lining' approach to bad news). Of course, Aristotle would not accept that every action or event leads to an improvement or a move toward a better state of affairs, for his vision of the universe and his understanding of human nature provided him with a variety of guides by which to judge action and consequence. For example, biologically he claimed that life involves nutrition and reproduction at its most simple, so an animal that failed to find the right diet or mate would have deviated from its immanent purpose. Similarly, if a man fails to attain *eudaimonia* (deeply contented happiness based on living the good life *qua* man), then he would have deviated from the highest purpose available to man, so if he fails to learn something that is in his interests *qua* man, such as moral strength, then fails *qua* man, although it may be said that he does not fail *qua* individual. Other people, it must be acknowledged, in Aristotle's system do not have a chance to become fully *eudaimonic* in the sense that a rational man can, since they do not possess the requisite abilities in the first place – slaves, women, and children. Nonetheless, each division of humanity can in turn attain its own potential given its 'limits.'

Taking a look from a different perspective: against Plato's arguments in the *Timaeus*, Aristotle rejected a consciously designed universe but did not reject teleology as completely as modern science has tended to do, although perhaps not as convincingly as is often made out or presumed (Cameron, 2004, p. 72). Teleological explanations presumably require intelligence behind the ends aimed for, although that is not necessarily the case: automatic biological processes are end oriented while we need not assume an intelligence behind them – do cells divide because of a desire to, or do they just divide? Aristotle's position is clear, though: 'It is absurd to suppose that purpose is not present because we do not observe the agent deliberating' (*Phys*, 199b27). Had he known of cellular division and had seen the films that are now readily available on the internet, he would have asserted that there was some element of deliberation involved, for even of the smallest of animals that he could perceive he believed to possess a soul, which at the simplest level that he could observe involved seeking nutrition and reproduction. Without a microscope to observe the world of uni- and multicellular creatures, Aristotle argued that purpose exists even when we do not detect it, a theory that critics have lambasted, for where would the deliberative intelligence reside if it is not readily detectable? Yet in one respect Aristotle is surely right: I cannot automatically *know* the purpose of the woman crossing the street except to follow her, watch her actions, and judge accordingly, yet her true purpose is hidden from me, and may remain so even if I ask her, for she may be a spy or mentally disturbed and possessing a complex of irrational purposes, but assuredly she possesses internal intentions to do something that would readily distinguish her from a robot crossing the road.

However, the language used by any philosopher generates problems of its own; for example, the words 'biological function' and 'biological purpose' can easily overlap with adherents of different schools of thought drawing on the same language but asserting different scopes of meaning particularly on nuances, and in reviewing Aristotle we must naturally be mindful of the problems of an Ancient language in translation.

Considering Aristotle's position, we note that causes, changes, and purposes are intrinsically wrapped up in each other for him; logically, they are held to be simultaneous. In every change there is both an active and a passive element, the active being the agent that acts upon the passive material: an 'active' teacher desirous of bringing about a change in a 'passive' pupil. The action and the effect happen concurrently not consecutively as modern theories of causation have it; for example, in speaking to the pupil, a change is effected there and then (or not!). And what is particularly characteristic of Aristotle's theory of cause and change is that both natural and human events and actions are said to be end oriented – they seek ends. In many instances, Aristotle anthropomorphizes nature: 'nature makes nothing super-fluous nor in vain' (*GA*, 744a36), but we can allow the philosopher his metaphors without tying him to a theory of intelligent design; after all, 'metaphor ... gives style clearness, charm, and distinction as nothing else can ... [they] must be fitting, which means that they must fairly correspond to the thing signified' (*Rhet*, 1404a8–11). So how does Aristotle extricate his own teleology from that of his master Plato, which asserts a guiding intelligence behind the world?

Teleology is a problematic theory, easily acceptable if we consider that the end of education is the formation of a good, virtuous character, say, but less easily acceptable if we believe that the purpose of fingers is to write literature or to play the flute, or, as Bill Cosby jokes, 'What is the purpose of air? To blow up volleyballs' (quoted in Perlman, 2004, p. 3). That is, the purposes of things are found in what they are used for. For Aristotle, there must, generally speaking, be a reason for things to exist: that I choose to eat so as to assuage my hunger, so the existence of the pig that filled my bacon sandwich is explained by fulfilling my demand for hunger. Except that there is ostensibly a huge logical leap in arguing this (as Mark Twain had fun pointing out), for it is arguing after the fact to explain the fact (the fallacy of *post hoc ergo hoc* – after this, thus this). However, while philosophically we again must be careful not to confuse purpose and function, Aristotle claimed that 'everything which has a function exists for its function' (*Cael*, 286a8), which sounds like a circular definition thus seemingly confusing the two. But the logical escape, for him, is discovered by alluding to purposes: that my fingers and thumb have the function of grasping pens is not the same as saying that their purpose as having evolved over millions of years is to grasp pens; the purpose can be described as incidental, or perhaps the purpose of my fingers can be described as potentially multifaceted and governed more by what I learn about how I can use my digits. Aristotle noted, though, that men are intelligent not because they possess fingers but they possess fingers because they are intelligent, as if intelligence helps to form fingers, a theory that the evolutionist Lamarck, writing in the early nineteenth century, later propounded in his first principle: 'In every animal which has not passed the limit of its development, a more frequent and continuous use of any organ gradually strengthens, develops and enlarges that organ ...' (Lamarck, 1914, p. 113). That is, habit produces new forms for the next generation to employ – Lamarck was being thoroughly Aristotelian and the theory certainly gave much impetus to biology teleology until Darwin's theory of evolution a few decades later and the cracking of DNA by Watson and company in the 1950s.

Yet philosophies are rarely rejected outright by science alone, for science is the application of philosophical thinking to the world, generally understood as inductive and based on repeatable experiments. The absence of repeatability does not invalidate scientific analysis; for instance, a medical treatment on one person may not have the same effects when applied to another: biological individuality (Williams, 1998, pp. 1–7) implies severe limits to forming conclusions from a range of disparate people. In biomechanics, the purpose of bone depends on its function and the individual's bones adapt to use – this is a highly Aristotelian way of looking at use and function. Form follows function: present understanding of the body invokes genetic expression and cellular interaction as causing Form, but 'function ... is the end point of joint structure ... [a]nd all components of human joints – bone, muscles, ligaments, cartilage, tendon – can adapt to functional demands' (Curlew, 2005, p. 70). Consider a young boy's body: how it will develop is not a given; what it will become is in part genetic (the Aristotelian actuality promoting the potential to become actual), in part environmental (efficient causes acting upon the body, e.g. diseases, traumas), but also in part how the child uses his body. These depend on his values and the values of his teachers that he picks up, particularly regarding the use of his self, which involves efficient (teachers) and formal causes (blueprint of good behavior), and cultural and filial expectations of what the child ought to know.

Function thus derives from the purposes or higher claimants to action and it is these higher ends that the minor functions serve, so evolved human intelligence produced fingers that are now incidentally useful for grasping pens. Except that Aristotle did not accept an evolutionary hypothesis, even though the ideas were around in the creation myths developed by some of his contemporaries, and he made note of an evolutionary mechanism concerning teeth. Consider the following:

> Wherever then all the parts came about just what they would have been if they had come to be for an end, such things survived, being organized spontaneously in a fitting way; whereas those which grew otherwise perished and continued to perish ...
>
> *(Phys,* 198b29–33)

It is an argument that would fit well into a modern biology book indicating a cogent theory of evolution, yet Aristotle rejected the theory. But does man possess function in the sense that an artist or musician possesses function? The question provided Aristotle with a means to explain the proper end befitting man *qua* man, and that is man's end as defined by the good is the 'activity of the soul in conformity with excellence' *(NE,* 1097b25–1098a16). That is, the mind, *nous*, provides the ultimate efficient and final cause to which man can aspire (see below), based on a formal cause of what life ought to be like and what means should be employed, for the attainment of such values is, of course, the remit of education. This relates to Aristotle's theory of the soul in which he averred that the soul is the cause of the body as the source of its movement, the end, as well as the essence of the whole body (*An*, 415b10–11). The soul (or mind) is the initiator of any action. While any action or event that initiates the process toward the end is active, the end is not: running for the sake of health is an activity, but health is not (*GC*, 324b14) – it is the cause of the running, meaning that is why we run. We wish for certain ends and then we attempt to fulfill them and we may err in our ways or succeed (*NE*, 1111b26; *Pol*, 1331b26); yet, once formed, we do not deliberate about the ends as such (that medical treatment should lead to health), but we discuss the means required to gain those ends (*NE*, 1111b12). Accordingly, if a pupil is to learn X, then X becomes the goal and the cause of learning X, and an appropriate procedure is then commended.

How is an educationalist to make sense of the philosophy? There are important strands to pick up. Purposes are things that are formed by us when we choose one action over another – when we choose to do something in order to achieve something else, but functions relate to how things work together (or fail to). That is, purposes relate to intentional acts rather than events in the physical world, which modern scientists prefer to consider as purposeless in the sense of not possessing any intelligence. When speaking of human action, such as learning lines for a play, we can readily characterize the action as being done for a specific goal, chosen by the actor as befitting a job description and formed by an intention to effect a result. So when we choose, we can say that we predominantly choose for the sake of something else, although I may be thoroughly mistaken in the effects that I do indeed produce, as Davidson, defending the broad Aristotelian view, noted (Davidson, 1980, p. 5). Sometimes one goal dominates all others, so I learn to swim to improve my chances in the sea or to get fit, I get fit to live well, I live well to contemplate – and the life of contemplation is the highest form of living for Aristotle; there is no higher value to which I can aspire. There are thus levels of function and values in purposes with the human mind presenting the highest on offer and anything below that, even though necessary in mind's service, rank lower. As we drop down Aristotle's great chain of being from man to the animals, we find several purposes held in common: plants and the human body both possess vegetative capacities, but once we drop below the level of living organisms to physical materials then the teleological play dwindles and the regularities that we perceive as occurring around us are of the order of necessary events rather than consciously chosen ones.

Yet such is not a complete or consistently accepted view: Aristotle was keen to draw our attention to the regularities of nature that the Ionian philosophers had begun philosophizing over, but he rejected the argument that regularities observed are there by necessity alone. Events, he believed, can only happen either because of chance or because of the sake of something else: the apparent regularity that we see around us cannot be the product of spontaneity, so there must be an ulterior purpose. (This argument, note, is still popular with creationists or supporters of Intelligent Design theories of the universe, although Aristotle would probably reject the mythic elements of such conjectures.) No distinction arises, Aristotle maintained, between events in nature and human actions: 'now surely in action, so in nature; and as in nature, so it is in each action ... action is for the sake of an end; therefore the nature of the things also is so' (*Phys*, 199a10–12). Emphatically, as noted above, the lack of evidence for a deliberating agent does not negate its possibility (*Phys*, 199b27). What happens is done for an end, and so there must be an ultimate end and 'that for the sake of which tends to be what is best and the end of things that lead up to it' (*Phys*, 194a30; 195a24–25; cf. also *Met*, 1013b26).

For life as we know it, there are purposes and ends for the sake of which our purposes aim; nevertheless, gradually, Aristotle brings us around to a Platonic vision of what the ultimate purposes are, for socially, the end of political life is the state (*Pol*, 1252b31), which is a necessary element to the proper life of civil people. However, while teachers believe that they have done their job when they can show their pupil working (*Met*, 1050b18), there is a harking toward the Platonic eternal: the end of all the processes involving 'that for the sake of which' cannot be infinite, he proclaimed (*Met*, 994b11). Yet when he turned attention to the ultimate cause of the universe, we find him upholding the existence of Pure Thought, or, to many advocates, God. This is because he believed that there ought – *in principle at least* – to be an Unmoved Mover, the initiator of all things that presently move, and this Unmoved Mover is a monistic, eternal, and unchanging actuality.

If we concentrate on just the material world, Aristotle argued, then we are faced with an eternal universe, for movement could not come into being by itself and neither is it destroyed: physicists still face the problem of whence the Big Bang, or in Aristotelian thinking, what if there is a something that can effect movement without itself moving? This must be an immaterial substance, eternal, but also possessing actuality rather than potentiality for bringing about movement (*Met*, 1071b3–22). Its essence must be as a final cause, an ultimate purpose which everything must eventually settle or rise to, and this must exist *necessarily* for Aristotle (*Met*, 1072b10). The Unmoved Mover does not create time as such, for the material world of our universe has neither beginning nor end; the Unmoved Mover is not an efficient cause as the sculptor is to the statue commencing it in period t_0 to complete it in t_1; rather, the Unmoved Mover is Pure Thought. In contrast, when we think, we think of objects, the objects of our senses and imagination, which reap ideas from the senses; if I think of acting toward an end, I bring into the universe a microscopic analogy of the Prime Mover – I intend to bring about X because I wish to and the wish emanates uncaused from me. Magnify this to the universe and we get a conception of Aristotle's Prime Mover – it is uncaused thought, thinking upon thinking rather than problem-solving as such.

Accordingly, it is the highest 'entity' that can exist for Aristotle. All the purposes on earth would make more sense if there were an initiator or theoretical principle greater than all that materially exists and which is evident to our senses. How can this relate to the physical world and its purposes? – as a good general with the order of the army: the two are inseparable, Aristotle noted. Those lower down in Aristotle's hierarchy are more likely to act randomly, purposelessly, that is slaves and animals, while those higher up exhibit purposes, increasingly ones self-created with increasing increments of rationality, until one reaches above the pinnacle of humanity to discover the Prime Mover. Man possesses the divine element of *nous* (mind), and the use of the mind is to imitate God (the Prime Mover).

The theory was and remains attractive to Christians and hence was very influential in Scholastic education (cf. Part 3).

Sensation and perception

Sensation, which distinguishes all animals from the plant kingdom (*GA*, 741a8), plays a critical role in Aristotle's theory of how we know things. Sensation is generated in the soul (*psychē*) via the body. This is an important premise in Aristotle's view of human nature, for he is giving support to what is called materialism, the theory that the human mind and body are inextricably linked and are not separate and distinct as Plato and other dualists held. In a characterization of Plato's Socrates view of education, the body is an obstacle to the power of the separate soul to understand things; for Aristotle, no such duality exists, hence the importance laid on being healthy. Although there is much emphasis on possessing good health, Aristotle does observe that some people are naturally healthier than others, while others have to work at keeping fit and others can never attain fitness no matter how hard they try (*Cael*, 292a25). But on average, human senses possess greater acuity than those of the animals, for they become the Aristotelian portal to knowledge and hence to the intellect; although while the senses are the path to knowledge, gaining knowledge is an achievement (Korsmeyer, 1999, p. 23), that is, a required effort.

His main thesis is thus that perception is a necessary condition of survival foremost and then, for humanity, knowledge (*SS*, 436b20) in the sense that we cannot know anything unless we have experienced things. As it stands, this is representative of the empiricist tradition, which claims that the senses are the only valid means to knowledge, but Aristotle's philosophy is effectively a modified empiricism, for he believed that animals and people are not passive receivers of sensations: to sense something is also to perceive it and that implies another cognitive process that leads on to thinking and reasoning. This entails that sensory perception is not a sufficient condition for knowledge, for we can formulate theories based on what we have known, which may or may not be valid – in particular, reasoning deals with universals while perception deals with particular percepts or data and so lifts our ability to know from just perceiving to the potential for understanding. Sensation, then, which is held in common with the rest of the animal kingdom, does not fully satisfy the function of man, which is rationality (*NE*, 1098a2–9).

Metaphysically, that which is perceived exists prior to perception (*Cat*, 7b35). This seems a commonsensical point to begin with, but it also allows a refutation of the idealist argument that *esse est percipe*, to be is to be perceived, which has the implication that things do not exist unless they are perceived. If a pupil is to perceive something, we do presume that it exists prior to perception; nevertheless, Aristotle did allow the possibility that 'when they go out of our consciousness it is not clear whether they exist or not' (*Met*, 1036a6; *APr*, 67a39), which would certainly fit in well with George Berkeley's idealism or the writings of recent postmodernists. Infants learn to expect (and we encourage them in this) that that which is not now seen is in fact still there, but philosophers are never keen to give such entities epistemological validity, for it is not certain that they do exist, especially from the perspective of the infant. When a mother disappears from the sight of a young infant, she may cry in desperation until her mother returns, but gradually forms an expectation that she will return. But Aristotle acknowledges in this sentence the philosophical problem with entities that have gone beyond our perception, although he does not countenance what we now call the solipsist argument that I can only be sure of my own existence and the things that I see are entities dependent upon my seeing them.

He also attempted to refute what is now recognizable as phenomenology, the study of appearances, in which adherents claim that all that we can know is from what we perceive, and because things are changing all the time (the Heraclitean *panta rei* or all things are in ceaseless flux); this was a view held by Democritus (460–370 BC) and Empedocles (490–430 BC) among others whom Aristotle studied and mused upon their theories. His own argument is that if perception is a necessary condition of knowledge, it need not be sufficient: I see something and I know that I see something, but I may be mistaken in what I think I see. It is an immediate and obvious retort (*An*, 431a8), so 'not everything which appears is true' (*Met*, 1010b1). But this argument does not denigrate the disclosure of truth as such but the rejection of the notion that truths are relativistic or ephemeral or even non-existent (each of those statements requiring at least one universal truth, though). Instead of rejecting the possibility of truth, he insisted that we should think deeper (such is the purpose of our mind, *nous*) and not to be put off learning philosophy. Consider an example: we observe that things' qualities may change both in the object and in our ability to sense (the sea changes color daily to my eyes and my vision becomes blurred if I have seawater in them), but there remains the underlying objective entity upon which we cast our perception – the sea (*Met*, 101b24).

Although our senses can be fooled by the alterations in the world around us, our reasoning indicates the possibility of an unchanging substratum which causes the sensation, even if the qualities alter. Understanding of that which is seen is different from perceiving – the child perceives a particular entity, a dog say, and perceives that here is an individual entity referred to as 'dog,' but that is a different matter from understanding that the next dog that comes along has something in common, a dogginess, rather than being a particular instantiation of a something wholly unconnected to the former, so one cannot understand through perception by itself (*APst*, 87b29): through the particular, perception of the universal is gained (*APst*, 100a16). An object of perception is indeed an object of knowledge, but 'to perceive is like bare asserting or thinking' (*An*, 431a8), so perception does not constitute knowledge as such (*Top*, 114a21). Knowledge belongs to understanding universals, which lie in his soul or mind, a truth, Aristotle argued, explained by the fact that when a man wants to think, he may without any intentionality toward objects external to his mind, but should he wish to sense something, there must be an object for him to sense (*An*, 417b24). Education's initial steps must therefore be with learning what exists via the senses: seeing, hearing, touching, smelling, tasting.

Empiricist reasoning is conducive to an epistemic and moral relativism, for if we rely heavily or solely on the senses to provide our knowledge, then the nature of the world or of people's actions cannot be judged as such; they can be studied and noted but ultimately, as Jeremy Bentham was to quip, pushpin is as good as poetry. Relativist philosophy was alive and well among the Greeks, and Aristotle rejected the relativist epistemology of Democritus, Empedocles, and Anaxagoras, who asserted that the senses provide the only means to the truth. Thereby, because each of us experiences a different view of the world, truth is subjective or relative to each of us, and because the world is in flux, no eternally true statements can be held of it. In a comment that is well worth repeating for modern students, who encounter the relativist argument that all is appearance and truth ephemeral: 'is it not natural that beginners in philosophy should lose heart? For to seek the truth would be to pursue flying game' (*Met*, 1009b37). In contrast, Aristotle held that in the things that change there is a something that is always there: 'for that which is losing a quality has something of that which is being lost, and of that which is coming to be, something must already be ... there is something whose nature is changeless' (*Met*, 1010a35). The study of the changeless is philosophical – it is the subject of his *Metaphysics* and appears as the quietly driven theme in much of his writings.

For Aristotle what is perceived, as we have just noted, affects the body, for it becomes body (*Cat*, 7a37), in that perception is of something moving and hence that impacts upon the body. This is a materialist epistemology of knowledge – perception involving a modification of the body in some manner, although it is entirely possible that an animate being may not be conscious of being affected (*Phys*, 244b10–245a2). That which is perceived is done so in three ways: by all the senses in common, by a particular sense, and in an incidental sense. The senses together may perceive movement, rest, number, figure, and magnitude (*An*, 418a18), while the particular senses may perceive color or sound alone. Seeing something 'incidentally' is when an object is temporarily colored differently or sounds differently; for instance, if we fill a guitar body with feathers it will produce a muted sound compared to when it is empty and acting as its sound chamber.

Interestingly, Aristotle refers to some basic perceptual experiments that are familiar to modern psychology students: of looking at a particular object or color and then looking away and retaining an impression of the initial object on whatever surface the gaze is transferred (*OD*, 459b3–23); he was also impressed by the fact that strong impressions such as a loud noise or fire can harm the perceptual organs, which ratified to him the effect of perception on the body. There is nothing in his analysis that a modern neurological book would dismiss, except that the knowledge that we now possess exceeds anything that Ancient Greek physicians were capable of knowing, depending, as it does, on the use of microscopes and electrical measuring devices. Entertainingly, Aristotle also noted an instance where a body can affect an object through looking at it: he believed menstruating women looking into a mirror could turn it bloodshot and cloudy (*OD*, 459b27) – where he got that information from we can only speculate!

The sensuous life given to animals is higher than the mere nutritive and reproductive life of vegetation, but it still does not warrant the complete adulation that empiricists may give the senses, or, for that matter, moral hedonists, whose definition of happiness is found solely in the pleasure provided by their senses. The five senses are grouped philosophically into the term 'perception' (*aisthesis*), and, as was Aristotle's philosophical disposition, he gave the senses their own hierarchy and wrapped them in teleological notions: sight is the highest, for it enables us to perceive a multitude of qualities in an object such as shape, size, number, and movement (*SS*, 437a5–9). Hearing is of next importance, since it enables the growth in intelligence, so of those who are afflicted with sensory deprivation, the blind are more intelligent than the deaf and dumb (*SS*, 437a11–16). The special senses' functions are specific and common, specific when they entail one stimulus (seeing is to sight, hearing is to sound), but they may also act in unison (*OS*, 455a14).

The senses possess purposes that fulfill their capacities: eyes are for the purpose of seeing, ears for the purpose of hearing; in some respects this may seem a banal statement, but recall that Aristotle's theory of biology needs to be contrasted with a reductionist mechanistic account, which holds that the function of the eyes is sight. The implications are different: for Aristotle, an animal seeks to survive, so it possesses (we would now say that it has evolved) sensory organs that enable it to survive. It possesses a purpose beyond the immediacy of a functioning tool – survival, he professed, is enhanced with the ability to perceive objects in the distance (*An*, 434a26). Overall, his is a theory infused with direction rather than chance and there are critics who read into Aristotle a thorough anticipation of Darwin's theory of evolution. But from what we have seen above, teleological descriptions may also invoke further purposes beyond the survival instinct or desires of an animal or person to secure certain values, and here the controversy begins.

To continue, though, all animals that perceive do indeed attain knowledge from their senses, but in a rising hierarchy from very little amid the plant kingdom upward to man (*GA*, 730a30–32). Nevertheless, perception is a state rather than an activity (*Top*, 125b17), which means that it is an elementary form of knowledge – or basal in the Aristotelian hierarchy of things – and so, while generally reliable, the senses do not require an effort to invoke them. They are passive in contrast to the activity of the mind, a theory that again falls consistently into Aristotle's hierarchy, for those entities whose knowledge is gained passively are lower down than those, whether it is the pursuit of knowledge or any other value. And so with human endeavors – those that are passive (watching television, for instance) are of less philosophical importance than penning a lecture or a play.

Perception naturally attracts philosophical attention, primarily regarding arguments on how valid it is as an epistemic tool, and once again we find Aristotle providing much of the analytical framework that remains familiar to modern thinkers. Induction – data gleaned by the senses – constitutes the first principle of knowledge, while deduction proceeds sometimes from induction and at other times from necessary statements (*NE*, 1139b27).

Pedagogically, this gives prominence to the Aristotelian emphasis on thinking once one has perceived; perception is not sufficient alone, so the pupil who is taken to explore a botanical garden certainly gains new sensations and is physically (we would say neurologically) altered, but whether he gains in knowledge is another matter. Often we have discussions with people who have seen the same event or thing and who draw different conclusions from it, a personal favorite example being commemorated in the famous 'Wittgenstein's Poker' incident explored by Edmonds and Eidenow (2001).

So, what is perceived is a particular thing, a concrete entity: this thing here, this cat, this woman. Such things are known by perception and thought, 'but they are always stated and cognized by means of the universal formula' (*Met*, 1036a6). That is, when I see a cat, I perceive a particular thing – of which there is no definition for Aristotle, but of which I know that it belongs to the universal criteria that we refer to as cat – presuming that I have encountered several in the past. No definition of an individual entity can be given, for the thing is itself, Mr. Hobbes the dog is Mr. Hobbes, a circular formula that gets us nowhere except providing us with an identity to distinguish Mr. Hobbes from Scotty the dog; when we refer to only one entity, we call it by its proper name rather than by any accidentals it may also possess (*Top*, 103a6–38; Book VII.1) (e.g. collar, perched on a wall looking at birds). Practical wisdom (*phronēsis*) in turn deals with the percepts we encounter (how should I deal with Mr. Hobbes – is he friendly?), while comprehension concerns itself with the universals (*NE*, 1142a25) and is the higher of the two pursuits for people.

Of the body's senses, the eyes and hearing are the most important for they are distant from the objects perceived and can obtain a more objective analysis of them, bringing forth the most information:

> The faculty of seeing, thanks to the fact that all bodies are coloured, brings tidings of multitudes of distinctive qualities of sorts ... however, it is hearing that contributes most to the growth of intelligence. For rational discourse is a cause of instruction.
>
> (*SS*, 437a6–13)

The sense of touch, while of less importance than that of sight and hearing, is nonetheless more acute in humans than in animals, he claimed, as humans possess more tactile discrimination: 'that is why man is the most intelligent of all animals,' and those of harder skin are less intelligent than those with softer skin (*An*, 421a22). Such a thesis fits the general Aristotelian philosophy of man's supremacy and that of a philosopher more so than other people, it sounds like. The calloused hands belong to the worker while the soft hands belong to the intellectual who reaches for the pinnacle of man's potentiality, the life of contemplation; those born deaf and dumb are relatively much more handicapped than those who are born blind, he observed, for again, the latter possess a higher sense faculty and therefore would be more capable, apodictically speaking, than those without (*SS*, 437a15). Correspondingly, the arts are arranged according to the hierarchy of the senses with the gastronomic arts, being the object touch and taste, lower than the visual arts, for the latter can portray the human condition and instruct in morality (Korsmeyer, 1999, p. 24).

The senses affect us emotionally and through our appetite can affect us physically, thus there is a moral danger present in touch and taste that is less present in sight, but we learn to employ reason to act to curtail the impulsiveness of what would otherwise be animalistic reactions. A beautiful woman may stir desire in a man but such a reaction is base relative to what the mind is capable of appreciating – harmony and beauty. It is difficult to indulge in the senses of sight and of hearing, Aristotle noted, for indulgence relates more to touch and taste, that is eating and drinking like a glutton (*EE*, 1231a15–26; *NE*, 1118a2–6). The formation and education of a virtuous character – pursuant of the good life – concerns learning to manage pleasures properly, not overindulging or abstaining from them, finding a characteristic Aristotelian mean.

From the ability to perceive, we move onto the next pedagogically relevant tier, the ability to memorize.

Memory, imagination, and experience

While some animals are incapable of memorizing, for most memory, according to Aristotle, provides a springboard into knowledge (*APst*, 99b35–99). Memory and learning become inseparable; indeed, Aristotle held, all teaching and learning comes from what is already known (*APst*, 71a1–2) so is highly dependent upon memory. In turn, teaching involves passing on what is already known and what is taught thus belongs to memory, in effect to previously sensed things.

Critical to learning, then, is the use of one's memory. In contrast to the passivity of perception, memory is an activity (*Top*, 125b19), the contents of which are recalled at will (*HA*, 488b26), which, like sensations, can alter the body (*MA*, 702a15). Much action can be internalized through repetition and association – 'many memories of the same thing produce finally the capacity for a single experience' (*Met*, 981a1). Consider the modern example of depressing the clutch to change gear or sitting upright upon a bucking horse – internalization of the skill takes time and practice drawing on previous experiences. Memory requires an effort to draw upon, as Aristotle recognized, for it relates to things perceived in the past which one now wants to draw into the present. Empiricists claim that all memories come from sensations, as does Aristotle, which is in contrast to theories of innate knowledge that claim a provocation can draw forth a memory from a previous life or from when the soul was floating in an ethereal realm – the fields of Elysium for the Greeks, for instance. Socrates (via Plato's rendition) championed this view that 'there is nothing that the soul has not learned' (*Meno*, 81c), but to an observational biologist like Aristotle the theory must have seemed inconsistent with people's memories and with their ability to learn. Having attained a sensation, the implication for Aristotle is that the memory must then be invoked: this is an action rather than a habit or a passive occurrence such as perception, he argued (*Top*, 125b17); it is defined by events that have passed, for the images of the things observed now exist only in the present, while things that are to happen involve expectations. The object of memory belongs to things in the past, but this implies, for Aristotle, that 'only those animals which perceive time remember' (*On Mem*, 449a24ff), which is an interesting but cavalier psychological thesis, for any experiment on animals that exhibit evidence of memory would not in itself construe a perception of time – associations of things in the present with things in the past does not in itself imply an understanding of the passage of time, just as perceiving this in front of me does not guarantee that I understand that I am perceiving. So, the sensation itself is not a memory, for the sensation has to be 'implanted in the soul' for it to become a memory (*On Mem*, 451a22).

Aristotle observed that some people are good at recollecting, and that these people tend to be quick-witted and clever, whereas people who are slow tend to have better memories (*On Mem*, 449b6), while the blind tend to remember better, since they are not distracted by the visible all around them (*EE*, 1248b1). Recollection involves a series of steps, preferably in the middle of a series of events or images, for invoking a memory involves an active running through of events in time until one stumbles across the desired memory; a good modern example would be to consider what processes we go through when we cannot find a set of keys or a wallet or purse or helping a student work through a series of forgotten mathematical steps. He also noted that mnemonic devices are useful as aids to memory. However, if one is in a passion, it is difficult for a memory to be imprinted on the soul for there is too much movement (affection or emotion) going on, while other people do not possess the requisite softness as it were for an image to be imprinted. The young are always in motion, so impressions are not made so well, while older people's minds have become like walls; the young are too moist, like running wax, the old too dry, he notes, drawing on his medical philosophy to help explain observable differences (*On Mem*, 450a29ff).

Accordingly, Aristotle was thoroughly empirical in his analysis of memory, but he also left us with an emphatic comment that the image that is recalled is a 'corporeal substrate,' that is a material entity existing in the mind, having been imposed there by the original sense perception. In this, he is not far removed from modern neurological understanding of the workings of the brain, although he added some physiognomical observations on the size of a person's head and their ability to recall – those with disproportionately sized heads have poorer memories because the weight of their heads presses down upon their perception organs, citing children and dwarfs (*On Mem*, 453a31–b7). Behind the observations, we must note, are the categories that Aristotle tended to impose, in this case physical differences explaining differences in memory, rather than a lack of memory training or habits, although his moral and psychological theories remind us that he was not so restricted by his materialism as Victorians hung up on physiognomy were.

Memory is intimately connected with imagination. The case of imagination is obscure, he wrote (*An*, 414b16), although like thinking it can certainly stand independent of the body in the sense that it does not need to be affected as it is by sensations, although he did describe it as a feeble sort of sensation (*Rhet*, 1370a28). But he also implied that a body is a necessary condition for possessing imagination in the first place (*An*, 403a8); some people, he hinted, live by imagination alone while others do not possess it (*An*, 415a11). Animals tend to follow their imagination without any further analysis of whether their imaginations are correct or not, while people possess the ability to judge their imaginings – and of course, the ability will differ among people. To imagine is like thinking but different from perception; sensations are always true, he noted, but imaginations are usually false (*An*, 428a11). They differ from assertions on what is right or wrong, for the latter involves a synthesis of thought or rational calculation (*An*, 432a10; 433b29). People can follow their imagination, then, and pursue erroneous actions (*An*, 433a10), for imagination may thus act similarly to any perceived sensation in creating a desire to act (*MA*, 701a5; 703b20); my imagined desire may promote an action to fulfill that desire.

Before moving onto mind, we must review Aristotle's thoughts on experience, for, as he saw it, from memory comes experience (*APst*, 101a2). From experience comes the principle of skill and of understanding (*APst*, 100a5–8), while upon experience come science and art (rather than relying on luck, say). Experience therefore leads us to form universal judgments of what we do and its causes, but to judge when to act is more of an art; that is, men who have much experience may achieve more than those who prefer theory over experience, for experience deals with individuals and art with universals and successful action in life is more dependent on experience than on theory. Relating that to medicine, the man with theory will not cure as well as a man who has the experiences and deals with a Callias or a Socrates. However, men of experience are usually not good at teaching what they do although they are much better at what they do than mere manual workers, who do not even think about what they do (these are like 'lifeless things' or automata). From which it follows for Aristotle that the only people who make good teachers are those who think about the theory behind what they do, giving consideration to causes and effects (*Met*, 981a1–9). Modern examinations, it may be maintained, especially for younger pupils, effectually promote the thoughtless over the thoughtful, for if a child manages to succeed in doing what the examination requires rather than learn, we can say that he is doing so thoughtlessly just like Aristotle's manual worker – my wife relates a tale of a child in her primary school tests who scored better for dotting his i's and crossing his t's but who told the same story each time he wrote one, compared to pupils who lost marks on the grammar but showed originality and breadth of plot.

The experienced, although they may not be able to explain why they do the things that they do, ought to be listened to just as much as to those who can demonstrate, implying, presumably through experiment or deductive logic, that experience 'has given them an eye they see aright' (*NE*, 1143b11); demonstrations deal with natural things rather than indefinite things (*APr*, 32b20). Yet experience pales in comparison with the pursuit of rationality, for it is of a baser and more commonly held ability – a horse gains experience just as a scientist may, but the scientist endeavors to learn about the causes that he is interested in rather than merely connect experienced associations.

Nous and *psychē*

The mind is the seat of human reason and for Aristotle it is the defining feature that distinguishes humanity from the rest of the animal kingdom; it is thus accorded an important place in his philosophy. While much that he wrote on life and humanity accepted a materialist view of the body, namely that its soul is material and inseparable from its organs, he also inherited from Plato a view of the mind as something ontologically special: the mind and understanding (*nous*):

> alone of our possessions seems to be immortal, this alone divine . . . mind is the god in us . . . We ought, therefore, either to philosophise or to say farewell to life and depart hence, since all other things seem to be great nonsense and folly.
>
> (*F*, B108)

The intellectual capacity is thus something unique to humanity and which sets us apart by partaking in what the gods presumably, or theoretically, possess. Despite the emphasis on materiality, we must remember Aristotle's vision of the hierarchy of life, which stretches upward from the more basic forms of life through to the more complicated with the pinnacle belonging to humanity; however, he also believed that there could, theoretically, be a stratum of beings above humanity – the gods – whose essential attribute was rationality unencumbered by the body (a very Platonic notion). While this picture should always be borne in mind with Aristotle, there is no doubt that the general thrust of his writing underscored the materiality and scientific comprehensibility of the natural world with perhaps a nod to his master or to generally held theology – the relationship between the two, incidentally, has fired philosophical imagination since his death.

As intelligence ascends through the animal kingdom up to humanity, so too does it through humanity. People are not equal in Aristotle's world: categories possess different levels of mental capacity, and while we may disagree with the implications drawn from his broad collectivizing, we can agree that there is a spectrum of ability (in different people and in the same people along different lines of activity or at different times); for Plato, the differences in people would be revealed during their formal education at which stage there would be a threefold split into the different classes that would inhabit his utopian Republic. For Aristotle the biologist-philosopher, such differences were, as with the rest of the animal kingdom, primarily in the breeding. Indeed, according to Jensen, Aristotle indirectly coined the term intelligence in the use that it has been given since as the assessment of a person's mental agility – his *dianoetic* was translated by Cicero into the Latin *intellegentia* (Jensen, 1998, p. 4).

It is difficult to explain why one person's mental abilities differ from another's, for the biological grounding upon which we are born (the expression of our unique DNA), which stimulates our neurological capacities can also be affected by environmental stimuli and intellectual exercise, while the cultural encouragement that we get to love learning may be countered by subcultures or a personal disliking for contemplation over action, of ignorance or inconsistency over knowledge and coherency. For Aristotle, though, humanity was to be considered initially through biological eyes and so he believed that he was correct in dividing people into broad *genii*: men, women, slaves, and children.

Categorizing people into groups follows a guiding theory upon which the data of humanity are to be grouped; as such, Aristotle's theorizing may be construed as apodictic or, literally, *de haut en bas* (from high to low), imposing an order upon the world's population – deductive rather than inductive, despite much of his writings on the inductive methods of experiencing and observing. In many respects, induction and deduction cannot be easily separated, for the deductionist will always require data from which to conceive theories, and the inductionist will at some point seek to organize material into more intellectually wieldy categories which have to be formed by the mind's operations. So when reviewing Aristotle's writing on men, women, and children, we are left wondering whether it was his theorizing that was at fault such that his prejudices clouded his observations, or whether indeed he proceeded from observation to assert a cogent theory of humanity's intellectual divisions. Aristocratic men naturally are the pinnacle of intellectual ability, followed by women and slaves – women and children differ naturally from their masters, he believed, for while the deliberative faculty is not present in slaves, in women it is present but 'ineffective' and in children (of good breeding), it is present but undeveloped (*Pol*, 1260a13–14) and children are inferior to adults because there is too much restlessness in their souls (*Phys*, 248a1).

To agree with Aristotle's broad generalizations would, in the present intellectual climate of the early twenty-first century, seem morally incorrect (commenting, for instance, on how his observations of things contemporary clouded his mind, which assumes that he did not think about them, possibly but not necessarily so) and recent critics tend to express embarrassment of his political notions. Yet it must also be recognized that his views (which reflected Ancient Greek prejudices) have been the mainstay of Western culture and many (but not all) other cultures right down to present times, so while we may condescendingly dismiss his prejudices, their import both in his philosophy and in human history should not be dismissed simply because the majority of us no longer believe in them (or would redefine them). Ideas change – not always for the better, and no great leap of the imagination is required to see how modern culture could unwind into more regular historical patterns and older prejudices. Perhaps, Aristotle would tell us, rightly so, for the notion of the equality of humanity is a deviation from the natural order of things: children are not adults, some people are not as intelligent as others, breeding matters. Such thoughts are found in conservative political philosophies that implicitly draw upon the Aristotelian (and other) influences, whereas the counterarguments are found in the classical liberal, libertarian, socialist, and anarchist philosophies of human nature, theorists of which may accept unequal talents but not inequality of political, legal, or moral status, which Aristotle does.

Nonetheless, while we can see that Aristotle upheld the prejudices of his time, he also sought to provide them with an intellectual rigor of sorts and his examination of the soul as mind (*nous*) is commandingly intriguing. His analysis of psychology can stand independent of the implications that he draws from his analysis (or, reading it differently, the imposition of his categories upon the analysis). In *On the Soul* Aristotle examines previous theories of the mind before exploring his own by noting that 'to attain any knowledge about the soul is one of the most difficult things in the world' (*An*, 402a10); notwithstanding a few comments on the divinity of thought, he dismisses the mind–body duality that is found in Plato, for the soul to act or to be acted upon requires a body (*An*, 403a6), and proceeds to explain his analysis of the soul as the essence of the body. When the soul and body conjoin, then, Aristotle argued, we find the most important attributes of all animals: we find sensation, memory, passion, appetite, desire, pleasure, pain. Unlike Plato, who divided the soul from its body, Aristotle claimed, as we saw above, that the two do correspond and are interlinked: the body cannot be simply dismissed as getting in the way of the mind's operations as Plato held (Cornford, 1957, p. 4). Knowledge is gained through the senses and it is of particulars as well as universals, rather than just universals. The senses are productive of pleasure, which can help the mind gauge that which is good or bad for the body, but, as we shall see later, pleasure constitutes a necessary but not sufficient condition for knowing the good. The senses perceive movement, and, positing a materialist view, Aristotle noted that too much movement in that which is perceived can cause damage and wreck the portals to knowledge. Body and soul are thus inseparable just as wax and its shape are inseparable, and in *On Sleep*, he emphasizes that that which is perceived affects the body and the soul jointly (*OS*, 454a7–10). A living entity necessarily possesses a soul as a substance (*ousia gar he kata ton logon*), corresponding to the account (or meaning – *logon*) of a thing (*An*, 412b6–11). Yet what does this mean and how does his theory relate to matters pedagogical?

Understanding the nature of the mind is a vital aspect of educational thinking, for after all it is the mind that is an integral part in any education, even if it is nominally physical training that is being learned (for any physical training necessarily engages the mind). Aristotle laid out much of the philosophical groundwork on psychology that naturally impacted on educational thinking picked up by his own students and later by his Scholastic critics and down to the modern era. The initial division of living matter and non-living matter provides us with the starting point for Aristotle, for that which is alive possesses something that inanimate material does not – that something becomes devilishly difficult to describe, with some philosophers preferring to avoid the debate by declaring that everything is material and so subject to the laws of the universe, whereas there are those who prefer to explain that living matter is animated by a soul but that soul is something unique and separable from the body it inhabits. Aristotle could not agree: for him the soul was the animating force but it was not separable; he rejected the pure materialism and psychological determinism of those who rejected soul's existence. He accepted that non-living material things are subject to external forces affected each in turn by the great flow of movement unleashed by the (eternal) motions of the universe, say, but the soul is its own mover, which reminds us that our audience or pupils are not bricks.

The soul (*psychē*) is the source of all movement in a living animal and all living things possess a soul (*OY*, 470a2). In modern times, the theory that all living things possess a power or quality that the non-living do not is called vitalism. Upheld by thinkers such as Henri Bergson among others, vitalism is readily dismissed by mainstream scientists, who reject it on the grounds that it is an ancient theory that modern science cannot accommodate, yet a simple rejection on grounds of its antiquity is not a valid philosophical procedure. Something distinguishes the living from the dead or inanimate materials and that something Aristotle simply termed soul; philosophically, we can leave it at that or demand further analysis and ask questions concerning the soul's whereabouts, whether it is separable from its living material, is it eternal or finite, and so on. If I am to teach a pupil, what presumptions am I making of her existence and potential? For Aristotle, it all hinges on the nature of the soul, how it relates to the physicality of the body, and its environment; for he was a materialist in much of his thinking, and if the soul is affected by material things then its will or the ability to learn will similarly be affected (consider how a class of children are affected by the year's first snowfall, or undergraduates after a night out).

Beginning with its function, Aristotle noted that the soul gives the animal its powers of self-nutrition, sensation, movement, and thinking; the soul is incorporated in the element of heat, for warmth helps its operations (*PA*, 652b11); the soul is also the master while the body is the ruler (*Pol*, 1254a35), and, as expected of Aristotle, he conjectured that the soul is provided by the male in all animals while the female provides the body or form (*GA*, 716a5–31; 738b25). Although he allows that thought can be distinguished from bodily activity, he does not accept that the mind is therefore physically separable: it is distinguishable as a definition in human language but that is all – a word does not necessarily indicate ontological status, except theoretically so, and thereby all the problems of dualism, the separate status of mind and body, disappear. If we think about 'that whereby we know,' Aristotle mused, we have two possibilities: the soul and knowledge. We know either through knowledge or through the soul that is, just as health and the body can be distinguished but not separated, but then Aristotle resorts to his teleological thesis that these things or some of them must be for the sake of something else and he relegates the qualities and abilities of the body to that of the soul: 'since it is the soul by which primarily we live, perceive, and think: it follows that the soul must be an account and essence, not matter or subject' (*An*, 414a12). Incidentally, each professional translation of this critical sentence presents confusion – for J. A. Smith also translates it elsewhere as 'a ratio for formulable essence,' while Hamlyn has 'a kind of principle and form.' The Greek is *hōste logos tis an eiē kai eidos*, loosely meaning, on my thinking, that the soul is 'in effect a sort of thought and form.' The soul is certainly not material and thus it is not an object in the sense of a material object taking up space, but its immateriality does not give it eternality; it remains the thing (*ousia*) that, Aristotle held, exists as the causation of all movement (*An*, 415b22). The body does not possess its own 'actuality,' for it cannot actualize itself into anything, so the soul is the seat of actuality (and hence Aristotle's *entelechy*), by which he means that the body cannot do anything in the absence of the soul – the soul is the body's driver. This contrasts with the several dualist theories such as the epiphenomenalist thesis which asserts that the soul is a passive repository of sensory experiences upon which personality accumulates, which resurfaces in recent claims that neuroscientists are still befuddled as to where memory is said to reside.

Since the soul is the body's driver, we must attend Aristotle's thinking on it carefully, for its nature – abilities and limits – defines what we are educating as teachers and what is being educated as learners and what in turn drives our curiosity.

Aristotle's description of life follows a hierarchy through increasingly complex beings, from the nutritive and reproductive, the appetitive, the sensory, the locomotive, and the thoughtful (*An*, Book II). Each category possesses the previous capacity and each capacity represents the soul's abilities, so the nutritive and reproductive constitute the basest forms of the soul's power, hence a plant possesses a simple soul. The pure empiricist account of the mind would rest on Aristotle's sensory-cum-locomotive divisions, thereby denying the initiation of thought, for sensation can produce association upon which movement can be motivated (horse sees grass, trots over, munches grass). But for Aristotle everything strains to reach a higher category of life, and so 'the most natural act is the production of another like itself [so] it may partake in the eternal and divine' (*An*, 415a28). Although living things cannot actually attain divinity, divinity, Aristotle's theoretical concept, is in effect permanent rest, but life for the animate is characterized by agitated striving. The mention of the divine falls into Aristotle's general thesis that all things belong to an ontological hierarchy that ascends through the aforementioned powers of living creatures up through thinking beings (people) and into the theoretical possibility of beings of Pure Thought – the gods or God. Controversy exists over Aristotle's own beliefs at that point, but to remain with the soul's abilities, he noted that 'the soul is the cause or source of the living body' in the sense that it is the source of movement, the essence of the living body, and its end (*An*, 415b9–11; *PA*, 645b19). The last reminds us of the teleological account of everything: 'for nature, like thought, always does whatever it does for the sake of something, which something is its end' (*An*, 415b15). In effect, the soul is the source of motion – of will – as well as the end for which all action is done, and for people the best end is the formation of an excellent character (*NE*, 1098a16).

The soul also knows: it knows that which exists, and since those things which exist are seemingly material and take up space, knowledge can only come to the soul via the body's senses (*An*, 432a6). Accordingly, everything that is, is a possible object of thought, but this implies for Aristotle that the mind itself is not actually any real thing in the sense that an elephant is – thought is nothing until it has actually thought (*An*, 429b31); it stands somewhat separate from the body in that regard, that when we think about something thinkable we are able to retain the thought of it in a very different manner in which a loud noise is only carried as a sensation for that instance and cannot qualitatively be repeated (*An*, 429a1–5). However, in a more controversial statement, Aristotle held that the thinking part of the soul 'must be potentially identical in character with its object without being the object' (*An*, 429a16) and 'the mind which is actively thinking is the objects which it thinks' (*An*, 431b16). This is an intriguing proposition, for if I think of an elephant, is the thinking part of my soul identical with that which I think – an elephant? That the thought requires a sensation seems reasonable, but whether the corresponding and later thought is equivalent is by no means certain, for the imagination tends to warp our original sensations or impressions. In a sense, Aristotle's thesis implies that which is thought that is necessarily identical with the object, at least potentially so (*An*, 429a16), insofar as I do not return my thought to the objects in my head, it is mine wholly and absolutely, but once I seek to clarify the object of my thinking with the original percept, it is no longer clear that my object is the same.

Nonetheless, he continues, the objects of the mind are separable from the objects of reality; particularly in the case of abstracts, they may be said to exist independently and as such in thinking of magnitude in the absence of a physical object, the thought is identical with the object of mind because both are in a sense abstract. Truth stems from this identity, while falsehood comes from combining ideas. The content of thought are images – thought cannot take place without images garnered from the world through the senses (*An*, 431a17; 432a6). Thinking, in Aristotle's philosophy, itself is impossible without any image to work on, and images come from the senses. Imagination and memory are linked in turn in the soul by the impressions that the senses have made upon the soul: all the images that the imagination forms are derived from memories, which is a thoroughly empiricist argument with a recognizably modern materialist foundation.

In turn, the images prompt a feeling of pleasure or of pain, which tells the mind what to pursue and what to avoid (*An*, 431b2–9) – and so our primary education is thoroughly immersed in the natural: 'Where there is sensation, there is pleasure and pain' (*An*. 413b23). This produces an interesting development to his psychological theorizing: although we are generally forming a picture of Aristotelian educational philosophy as one that underlines the intellect as the highest form of activity for man, here we have an emphatic indication that primary action at least is governed hedonistically – by pleasure and pain.

Thus, as we go beyond mere instinctual reaction, movement is generated by the operation of either appetite or imagination, which calculates the end of an action and which in turn stimulates appetite (*An*, 433a20). This also implies that pure reason – the unallied realm of thought – cannot initiate movement, for it deals with speculative notions, so knowledge alone cannot motivate a man to do anything (*An*, 433a7), but when thought is connected to achieving an end, then it may be said to engage the agent in action alongside appetite, for where there is no appetite, no desire for a different set of circumstances, no action will occur. Desire includes wishing, impulses, and appetite (*MA*, 700b21). Although pleasing things indicate to the mind what ought to be pursued and what painful things ought to be avoided, a person becomes bad by pursuing pleasures or pains which he ought not (*NE*, 1104b20–21). But since there are pleasures of the body and pleasures of the mind, Aristotle is able to bring his audience back round to the importance of the intellect as being of higher value than mere sensation and a theoretical imposition of the motive according to a moral analysis, so we return to teach others what we ought to do.

Sensation is necessary and vital to Aristotle's theory of knowledge and hence of learning, but, we shall discover, it cannot be sufficient – logic and deductive processes are also important.

Thinking

Typically, Aristotle moves beyond the acts or thoughts that have purpose as such, that aim for another end, to describe the higher values. The higher values are those that are done for their own sake. When thought is purposeless but does unravel truths then it is purer in a sense. Action that follows the right aims and pursues the right means to those ends (practical wisdom – *phronēsis*) is accorded a lower status than the pursuit of rationality (*theoria*) or the 'activity of soul in conformity with the best and most complete' (*NE*, 1098a16); in other words, Aristotle converges onto a theory of perfectionism, a nod as it were to the Platonic system in which he was initially immersed.

From induction, we begin to learn of universals – that this horse is similar to that horse on grounds of their horsiness when their incidentals are removed. This involves an intuitive leap – grasping universality rather than forming a probability statement or merely resigning oneself epistemologically to the fate of seeing each entity as a unique instantiation rather than as a something that possesses commonalties with other things: this is the initiation of thinking. While even a non-vocal infant grasps that this red ball is similar to that blue ball in both being balls, some empirical philosophers are not keen to claim any justification for a separate entity 'ball' on that account, there is only ball 1 and ball 2; but consider what Aristotle says: 'when one of the undifferentiated things makes a stand, there is a primitive universal in the mind (for though one perceives the particular, perception is of the universal – e.g. of man but not of Callias the man)' (*APst*, 100a15). The mind leaps to the universal when faced with numerous examples – the 'ah-hah!' moment of cognition perceptible in pupils' faces.

We can also learn of universals through deductive or scientific reasoning. Thought is continuous rather than discrete and does not possess a magnitude (*An*, 407a7). Drawing the two together, the intuitive science based on induction and the ratiocination of deductive reasoning, we have the path to philosophy: to thinking at its highest. And so philosophy seeks the truth as it stands, not as it exists instrumentally for something else, for it aims to disclose eternal truths (*Met*, 993b20–30), truths in themselves we could say, and, analogous to Plato's famous metaphor of the cave (*Rep*, 524), 'as the eyes of bats are to the light of day, so is the reason in our soul to the things which are by nature most evident of all' (*Met*, 993b10).

Yet the investigation of truth is both easy and hard: 'no one is able to attain the truth adequately, while, on the other hand, no one fails entirely, but everyone says something true about the nature of things' (*Met*, 993a27). Not all that is thought is logical, some products of thought come about by chance, but such thoughts are aimless and apparently of no worth (*APst*, 95a3–9). This presents an awkward moment in Aristotle's logic, for if the purposelessness of thought is at once useless *and* the highest form of thinking, there must be something to distinguish Pure Thought from those images and thoughts that are unallied with life's aims or which are simple daydreaming. Yet at times random formations can provide insight and truths at unexpected moments.

The theoretical sciences – mathematics, natural sciences (sometimes translated as metaphysics), and theology – are of higher status than the applied sciences since they seek eternal truths, that is to deal with being *qua* being, rather than being as a particularity. They deal with causes, and causation can be due either completely to nature (as modern science would hold) or to a prime mover. If nature is the cause of all movement (energy we could say) and no prime mover exists, then, for Aristotle, the natural sciences become the most important sciences of all; otherwise should there be an unmoved mover then philosophy (not, interestingly, theology) constitutes the highest intellectual endeavor possible (*Met*, 1026a28–32). Philosophy contemplates truth and this activity is done for its own sake, indeed loved for its own sake rather than for any other purpose; reason's activity, contemplation, is superior to all other forms of activity and therein lies the complete happiness of man (*NE*, 1177b17–26).

As we rise up through the levels of capability, we have been converging onto the highest abilities evident to us, namely thinking. Thinking divides between that which is interested in things useful for us and that which is useful in and of itself, usually divided into active and passive intellect, active intellect dealing with science or metaphysics (whose goal is truth alone) and with deliberation (whose goal is practicality – practical wisdom, etc.). Active or Pure Thought cannot be moved by anything else, so it is humanity's divine spark, that which we share with the gods. Interestingly, despite a general empirical and materialist disposition, Aristotle defines active thought (or Pure Thought as it may be better understood) as something that is separable from the body (*An*, 413b25; 429b5). Critics admit that it is an awkward passage that barely connects with the rest of his psychology (Barnes, 2000, p. 108; Copleston, 1985, p. 331). Perhaps this was for his audience, or an echo of Plato, or perhaps his reflections were to allow the introduction of the theoretical level of beings higher than man who are Pure Thought unencumbered by body: it would after all keep the hierarchy tidy, yet this Pure Thought, unencumbered by the memories of life, would not end with the life of its possessor as memories and desires and fears would, for it is eternal: it also emanates from the outside (*An*, 408b24–30; *GA*, 736b28), which begs the question – whence?

Thought is for a purpose (*An*, 415b15); thought is of a something that exists (*An*, 427a21); it is part imagination and part judgment (*An*, 427b28); but while we are capable of calling upon our imagination at will, we are not free to form opinions concerning truthhood and falsehood, which in turn require a synthesis of thoughts (*An*, 427b16–21; 432a10). It is, however, something that is not passive but active (and thus higher than the passivity of perception), and when it turns on itself, can think about thinking – then its objects are the same as what is thought, but when I think of an object external to me, my mind probably does not possess a true image, for it requires the use of memory, infused with imagination, to produce. So 'thought ... is what it is by virtue of becoming all things' (*An*, 430a14). When what I think of is identical with the object, then I possess knowledge. While senses produce the form of sensible things – I feel the shape of the ball – thought produces the form of forms (*An*, 432a5), the universality of the idea of ball; and since there is nothing outside the world of experience, the content of our minds is always based on sensible things, 'hence no one can learn or understand anything in the absence of sense' (*An*, 432a6).

This last comment is a reminder that Aristotle demands we return to what we can know in this universe – that which lies beyond the realm of the senses cannot be known and only be conjectured. Sensory data pose a limit to our knowledge, then, although the mind strains to understand the nature of things behind the data – the nature of their being, or metaphysical questions, and although the mind is able to intuit universals and to follow the logic of what we know from our basest to our highest abilities and beyond to the realm of thought, thinking without bodily form, such leaps are just that. These are things that remain theoretical possibilities, but not actualities in the sense that we could ever perceive them.

Thought, as noted above, can never work alone to cause action; it always invokes appetite (desire) (*An*, 433a23) and so is fundamentally connected to the body and has its affects. This in turn leads us to Aristotle's thoughts that discuss the ways in which appetite can let thought down, for thought can never be wrong as such, but desires can be misplaced (*An*, 433a26). This is because while thought (and its ally, desire) is unmoved by anything else, appetite's goal is the apparent good, while thought's goal is the real good, but desire is dependent on opinion, which may or may not be right; thought, however, is moved by the object of thought (*Met*, 1072a26–30).

Forms of wisdom

From sensation, memory, experience, and mind, Aristotle takes us higher on the ladder of ability and learning and into the reaches of wisdom. Wisdom constitutes the highest that education can take us – to become in effect intellectually self-sufficient is the Aristotelian ideal for man. As an ideal, however, the purely wise man of thought remains for him a guide not a reality, for we are, he acknowledged, too implanted in human nature to succeed in striving so high. Perception alone, we have seen, does not bring understanding (*APst*, 87b29):

understanding comes only through learning the universalities involved in what is perceived. At this junction, between those aspects of learning that humanity shares with some of the animal kingdom, and those which are peculiarly man's, we find we may enter philosophy's halls – for here, once thought is engaged, logic may be taken up (or rejected) and we may begin to distinguish good from poor thinking, truth from falsity, and wisdom from ignorance.

Plato's Socrates had sought to separate belief from knowledge in his discussions with Athenian citizens, and Aristotle in turn sought to provide a securer logical basis for arguing and building up a theory. He was the founder of formal logic and wrote a treatise in *Sophistical Refutations*, as well as his outline of logical methods in *Prior* and *Posterior Analytics*, and the *Topics*. His logic was relevant for logic's sake but also because it has been taught and learned as an essential element in scholarly education since his time.

For instance, consider a non-controversial philosophical idea that an opinion is generally held to be a proposition that may or may not be correct: it is often introduced with 'I believe P' whereas truth is simply 'P'; sorting out people's thinking is nonetheless a difficult task, for, as Socrates discovered, people speak as if they are certain of what they are referring to, whereas often they are only believing that what they say is true. A mark of the educated man is to be able to judge arguments, and particularly the wise man will be able to judge well on all topics (*PA*, 639a1–12); he can also differentiate opinions from statements purporting to be truths. An opinion differs from understanding, Aristotle argued, for understanding necessitates the truth (so long as the logic is valid, it must be noted), whereas forming an opinion is like perceiving something – it is an immediate belief that agrees with appearances (*APst*, 89a5). But these can be misleading: 'many things which do not exist are objects of opinion' (*Top*, 121a22), for opinions are to do with things that exist and which do not exist, hence they do not necessarily imply truthfulness: take an enjoyable look at Aristotle's *On Marvelous Things Heard*. Indeed, the man who has opinions and not knowledge is, he intones, like a sick man to a healthy man (*Met*, 1008a30), for opinions and beliefs may be wrong since they often involve contradictions and so cannot be right. In contrast to opinion, knowledge deals with that which is necessary knowledge; that is, its truth cannot be otherwise, though other knowledge does depend on beliefs about what is the case rather than what is the case regardless whether we believe in it or not (*APst*, 71a12).

Specific education would thus, along Aristotelian lines, draw our attention to the importance of teaching pupils (perhaps, if we may extend his thoughts into early education) the difference between opinions and verifiable statements, such as 'I believe Shakespeare meant this here,' and the more objective 'Shakespeare meant this here.' The latter form is much more readily discussable, and unlike opinions helps to produce knowledge, the necessary condition of wisdom. In itself, such a proposal is not controversial: it is a useful exercise to distinguish between what is and what is believed to be; however, people do get emotionally attached to theories that are seemingly scientific or logical, which today demands a greater alertness on the content of what is claimed over the hedging of theories behind statements such as 'I believe X.' This is particularly true and deserving our critical attention when theories are uttered by experts or well-known personages in their field and are so dressed in sophistic clothing – especially if we think about slick campaigns or lobbying – as to seem true.

Wisdom begins in our curious nature, which forms an agitation to know and to grasp meanings and relationships. This Aristotelian restlessness is a disposition of the human soul (*Top*, 145a36), and accordingly its activity, a motion to discover, must come to a rest in knowledge (the satiation of its entelechic drive) until curiosity burns again and our soul becomes once more unsettled. While the philosopher may agree with Aristotle, is his theory a description of a universality, or a prescription as to how we should live our lives with respect to learning? Often, we encounter the epistemic barrier, 'don't go there,' either because a too enormous shift of perspective would be required and/or there is too much emotional investment involved in a held opinion for the person to alter his or her thinking without fear or trepidation. For Aristotle, such barriers would entail a relinquishing of mind to emotion or to a preference for ignorance and would be inexplicable for those surely capable of reasoning well (the well-educated civilians of the *polis*) but explicable for those whom he deemed incapable of reasoning beyond a certain level (his infamous trinity of children, women, and slaves).

The knowledge that is the realm for the wise is based on five states: art, knowledge, practical wisdom, comprehension or intuitive thinking, and philosophical wisdom (*NE*, 1139b16–18); he does not deal with them all in what follows in the *Ethics*, so we shall attempt to build upon the thesis. Education is a practical art, for it aims to build character and secure the foundation for the pursuit of happiness both in the state and in the individual (Burnet, 1903, p. 1).

When we consider a perception – of a sound, a movement, or a scent – we may agree that this provides the mind with the data of life, but knowledge, for Aristotle, is something higher. Knowledge belongs to the mind, yet knowing something is not the process as such: it is the end result of our curiosity that leads us to seek and to perceive, and when I say that I now know (the answer), then my philosophical restlessness, 'the deepest craving of human beings' (Verbeke, 1990, p. 11) is satiated and my mind comes to a rest, as it were (*Phys*, 247b3–19). A reason that Aristotle gives for knowledge providing soul's rest is that it deals with things that are necessarily true and which are thus eternal or universal in nature (*NE*, 1139b19–34), and what is eternal is – theoretically for Aristotle, remember – at rest.

Yet what does this mean, philosophically speaking, for our learning on earth and thus what connection can we make to the world of education? If we take up Aristotle's theory, then once I know that $a^2=b^2+c^2$ and have worked through a proof, then I know it, and the knowledge cannot be challenged further. The Pythagorean solution to orthogonal triangles is thus eternal and universal, and why should my mind be further unsettled? Well, I could break out of two-dimensional mathematics by asking what happens when I bend space and so become restive once more, but non-Euclidean geometry sets us off down another curious path indeed. But we can ask whether that makes the Pythagorean solution universal; arguably, it is within its confines – philosophers, of course, are curious as to what constitutes universally valid propositions, a subject that logic ostensibly deals with (as Aristotle elucidated), but it also invokes in its own right metaphysics and ontology. For instance, if I agree that there is a proposition P and then relate it to proposition Q, I am saying something at least about the world. But there we may jog off into the logical discussions of other books. Specifically regarding educational methods, his thesis provokes us to inquire (and to encourage pupils to inquire) what the ultimate aim of education can be – should it be the search for universals? Inquiring into their nature is the stuff of Aristotle's metaphysics, which he generally erred on asserting that they were the thingness corresponding to a group of similar entities rather than an ontologically separate and existing set of Ideas as Plato held. But what if such Aristotelian universals are very limited in number or cannot uncontroversially be formed of any similar entities? The latter is the skeptic's retort of particularist thinkers: all that I know can only be particular entities and hence any attempt to mold individual entities into universals is a hapless task; no two snowflakes are the same, they may assert. To which Aristotle would respond, at least we both know we are looking at a range of things called snowflakes.

Elsewhere, Aristotle admits of a range of human potential in his thoughts on politics and society, and presumably only the best thinkers should set their intellectual targets on knowledge in this sense – it is a reminder that wisdom's halls are limited to the best among us, which has repercussions both political and ethical in turn that we may wish to acknowledge or denounce.

Art

While experience is a higher form of activity than just sensing, for it involves memory and learning, it becomes an art in the craftsman; art, for Aristotle, is the practical wisdom of dealing with particular circumstances and individuals (*phronēsis*), whereas science reaches beyond the need for practicality and deals with pure knowledge or understanding things for their own sake (*theoria*). Actions are learned in order to pursue the higher end of the art – healing is learned to practice medicine, for instance. Only people are capable of art, even though we may wonder at the intricacies of a spider's web, which is not art for there is no deliberation involved: the presence of deliberative action thus defines art for Aristotle (*Phys*, 199a20–24). Building upon experience and deliberation form the conditions of practicing an art, and this trips into a most important area of Aristotle's philosophy found in the *Nicomachean Ethics*: that one becomes just by doing just things, or one becomes proficient at an art by doing that art. He distinguishes the moral perfection that a man may attain from the art that he practices, but both have in common the need to do in order to become, the former to act and the latter to make: 'art is the reasoned capacity to make, involving a true course of reasoning' (*NE*, 1140a10), while in the doing there is no other end except the doing (hence the 'lifelessness of manual labor') – in playing the harp, the end is playing the harp. Art is involved with making and is contingent upon pursuing a correct method of reasoning (*NE*, 1140a10–23).

Art in turn may imitate nature (what may be called technology or technical art) and may indeed complete what nature cannot (*Phys*, 194a22; 199a16; *Pol*, 1337a1). A spider spins a web and so produces a form out of matter, and the end (and so the cause) is the form of the web that it produces, and this is analogous to a person making a hammer or a musical instrument, for instance; so, he reasoned, just as a person may make a mistake and not achieve the end sought, nature too may err (*Phys*, 199b1), which relieves him of the problem implied that nature does everything for the best, for patently it may create monstrous creatures or destructive forces that annihilate life. Reversing the argument, though, Aristotle used the fact that an artisan aims to produce something to justify, more controversially, his belief that nature also aims to produce something. That is, nature, is teleological: everything that comes to be in effect comes to be from something (*Met*, 1032a12) and why it comes to be is explicable in terms of having a purpose (see above).

Nonetheless and less controversially, technology (from the Greek *technē*) augments that which has been provided by nature, as the hammer extends the hitting power of a man's fist. Man is thus capable of improving his natural endowment and this is what art and technology strive to do.

Fine art, incidentally, is an imitation of nature, and Aristotle's theory of art has to be contrasted with Plato's, for his master argued that just as the world of appearances is a second-hand version of the true world of Forms, so an artist's work is a third-hand rendition of Forms; the artist seeks to copy the world of appearances. Aristotle, Copleston notes, was more inclined to argue that the artist actually seeks to find that which is universal in his art, whether it be literature or sculpting (Copleston, 1985, p. 360); in other words, the artist invokes a philosophical, educative enterprise. Again, Aristotle refers to a natural tendency to artistry in a broad sense, for he observed that to imitate is natural for man as we see it in children, and adults in turn delight in artists' representations; this is further explained by our love of learning, which 'is the greatest of all pleasures not only to the philosopher but also to the rest of mankind, however small their capacity for it' (*Poet*, 1448b6–11; 13–15).

Poetry is a particular kind of art that uses meter and forms of language; however, Aristotle is quick to note that it is not just the writing of verses that makes a poem but its content, for the work of Empedocles, although he wrote in meter, remains a physicist's text rather than a poem (*Poet*, 1447b18). The artist aims to exaggerate for his purposes representing people as either much better or much worse than they really are (*Poet*, 1448a3–4) and through exaggerating or idealizing, art captures universality in character and action. Comedy is an imitation of men worse than the average, while the ridiculous is ugly: it represents deformity and deviation (*Poet*, 1449a32); similarly, there must be poetic justice in a plot, for a good man must not fall to bad fortune or a bad man rise to good fortune (*Poet*, 1452b34). He proceeds to explore what he thought made a good plot and good character, which is beyond our remit here, but suffice it to note that in the grand scheme of his philosophy, fine art finds its place as representing the essences or universalities that we understand.

This particularly relates to the universal concept of beauty; however, Aristotle's definition of what is beauty slips and slides and no exact definition is forthcoming. In the *Rhetoric*, beauty is the good; in the *Topics*, it is what is pleasing to the eye, which suggests a materialistic account of an entity causing a concomitant stirring in the body; but in the *Problems*, 'not every kind of beauty is pleasant,' for we may look upon handsome men and enjoy their beauty without possessing a desire to have sex with them (*Prob*, 896b10–24); while in the *Metaphysics*, beauty is not the good as such (1078a31) but something that possesses order, symmetry, and definiteness, which allows a nod to the Pythagoreans and the theory that mathematics demonstrates a beauty of its own (*Met*, 1078b1). Art remains a human endeavor that proceeds from the soul while nature's movement begins in itself (*Met*,

1032b1; 1070a8). It is a manifestation of that element – reason – which Aristotle refers to as the divine within. Needless to say, his aesthetical philosophy continues to encourage philosophical debate.

The implication from Aristotle's explanation of art is that there are good forms and poor forms – those that pursue the 'correct form of reasoning' of evoking universals in our enjoyment possessing, by implication, a higher value than those that do not. Accordingly in teaching art properly, Aristotle would have us address the question of what makes some artwork better than others: his *Poetics* was certainly a tract on what it is that makes art excellent, berating some playwrights and praising others as producing what we would now call 'classical works' – works of art that we enjoy returning to again and again for, if we look upon them through Aristotelian eyes, they capture something eternally laudable and perhaps indeed touch that divine spark that connects the prehistoric artists of the cave with their modern counterparts.

Practical wisdom

In contrast to the technical skills required to make a good pair of shoes or a good flute or even a healthy body, which belong to the lower orders of society or of the mind, practical wisdom belongs properly with the aristocracy. Practical wisdom (*phronēsis*) deals with our awareness of the highest values that we can pursue: its object is the pursuit of the good life (*NE*, 1140a28). Accordingly, since it does not deal with the skills of life, it involves deliberation (*bouleusis*), which involves reasoning and should be done relatively slowly, for it differs from conjecturing, which may be swift in its operation (*NE*, 1142b1–15); it is about things that happen with some degree of frequency, but in which the event is obscure (*NE*, 1112b7–10). With regard to action, deliberation is about thinking what ought to be pursued and then thinking about how best to secure those goals; specifically, it discloses which acts are good in themselves rather than which are good for the pursuit of another end (*NE*, 1140b6) – it is not a state of understanding as such, as when I suddenly realize that the morning star is the evening star that is Venus, which is not practically oriented, but rather the wisdom of doing the right thing. Education is thus practical wisdom.

Much practical wisdom involves interacting with others, so political wisdom is a form of practical wisdom, for its aim is the common good as befitting man in general rather than the pursuit of one's own interests; these in turn require a wisdom concerning how to manage the household as well as a political wisdom, for without good government or good household management, it is difficult to see how one can pursue one's own interests well (*NE*, 1142a9). In itself, practical wisdom cannot be the best pursuit in the world, since it deals with men and man is not the best thing in the world (*NE*, 1141a20). Evidently, some animals also possess practical wisdom, knowing with foresight what is in their best interests, but because it deals with a wide range of possibilities affecting us and a wide range of options ahead of us, it does not constitute proper wisdom – so philosophers such as Anaxagoras and Thales knew admirable or remarkable things, but in general their knowledge was useless: it had no point, even though it dealt with the higher reaches of the mind (*NE*, 1141b4).

To possess practical wisdom is to engage in virtuous behavior, for it involves reaching for the best ends the right way; to act well without considering the ends is to be merely clever, or villainous if aimed at evil ends (*NE*, 1144a26), but it hardly constitutes being wise. Educationally, then, we would expect the Aristotelian to explain the relationship between means and ends and hence to avoid an absolute deontology and an absolute consequentialism and perhaps to seek the balance between them. Indeed, we later read of Thomas Aquinas attempting to promote such a reading of Aristotle in his medieval tome the *Summa Theologiae*. At a level below philosophical wisdom, practical wisdom is necessary: it forms the bedrock of higher wisdom but also reminds us that Aristotle preferred to reconnect his philosophy back to life and the appropriate actions required rather than remain on the abstract realm that has become the stereotype of the absent-minded professor – such a character, for Aristotle, would epitomize a failing or deviation from human potential, not its apex. Being practically wise involves forming good character, for it invokes knowledge both of good ends and of the proper means, and in acting upon one's ends properly, virtuosity or moral excellence is promoted, which contrasts with the indolent or fearful pontificator of great acts, or even the man who acts without thought.

Philosophical wisdom

As we reach the pinnacle of Aristotle's hierarchy, we attain the level of philosophy – the love of wisdom. Wisdom, we have seen, stems from experience and from understanding how the means fit the ends sought after, though there is, for Aristotle, a tier of activity that does not assume a utilitarian or end-oriented path, but is done for the sake of itself. This is akin to the realms of what we would call pure science and pure mathematics – studies done for their own intellectual sake rather than for the production of a better rocket or car; philosophy, then, deals with justice rather than the just nature of this or that act (*Prob*, 917a3–5), that is with the universals that we encounter or begin to understand rather than the particulars (*Met*, 1061b25).

The value of philosophical teaching, he wrote, cannot be measured in money (*NE*, 1164b3–4). To his pupil Alexander, Aristotle wrote:

> Many a time, Alexander, has Philosophy seemed to me truly divine and supernatural, especially when in solitude she soars to contemplate of things universal and strives to recognize the truth that is in them ... [it is fitting for him,] the noblest of rulers, should pursue the inquiry into the greatest of all subjects and that philosophy should entertain no trivial thoughts.
>
> (*OTU*, 391a1–3; b6–8)

Indeed, it is owing to their wonder that men first began and still do philosophize, and as man's curiosity deepened it shifted from dealing with scientific problems to dealing with science in order to know for its own sake (*Met*, 982b12). When philosophical areas fall into place, philosophy first defines existence and essence (i.e. metaphysics) and investigates being as being (*Met*, 1003a22), but overall, philosophy is 'knowledge of the truth' (*Met*, 993b20).

Yet even here, at the pinnacle of man's potential – to philosophize – Aristotle the biologist does not disappear: philosophers are a type whose form is promoted by a certain imbalance in the humors that affect the body. In particular, philosophers (and other eminent men) tend to be morose due to too much black bile production; entertainingly, the atrabilious temperament is flatulent but lustful (also a condition produced by red wine, he noted) – philosophers are accordingly (due to this excess of air) thin and their veins stand out due to the abundance of air or breath in them. These causes can produce a wide range of effects (cold black bile becomes dull and stupid, hot black bile erotic or clever); if it affects the mind, then the person becomes inspired, or if it calms down then a practically wise person is produced. The atrabilious lustful character stands in ironic contrast to the image of Aristotle passed down to Diogenes Laertius.

He proceeds to examine the kinds of characters that philosophers become, whether they are proper philosophers or those who merely seek refuge in philosophy for some reason, types that we may recognize as still around us today. The true philosopher investigates truth (*Prob*, §XXX.1), whereas sophists and dialecticians are hampered by a wrongly placed desire not to discover truth (according to Aristotle, that is); in the case of the sophists, they are said to deal with appearances only, whereas the dialecticians of the Academy are too promiscuous in embracing everything (*Met*, 1004b16–23). Today we may call the latter spin doctors and skeptics or nihilists, but the same problem underlies their work – it is rarely a search for truths. However, there are others who take refuge in theory 'thinking they are philosophers' and they are similar, Aristotle notes, to people who upon receiving a medical professional's advice, do none of the things they are ordered to do (*NE*, 1105b6–7). Hume was obviously aggravated by similar people two millennia later: 'Disputes with men, pertinaciously obstinate in their principles, are, of all others, the most irksome; except perhaps, those with persons entirely disingenuous, who really do not believe the opinions they defend ...' (Hume, 1983, p. 13). We would thus expect Aristotle to teach his pupils to proceed against dogmatism as well as epistemic nihilism and, more interestingly, to guard against living for theory alone with the implication that they remove themselves from the necessary chores or indeed pleasures to be found in life.

Recall that Aristotle's philosophy is to deal with the first principles of thinking; it then proceeds, initially from induction and then through and also alongside deductive processes to seek the truths of matters human and natural. As a discipline in itself, it raises the mind higher than the appetitive desires that tempt it elsewhere to study and to contemplate – the bedrock of the contented life. The philosopher 'must be able to state the most certain principles of all things' (*Met*, 1005b10).

The wise man

The wise man, Aristotle's apex of ability, is contemplative and presumably happy, despite the atrabilious character that seems to be symptomatic of the philosopher! This wisdom is not for all to attain, and perhaps only the greatest minds to attain periodically, similar to Buddhist monks, who meditate to feel the great void (which the present Dalai Lama mentioned in a talk that he had felt only a few times). The contemplative life involves thinking about the eternal or pure things (*theoria*), and in turning his thoughts to universals and eternal things the philosopher transcends to some extent his humanity, for *theoria* – contemplation – properly belongs to the gods as divine *nous* or Mind; it is accordingly superior to other forms of good activity for its pleasure is found purely in itself (*NE*, 1177b20–34). It is also self-sufficient, for it does not rely on others, although conversation may enable the philosopher to think better or pursue different paths.

Intellectual self-sufficiency is also an important element to Aristotle's economic theories, for he, like Plato, believed that the self-sufficient state is the best kind of state, rather than one that is dependent upon others for trade (*Pol*, 1326b27). Since that is rarely an achievable condition, trade is deemed to be a necessary evil – echoing Aristotle's distrust or distaste of things *banausic* (commercial), although in general he supported private property and wealth accumulation as having good moral effects and attempts to restrict property and wealth having bad effects. Similarly then, given the economic autarkic ideal, the philosopher should aim for intellectual self-sufficiency – to be able to work things out himself, so when the economic necessities of life have been adequately supplied, the leisurely

philosophical life proper to the wise man is within reach; not that the
happy wise man requires much, for 'we can do noble acts without
ruling the earth' (*NE*, 1177a27; 1178b33–1179a8), which may have
been a guarded criticism of Alexander. The self-sufficient life makes
life desirable for nothing is lacking (being provided for, that is, by
workers) and so we expect this to be the happiest of all states: the
complete good is this self-sufficiency (*NE*, 1097b8–16; 1177a33). But
Aristotle, always with an eye on this life, is quick to note that this is
not a solitary life, for, although the contemplating philosopher would
aim to contemplate the eternal things alone and 'his own society is
good enough for him,' man is a social animal and friendship is one of
the greatest values that we can enjoy – so the happy philosopher will
live with friends (*NE*, 1169b3–21; 1244b7). His friends are few and
equal to him, which means that he can neither teach them nor learn
from them (*EE*, 1245a16), their relationship implicatively providing
another need that is natural to man. Extending his analysis of the
sociable wise man, he also notes that in the ideal state, political justice
is suitably found among men who are self-sufficient (*NE*, 1134a26),
for we judge better when we are intellectually and economically
independent than when we are in want (*EE*, 1244b19) and so
dependent on others; in the mind of Karl Popper this was nothing less
than a justification of what became feudalism (Popper, 1986, p. 3).

Such is the ideal to which we should once again reach and
accordingly teach our pupils. It is not, however, an ideal for young
people while they are still young, for they are not capable of judgment
and intellectual independence, for that can only belong to the more
mature mind. Naturally, we can ask when that is – Aristotle, it must be
assumed, is thinking of middle age: the years following the turmoil of
youth and before the hardening of the mind to new experience. It is, as
with much that Aristotle writes, a commonsensical proposition but
leaves us considering the implications of the nature of the
philosophical man: is he one to whom we owe allegiance, for instance,
or merely one to whom we should listen but without any formal
understanding as to the youth's subservience? The vision is a
conservative one, in which the wise should be heard, but Aristotle
did not believe that his wise man should also be king: he is there for
advice, for that is his specialty and that is all – Plato had evidently

failed to reform politicians into philosophers or philosophers into politicians. The downside is that such a conservative morality may forego the aggressive competitiveness of youth, who may provide the solution to social, political, or economic problems that the more conservatively minded aged would not risk.

The philosophical man becomes the Aristotelian guide for education – the intellectual leader to whom we turn for sagacity and honesty in all affairs. It is a particularly edifying or comfortable vision in some respects but also one that seemingly reflects Aristotle's conception of himself. Nonetheless, empirical research on human societies may sustain the notion of wisdom belonging to the elders, but only up to a point, perhaps, for much innovation does come from youth particularly in the fields of mathematics and physics; how this may pan out in years to come is an interesting issue for psychologists and sociologists to pursue as Western societies' aged populations increase.

The active and philosophical life

The good life – the *eudaimonic* life – is the same for the individual as it is for the state (*Pol*, 1324a2–3). To the modern liberal of various persuasions (social democrat through to the libertarian), such a thesis strikes one as odd, for liberalism views the state as being a separate, institutional entity and the life of the individual similarly removed from the instrumental mechanics of the state. Communitarians, on the other hand, have sought to remind us of the intimate links between abode, responsibilities, rights, and the policies and bureaus of officialdom; in so doing, they bring forth Aristotle's political philosophy, which merges the individual's life and its potentiality with the intricacies of society. Against the skewed comment that 'the main difference between Aristotle and his predecessors in theory lies in his greater consideration for the individual' (Dobson, 1932, p. 79), for the Greek the liberal separation of the individual from his social milieu would be unconscionable, a regression to a barbaric, outlaw status, or frivolous in the sense of Diogenes the Cynic, who rejected social mores and rules (but only to live among them to ridicule them – he was no hermit).

The free citizen, for Aristotle, thus faces a choice: would he be happier as a serving member of a *polis*, or as an alien worker or migrant, one cut off from the state? What about the philosophical life – is that the best kind? Historically, he noted, people sought to be both statesmen and philosophers, to be engaged in political life and also to distance themselves so that they may pontificate. When young and strong, they must serve in the military, but when their strength fails, they should become politically active and adjudicators or become priests, for it is fitting that the gods are served by those higher up the social ranks than those from below.

But can the statesmen find happiness in ruling over neighbors, or in tyranny, or just in the active participation of the *polis*? The militarily minded state cannot provide the conditions of the happy life, for its aggressive stance – implied in the constitutions and culture of such people as the Spartans, Cretans, Scythians, Persians, Thracians, and Celts – is in itself unlawful: might does not necessitate right, nor is it right that a people inflict upon others pains and misery that they would not have inflicted upon themselves (*Pol*, 1324b29; 33–35). Yet if we think that Aristotle may have suddenly become a cosmopolitan-minded pacifist, he reminds us that it is only natural to rule over those whose nature determines them to be ruled: in his egalitarian moments, he is only thinking of those peoples who are 'naturally equal.' Just as all freeborn citizens are each other's equal, so too are certain *poleis*; others, those of the non-civilized peoples who do not possess a polity with its impartial laws and balance of interest, are fair game: 'just as we ought not to hunt men, whether for food or sacrifice, but only those animals which may be hunted for food or sacrifice' (*Pol*, 1324b40–41). Since the autarkic state could be very happy, any constitutional provisions for war are incidental – they are admirable as instruments for preservation but not as ends in themselves: the happy state must be one that does not wage war for its own sake.

Happiness is to be found in action, but this is not found in ruling over slaves, for to issue orders for slaves is not in itself a noble endeavor; it is low-level action compared to other kinds of action in the Aristotelian hierarchy. Mastery does involve some nobility, for he who cannot rule over his wife and servants does not show much nobility (*Pol*, 1325b2–5), but the kinds of action implied are not those meted out in routine tasks, rather those in which ruling implies a higher end – the good of the state, for instance. The isolated state has much to act upon anyway without having to subjugate others: it has its own internal relations and associations to organize, and this is similar to the individual, who, alone, also has much to mentally organize.

The man of excellence, of course, possesses the character to be happy, but without action, he cannot attain proper happiness – and to act, he requires power. But, like the power of the state, it does not have to be directed toward other people in the sense of seeking to subject them, and the power of action can be directed internally into thought: 'thinking and speculation that are their own end and are done for their own sake are *more* "active", because the aim in such thinking is to do well, and therefore also, in a sense, action' (orig. italics; *Pol*, 1325b19–22). Freed from manual work, the citizen has the potential to pursue the life proper to man – contemplation.

Upon contemplation – immersed in the right kind of state – proper happiness is to be cultivated. Happiness depends on aiming for the right end and going about it the right way, and while subjectivists in the theory of value dismiss judging of ends in favor of focusing on the practicability of the means, it is not surprising that Aristotle's hierarchical view of life implies a hierarchical view of ends too; that is, some ends are better than others. Happiness is 'the complete utilization of virtue, not conditionally absolutely' (*Pol*, 1332a9), conditionally implying those things that are necessary, such as the infliction of just chastisement, which removes an evil, while the pursuit of honor and advantage are absolutely noble actions. It does not depend on wealth as such, for that is to invert the logic, just as if we were to applaud the lyre player for the lyre rather than the player. And the pursuit of happiness should not be left to chance and fortune but to deliberation and knowledge, hence the importance of the state being set up properly to ensure the correct framework for moral advancement. The citizen can only become excellent or sound in a properly organized state, one that is neither too big nor too small, as noted. Given the framework, the citizen can only become sound because of three things: his nature, his habits, and his thinking. A man's nature depends on his birth: he must, indubitably for Aristotle, be born a man but also a man with certain characteristics and qualities, which, if they are good, should be augmented by his habits – for habits can work against a good foundation. But man can also reason, so his thinking must be such as to complement good character and excellent habits, so an explicit education may be described.

So the highest life proper to man is a difficult path to get onto and to sustain – right action is, as we have seen, dependent on right intention and the proper means, so two things can go wrong: we can choose wrongly or follow the wrong path to our values. In contrast to Socrates' belief that a man can never knowingly do wrong, Aristotle evaluated the reasons why we can go wrong in action, why we may fail to secure the good. The theory of *akrasia* or moral incontinence is the final pillar to Aristotelian philosophy and one to which educationalists have often returned.

Akrasia – moral weakness

Being wise, in Aristotelian theory, is something learned and cultivated over time. But that wisdom, in part the understanding of practical wisdom and the application of good judgment, also implies that the holding back from appetite and desire – from emotional responses and lustful wants, say – is vulnerable to alterations and to what Aristotle called the weakness of the will, or *akrasia*. The emotions and appetite are not separable from our wisdom, but it is critical for us to relegate them appropriately, rather than extinguish them completely. The problem of *akratic* behavior provides education with much to contemplate, for how and when we begin the learning and habitual processes underpins much pedagogical analysis. Had Aristotle known more about the psychology of the young mind – perhaps if he had observed infants as much as he had other animals – then arguably he would commend beginning at the beginning: from day one of the newly born's life. Otherwise, we can imagine his asking, 'When would it begin if it had not started at the most obvious time?'

The problem of *akrasia* is central to Aristotle's ethical theory; he was responding to Socrates' argument that man does not willingly err, for if he knows the right thing to do, then he does it (*NE*, 1145a25–27). It is an awkward logic, for that would mean that anything I do is the right thing, because otherwise, I could not have done it had I known it to be wrong. It also quickly leads to inconsistencies or contradictions, as my action now may be opposed to my action tomorrow and yet both cannot be right, unless we accept a situationist ethic in which today's killing is wrong but tomorrow's is right. Such concerns prompted Aristotle to refute Socrates, but then he sought to explain why it is possible for a man to knowingly do wrong.

Aristotle's relentless thesis is that we are constantly subject to our appetite and desires for things and these, which are particularly strong in youth, have to be controlled carefully by our rational element, which is particularly weak in youth, so that we do not live our lives through our emotions. In turn, what we do is judged – praised or blamed for its intentions or effects – and so we may become bad or good people. There is much that is commonsensical in Aristotle's analysis, for arguably we can only praise or blame those actions that fall within our capacity, actions which he calls voluntary (*hekousiois*); those actions that fail to do well because they do not stem from choice are what he calls involuntary (*ankousiois*): no praise or blame can then be accorded. To consider what is virtuous thus warrants a separation of voluntary from involuntary acts (*NE*, 1109b30–35): an involuntary act, for Aristotle, is when there is an external force acting upon the agent such that he or she could literally not do otherwise, but he also adds that it includes those acts the agent does in ignorance (*agno-oon*). While the first is perhaps obvious, the second is less so.

For example, John rugby tackles George who falls onto Sam, who breaks his clavicle: George is thoroughly innocent of blame and cannot be chastised for his action for he was compelled to fall; he had no choice in the matter of falling, although we may make some minor judgment of his manner of playing which led up to his being in a dangerous situation vis-à-vis Sam, but if we focus on the forces involved in the tackle, he is blameless, for he acted involuntarily in breaking Sam's clavicle. John's actions, however, are voluntary in that he chooses to tackle George and is the instigator of the clavicle breaking; however, whether he intended to break Sam's clavicle or do injury to him is another matter – for here, John may be blamed of ignorance, of not knowing that his act would cause injury, but to what extent should he have known? Aristotle sought to delve deeper than the Socratic thesis and presented a useful if simplistic analysis. But what if John were drunk when he tackled George? Then his causal culpability is reduced somewhat, for were he sober he would not dive in so dangerously, let's say, but his moral culpability remains, for he chose to drink before engaging in some rugby.

In his own examples, Aristotle considers a tyrant offering a bribe to an agent to do something evil, using the agent's family as collateral. Aristotle recognized that a debate may ensue as to whether the agent's consequent acts are in fact voluntary or involuntary. Similarly, when a captain of a ship throws the cargo overboard to save the crew and its ship, it is an action that he would prefer not to do, but compared with losing everything it is commendable. The action, he allows, is relative to the occasion and one that any sensible man would do; yet since the agent would prefer not to act thus, the action is also involuntary. The end is important: is the agent seeking a noble end in committing his moral error or merely a trivial end? Naturally, the more noble the end, the more we can understand the agent's otherwise moral failing, a move that points his ethics in a consequentialist direction, or one that was expanded on by Thomas Aquinas – the problem of double effect, that as long as the intention was correct the moral failing within the act can be viewed as collateral damage (an argument used by 'just-war' theorists to explore attacks on military installations that would knowingly kill civilians). However, Aristotle held there are some acts that we should never do; there is a limit to our transgression or immorality and we should rather face death (*NE*, 1101a26).

Between voluntary and involuntary is the non-voluntary: this category allows us to study those acts that are done in ignorance, which, had we known better, we would not otherwise do. We can act in ignorance and of ignorance: the drunk acts in ignorance, for he has lost his faculties, as it were; the wicked man, though, is ignorant of what he does and what he ought to refrain from doing (*NE*, 1110b28–29). Assume that a man is not mad: then he can know who he is, what he is doing, what or on whom he is acting, what he may be doing it with, what end he has in mind, and the manner in which he is doing it. To not know these suggests madness, Aristotle observes. But then the subtleties begin, for a man may not know what he is doing such as the man who let off a catapult, Aristotle relates, who was just showing how it worked; or one could be mistaken in assuming your son to be an enemy in battle, or give a man medicine to help but which really kills him. Such acts are painful and must involve regret, but are involuntary in the sense of being done out of ignorance (*NE*, 1111a11). But what if a man acts in a passion – he angrily takes a swipe at his friend and hurts him, for he is in a rage? Here Aristotle maintains that the passions belong to the man and so cannot be called involuntary: they are within our range of choice.

Choice is nevertheless a distinct category from the voluntary, for while children (and the lower animals) may act voluntarily, Aristotle contended that they are not *choosing* as such. Choice is voluntary but more than that: when the weak-willed man acts, he is said to do so voluntarily but not with choice, while the moral man acts with choice rather than from appetite. Appetite explains to us what is painful or pleasurable, but choice, as Aristotle defines it, is not involved with appetite as such, so it does not deal with pain and pleasure temptations; choice is not done through anger nor through wishes, although these do impinge on how we choose in the sense of ends aimed for, so we wish to be healthy but choose to become healthy – choice is limited to what is in our power to effect. Holding an opinion is different from having a choice, and having good opinions on something (i.e. that are true) does not mean to say the agent will act morally (*NE*, 1112a5).

What we choose to do determines whether we are good or bad, regardless of our opinions on whether we think we are doing the right thing; choice is praised for being related to the right object or for being right – we choose what we best know to be good. Choice involves rationality and thought (*NE*, 1112a16), so it is again elevated above the hurly-burly of desires, emotions, and particularities. Deliberation is what the sensible do rather than the mad, which is fair enough, but then there are limits to Aristotle's world of deliberation: we cannot deliberate about the materiality of the universe or the incommensurability of the diagonal of the square (i.e. irrational numbers such as $\sqrt{2}$), nor the regularities of the universe or the political constitutions of other peoples, and we often need advice when deliberating (*NE*, 1112a18–b11). In other words, we cannot deliberate about that which we cannot alter by our own actions. This is a very narrow understanding of deliberation and (perhaps) Aristotle's goal here is to separate it from contemplation – thought of thought, reaching into the sphere of the divine.

The more famous aspect of Aristotle's educational thinking is the political agenda that seeks to instill good moral habits in the youth – the virtues of liberality, magnificence, magnanimity, good-humor – that will eventually supplant the present elders and teachers. So from the heady heights of *homo philosophicus*, we return to the political agenda of Aristotle's education and move through the explicit educational reforms and proposals he made and for which his thinking still remains attractive and influential in ways subtle and explicit.

Chapter 4

Theories on Education

Education in the *polis*

Education is inevitably a political subject, even for the anarchist who believes that it has nothing to do with government, for it involves thinking about, among other things, the relationships of learning to society and of society to learning; of children to elders; of teachers to the perceived needs of the present and the future; of appropriate forms and methods, even if they should be wide ranging rather than narrow and subservient to state interests. We may reject the state's role in educating children and call it a gross violation of liberty; we may accept that the state has a minimal or a large role in setting standards; or we may accept that the state is education and education is the state. Hellenic education was indeed, according to its traditions and justified by its intellectuals, embedded in the existence and functions of the state – the *polis* – and its moral and religious order (Acton, 1948, p. 45). But they did not believe that that constituted a tyrannical or despotic burden, for teaching was generally a voluntary affair of various institutions such as the family, tutors, and small schools, yet should that education have veered away from respecting the *polis*, assuredly the elders would have acted to close them down. Yet when we cast critical eyes upon the political nature of the *poleis'* populations, the obvious drive of Hellenic education was to ensure the survival of its citizen elite (MacIntyre, 1998, p. 83). Likewise, when the Hellenic model has been resuscitated in school systems, it has usually been to defend or to procure a divided political system justifying the advancement of those in positions of power over those who allegedly are there to serve them. It is a vision that Aristotle in turn defends and justifies – unsurprisingly given his disposition to describe and defend theoretical or observed hierarchies.

For the Hellenic citizen, being part of the *polis* was essential. In contrast, he who is without a state, Aristotle opined, quoting Homer (*Pol*, 1253a4), is in a sorry state of being an outlaw (literally) but also a barbarian, an uncivilized man whose attainments are necessarily thwarted by the lack of social institutions. Another implication is that it is only within the confines of a political existence, under the aegis of the protective state, that a man (or at least some men) can attain his proper status and develop those capacities that lie latent within his being, namely excellence of character and happiness (*eudaimonia*), particularly through the philosophical life, and this is the angle that Aristotle took in explaining how a political education ought to be managed. Of course, Aristotle was a well-regarded teacher, but he was not properly a citizen of either the great city of Athens or that of Pella in Macedonia: accordingly, he was a Hellenic nomad, welcome, probably like his aesclepiad clan, as an itinerant professional. Moreover, his homeland as well as his adopted city would not have been absolutely secure places for his political safety – he was at times a political refugee, albeit one with many lines of sympathetic routes to exploit. Yet in his writings on the state we have a man justifying the position of the elite with whom he dealt, as many an intellectual, patronized by the politically powerful, has done since.

The attraction to the state was intrinsic to Hellenic culture. Yet before we fall sycophantically in love with its ideals, it should be noted that those ideals have been passed down to us through its patrons, artists, and intellectuals, who of course enjoyed the benefits of the *polis*, rather than the thoughts of the slaves, women, or conquered, who did not. Aristotle took it up as a natural institution, but constantly seeking the wherefore and purpose of things as was his wont, he also sought to explain why the state is a natural outcome of social interaction, as well as justifying it in turn to be a natural form for society that has a rightful purpose. Contrary to other political thinkers throughout the ages who have looked upon the state as an instrument of the people, contingent upon doing well by the people, perhaps formed (or should be formed) by an implicit or explicit contract, Aristotle presented a naturalist theory of the state, which views the state as a natural development of human interaction: from the sexual urge to mate comes the family, and from families associating there emerges the clan, and then clans are naturally disposed to form a political agency. Yet the resulting government is not a government of people as such but of law – his was one of the first philosophical voices to assert the primacy of law over people and thus of the subjugation of rulers to the law (Hayek, 1963, p. 165; *Pol*, 1287a19). Speech and the conceptions of good and evil, just and unjust, differentiate man from animals, and so sharing a common view on such matters underlies the formation of the state (*Pol*, 1252a10–18). But following what may be a benign thesis on the naturalist emergence of the state (not one that should go unchallenged) is Aristotle's argument analogous to the naturalness of the urge to procreate, namely the naturalness of some to rule over others: this is natural because both wish preservation (*Pol*, 1252a25–31).

Among the barbarians – those who are not civilized in that they do not possess a *polis* – women and slaves are equal, but in the Hellenic polity, some men rule, others obey, men rule their women, and slaves are ruled by their masters: Aristotle's is a patriarchal and hierarchical view of society, which provides a foundation for his system of education: that it should be designed for the aristocratic youth, who will be trained to serve their *polis* well and thereby perpetuate their interests. In this, Aristotle was being broadly Hellenic, but we must not forget that his Lyceum existed to educate the citizens far beyond the normal expectations of political and cultural life – he was, after all, a philosopher, because, as he noted, 'the state or political community, which is the highest of all, and which embraces all the rest, aims at … the highest good' (*Pol*, 1252a4–6).

Once the state arises, according to Aristotle's archetypal history of the *polis*, it may have historically followed a natural progression from kingship, when one man possessed the character capable of leading his people well, to aristocracy, when more people joined the ranks of the politically talented, but these tended not to remain good, for they may have abused their rank and so the society fell prey to tyranny, and from tyranny to democracy as the power of the multitudes increased relative to the great and the few. The next logical step was the formation of constitutional democracies in which the freeborn are to play a role and take turns serving in office, their powers restricted by constitutional arrangements (*Pol*, 1286b). But, being attached to the Macedonian court, he was not averse to proclaiming the benefits of monarchy, should an outstanding family or individual be found among a people, for such talents would meet the requirements of justice and the people should obey such a character always (*Pol*, 1288a16–29).

For those who were citizens of the Hellenic *poleis*, the city state was naturally the focal point of political affairs (so well represented by the Athenian acropolis, which was a common feature of the Hellenic *polis*) and much of their culture – their common interest, as Aristotle observed, that brings them together (*Pol*, 1278b21). Appropriately, Aristotle's theory of education is intimately connected with the Hellenic and his own conception of the *polis*, so it is critical to our purposes to possess an overview of his political theory while relating its connection to education.

The concept of citizen is fundamental to Aristotelian and indeed Hellenic politics and educational thinking. Although the definition of citizen will change according to the polity, Aristotle sought to universalize its meaning as one who shares in the offices of government and justice (*Pol*, 1275a19–21), and so the state is an association of citizens taking turns in political action (*Pol*, 1325b6–7). In turn, the state should make its citizens into a certain character, namely good and capable of noble acts, he argued (*Pol*, 1099b31): and so education gets its entrance call, to which we shall return. Appropriately, for a philosopher who prefers the mean between the extremes, democracy presents the best form of *polis* in that it enables all free men to participate in politics, which is their natural due, since the best form of government should provide its citizens equal access to its offices. Such an argument was, however, given Aristotle's relatively precarious position vis-à-vis the Macedonian hegemony, somewhat surprising: while we have come to expect to understand his predilection for hierarchies, a subtle shift to expressing democratic forms as the ideal is unexpected – it becomes, though, a central feature of his political philosophy rather than an anticipated glorification of a great mind, a philosopher-king, say, in the Platonic tradition. It acts to remind us that Aristotle, for all the pomposity that can quickly be associated with him for demeaning the abilities of say 90 percent of the human population, nevertheless seemingly did not have much confidence in the abilities of one person to rule or to negotiate politics well.

In justifying and exploring the purposes of the state, a philosopher typically uses rational analysis rather than just historical exegesis and in so doing begins what may be a subtle shift from positive to normative analysis, from description to prescription; and while he was also a historian or compiler of political constitutions, in the *Politics*, we may look upon Aristotle writing as a philosopher, securing the best form of state for man. And so lifted from the historical context, the main element of Aristotle's theory is what is known as a political rationalist theory of the state; that is, the good state can be envisaged through the application of reason and hence existing states can also be criticized or amended through reasoning. However, he was not a utopian thinker as Plato had been – he accepted the nature of the Hellenic *poleis* but did not seek a blueprint for a future state by which to guide and judge present policies, for after all, are utopian visions of the state satires or blueprints? While at the Lyceum, he was the first to compile a collection of constitutions; this would have been useful for comparative analysis, which is evident in his writings, but it is important to note that Aristotle was not seeking the best constitution to which all others should be compared, for he was fully aware of the diversity of human organization and hence of the futility of designing a political utopia in the manner of his teacher, Plato: as with his ethical thinking, politics ought to be contextual. So at times he writes as if the good *polis* was thus what would be good for a people, rather than for all people. This would draw attention to the empirical and descriptive or historical leaning in his thinking that we encounter in his biological writings; however, his researches do not in themselves constitute an abandonment of the apodictic vision that the political – howsoever constituted – forms a great part of the good for man.

So pure rationalist designs to better the state were not lacking in his *Politics*. Following Plato's emphasis on the application of reason to political affairs, Aristotle asserted that the state should provide the wherewithal and the education to help its citizens develop to the best of their potential. This would seem to be a logical inference since Aristotle adduced that the state is a necessary condition for the good life and aims at man's highest good, and hence the state should engage in securing the proper foundations for its citizenry (as he does argue). However, the connection is not necessary at all: we can admit the need for a political entity of sorts to exist either as a tool or as a guardian of the people's rights or laws without adding that the state should also produce educational services. Alternative visions of the state may argue that the nature of politics is inherently irrational, namely that people within or without power tend to be irrational or cannot be trusted to be objectively, impartially, or scientifically minded in all that they do – a counter that Aristotle may have accepted since he turns to promote a more democratically inclined constitution. Hence, according to these views, people are best left to evolve their own codes of conduct between themselves including forming their own educational plans, either through and within the family or through the purchase of teaching or schooling services, which is what indeed many Hellenes did do. But this is antithetical to Aristotle's understanding of what polities are for and of his hierarchical understanding of human nature – that some kinds of life are inherently better for people than others, and while he retreated from Plato's dream of philosophers ruling states he maintained a preference for philosophers advising states. The state, he reasoned in the *Politics*, is in the best position to decree what is in the best interests of the citizenry, for the state is the citizenry (defined narrowly), but also the citizens owe their existence and their potential for happiness to the state and so too they should willingly and rationally accept state provision and direction of education.

Although Aristotle's philosophy is often deemed to be rationalist, in that he proposes a series of ideas through which life is to be described and prescribed, we have also noted that his allegiance to rationalism is not absolute. As a medical thinker he certainly agreed with the rationalist Hippocratic tradition of the four humors mirroring the four elements of the world, but experience was also Aristotle's great teacher and this acted to give a balance to his thinking (leaving intellectual descendants to take up one arm or the other as they saw fit, while modern commentators prefer to stress the inconsistencies therein). We could say that Aristotle presented a modified rationalist theory. Since humanity is naturally divided into people of unequal character and abilities (men, women, children, slaves), there exists a broad blueprint for citizenship and politics, i.e. free men (*eleutheroi*) should rule. But the form that should take is dependent on many factors: constitutionally ordered democracy is best, for the collective judgment of the citizenry of laws, etc., is of much higher standard than the judgment of single people (*Pol*, 1282a36–37; 1286a33–35), so long as the people are not intellectually slavish – an ideal that echoes loudly in Rousseau's political thinking, but which also returns us to the primary premise of Aristotle's theory of politics that puts much emphasis on the importance of education for citizenship and political engagement and responsibilities. Indeed, the best form of constitution is one that is so ordered that any citizen within it may prosper and live happily (*Pol*, 1324a22–23; 1328a). Moreover, he was particularly critical of purely rationalist utopian reforms proposed by Plato, Phaleas, Hippodamus, and of Sparta: 'to set down in writing the whole organization of the state, down to the last detail, would be quite impossible,' for constitutions can only apply to the universal while action deals with particulars that cannot be described beforehand (*Pol*, trans. Sinclair, 1269a10–12). But most emphatically, there must be rule of law to which all are subject (*Pol*, 1292a32); these laws ought in turn to be good by serving the interests of the polity – they are not to be regarded as enslaving devices, but rather as means to self-preservation (*Pol*, 1310a34–35).

The Aristotelian *polis* fits into his general teleological philosophy and is thus a community which has an end – the end being the good. In itself that is a powerful and influential thesis which sits behind most Western political assumptions: we expect political elites to explain their end game to us and to strive to adjust our society through its laws and educational systems to achieve that end. On the other hand, it is not an uncritically accepted theory, for we may also ask why the state should take on the personification of the captain of a ship (as Plato and many since have held), when the plural nature of society may suggest a plurality of ships and no allegiance to any one 'captain' or vision. Aristotle proposes, however, that the state intrinsically possesses aims, so the state should aim for the highest or best ends befitting a civilian population (*Pol*, 1252a1–2; 1278b24); that implies that the state's ends should transcend that which is the good that individuals may pursue, for the good aimed at by a political entity is justice, which is also known as the common interest (*Pol*, 1282b16), and so we can readily see how thick the connections are between the Aristotelian state and education. But like many political philosophers, Aristotle does not accept the state as a stand-alone entity, a set of institutions to be accepted without thought; instead, he turns to its origins, which again provide us with more explanations as to why political education was so important to him.

Emphatically, the state should not be a totalitarian organization; against the Platonic utopic vision – a vision built on Spartan culture, Aristotle's state is very conservative and admits much plurality from its filial foundations upward through its clans and associations. Built up from households, the *polis* should recognize the plurality of these households (*Pol*, 1261a16; 1277a5) and their private property, which implies that the ruling families are to be treated as equals, members from which take it in turns to rule. Plato's communism – especially the community of wives – is rejected as unworkable: a state cannot be unified in the communist sense of all being equal, for patently, according to Aristotle's philosophy, all men are not equal – the state consists of different kinds of men (*Pol*, 1261a23). The proposed differences between people logically have implications for the forms of education and training that people will undergo. Communism – or a broader ownership of property – would also be dangerous and undermine the strength of the aristocratic *polis*: dilution of ownership lends itself to carelessness, for if someone else is presumed to be looking after the property or a child, it will not be cared for. Similarly, if all women are to be free of household ownership (i.e. property of their husbands) and children to be brought up anonymously, this will act to weaken the social bonds between peoples upon which the *polis* is heavily reliant; without those bonds that are expressed in such phrases as 'this is my son,' the state will weaken, which is not what Plato was assuming would happen, Aristotle argued (*Pol*, 1261b16–1263b25). Nonetheless, he warned against such inequalities of wealth that a private system could produce, which could prove politically dangerous: as it was for Sparta, whose inequalities eventually weakened the *polis* such that it was defeated at Leuktra. Following the general principle of the mean between two extremes, Aristotle lauded the *polis* formed mainly by the middle classes rather than those of either the haughtily rich or the envious poor.

It seems another extraordinary turnaround by Aristotle to uphold a middle class (and democratic) state over the aristocratic state that appears from much of his writing to be so much the highest form that a society could reach. Nevertheless, the theme that resounds more is the importance of securing the moral path between the extremes that life, interaction, and politics present, since as a principle, if the governors of the state serve their own ends rather than those of the state for a while, they deviate from what is the proper end of government (*Pol*, 1279a25). Hence any purpose for education to serve the needs of the *polis* needed to be further underlined, and Aristotle presented reasons why each form of government possessed a danger to revert to a more fearful or disastrous form. So kingship aims to serve the state through one man; aristocracies through the service of the best; and polities or constitutional governments through the service of the citizens. Each properly formed constitution aims, in principle, to serve the entire state, but when kings deviate to serve their own ends, they become tyrants; when aristocracies deviate, they become oligarchies; and when properly formed constitutional states deviate, usually through the rallying of demagogues, they become democracies, which is the least problematic of the three deviations (*Pol*, 1289b3–4; 1304b22).

Ideally, the statesmen should serve the *polis* with the end being justice – benefiting the commonwealth according to the various stations and virtues of its people (*Pol*, 1283a, 18). But should any individuals surpass their fellows in all characteristics, it is important for the polity to possess a safety valve: such Aristotelian great-souled men (or in modern philosophy Nietzschean *Übermenschen*) are to be ostracized – a hint that Socrates, perhaps, was too good for the Athenians or Alexander for the Hellenes while recognizing the limitations of ordinary citizens to understand and deal with such demigods in their midst. So while education seeks to improve a man's talents and abilities and to train him to be a man of virtue, the importance of balance overrides, hence, Aristotle noted, even the legendary Herakles was left behind by his crew (*Pol*, 1284a21–25). Any shift away from the balanced or harmonious state is antithetical to the Hellene, he inferred, just as tyranny – the slavish toleration of masters – is natural to the barbarian (*Pol*, 1285a19); in turn, the best constitution is that which balances many political and economic considerations, for the virtuous system is a balance between two extremes. Realistically, most people are not going to be of great character, and their educational abilities will not glow; the extreme political states are imbalanced and subject to upheaval – the children of wealthy aristocrats may never appreciate being ruled while the children of those lacking great qualities may become too subservient: the result would be a state 'of slaves and masters, the former full of envy, the latter of contempt' (*Pol*, trans. Sinclair, 1295b15–23). Likewise, the youth of the ideal Aristotelian state should suffer policemen in their midst to keep them deferential toward the proper order of things (*Pol*, 1331a36ff).

Any existing or resulting imbalance is not favorable to the state, so the best form of state is one that is ruled by an educated middle class and which also has a large middle class. It should not be too large, either, for capacity to do things is more important than sheer size, and it is difficult to secure good constitutional practice in a large state; order creates beauty, and the orderly, medium-sized state permits the people to know each other and thereby have an impact and control on the officers. The ideal state should be economically self-sufficient and that would imply possessing enough land so that its inhabitants can live the life of the free man, but better in moderation than in luxury (*Pol*, 1326a25ff); invoking a determinist thesis, which pervades much of his medical thinking, the climate should also be temperate rather than too hot or too cold – for the Hellenic climate is (of course) the best for producing a spirited and intelligent race living under the best constitutions and capable of ruling those who should be ruled (1327b29–32).

Let's return to why educated man should also be political man, that the twain shall ne'er be rendered. Man is by nature a political animal, Aristotle famously noted (*Pol*, 1253a2–3): his nature predisposes him to join a state and to live within that state – to reject the life of the *polis* is therefore to reject his very nature, so anarchic societies have always been rejected by Aristotelians as lawless and war-mad people or as isolated pieces on a games board. The educated man, knowing that his fortune rests with that of the state, therefore should understand what his state's interests ought to be and be prepared to promote the interests of the *polis* both economically and, necessarily so if a mercantilist policy is pursued, in terms of the balance of power of *poleis*.

Again, rather than just accepting the status quo, Aristotle also turned to justify the internal nature of the typical Hellenic state so its educated citizens know that they belonged to rightful society. In particular, and especially so from our modern perspective, patriarchy and slavery needed justifying: Aristotle was no thoughtless bigot, and while we may excuse his remarks to some extent, we must also acknowledge that he sought to provide an explanation as to why some should rule over others. It is a strange justification. A slave is owned by another man; this is a mere definition, but since life is about purposeful action, the citizen requires tools for his purposes, and slaves can be considered tools in that regard. Aristotle furthered the point that nature divides people into rulers and the ruled, and that this is both necessary and expedient (*Pol*, 1254a21–22); that is, slavery reflects nature (in that the mind rules the body) and is also useful. Similarly with respect to women: nature has molded them weaker, Aristotle avowed, hence they should be subservient to men (*Pol*, 1254b14). Accordingly, the educational requirements of the state should reflect the basic divisions of people thus outlined.

Yet contemporaries were not in agreement: Plato thought that women should be educated, while later thinkers (particularly the Epicureans) were to argue against slavery. So why did Aristotle argue so – was it because he was so integrated with Macedonian politics? Or was he so much a man of his time? Or was a consistent or apparently consistent extension of his understanding of nature learned through biological eyes? In the past century, political writers have taken Darwin's theory of evolution to justify aristocracy on the grounds that some are fitter to survive than others; in politics, eugenicist laws were passed in the United States that sought to improve the American race by sterilizing those deemed weaker by those in power. In many respects the so-called Social Darwinist philosophy was an echo of Aristotle's earlier biological thesis that some are stronger or more intelligent and they have the natural right to rule over others. For those who breed animals, selective breeding is commonplace, and it seems a logical step to assert that 'good breeding' should be employed among humans – biologically it makes sense. However, there is first the broad and deep treasury of human culture of ideas and behavior that is also passed on from generation to generation and which cannot be captured in genes – Dawkins calls this 'memes' (Dawkins, 1989).

Second, there is the moral import of humanity. Aristotle stressed how different man was from the animal kingdom; if so, the humanist retorts, then each person deserves equal moral standing, regardless of strength or intelligence. Here Aristotle reverted to nature: evidently, some people are not as intelligent or as strong as others, so they are not fully moral persons in the highest sense; just as man differs from animals, so men differ from women, and because man possesses rights (he would not have used that term) over the animal kingdom, then so too must the stronger man possess rights over the weaker man (the enslaved) and women:

> Where then there is such a difference as that between soul and body, or between men and animals (as in the case of those whose business is to use their body, and can do nothing better), the lower sort are by nature slaves.
>
> (*Pol*, 1254b15–17)

This kind of relationship suits both sides, he argued, unless the relationship has been forced upon them by the law. Nonetheless, it was not so thoroughly natural as to be without potential problems, for later (*Pol*, 1330a25) he warns that the slaves ought not to be from the same people in case they urged rebellion!

This is a far cry from Kant's kingdom of ends in which each person is an end in him- (or her-) self, and no one should use any other as a means to an end, which is the hallmark of modern political morality. Indeed, the supporting intellectuals of the Enlightenment asserted that all men are equal, which is evidently not true if we don an Aristotelian hat and observe behavior and thought, but the Enlightenment demand for moral equality (and thus political and legal equality) overwhelms physical or intellectual differences, hence, pedagogically, much of the modern thrust in Western democracies has been to encourage a comprehensive, egalitarian education rather than a selective system that seeks to reflect innate differences between people. Interestingly, in contrast to Aristotle's vision, Plato advocated a selective education in his utopia, but this was to be based on merit rather than on parentage – one can read into this controversy the simplistic 'nature versus nurture' debate, with Aristotle arguing for nature and Plato nurture. But things in the works of philosophers are rarely that simple: their thoughts are too deep and wide ranging for simplifications to stand up to too much scrutiny – Aristotle also proclaimed the importance of education in forming the moral citizen.

Slaves may gain knowledge and in turn educate, for it was not their education or intelligence alone that made them slaves, but their character (*Pol*, 1255b21): he related of a Syracusan teacher who was paid to teach slaves in their duties and tasks; such menial tasks are inherently servile, for masters do not learn such things – they learn how to command slaves. He hinted that slaves should be presented with the possibility of gaining their freedom as an incentive to avoid rebellion and to work well (*Pol*, 1330a33), which suggests an awareness of the incentive freedom may have on most people, yet did not pursue the notion further to consider all men being born free: such an idea would have been preposterous for him.

Moving away from slavery, Aristotle argued that the rule of the statesmen over people is different from that of the master ruling over the slave, for the statesmen rule over free citizens (*Pol*, 1255b19). Women and children within the household are free in the sense that the slaves are not, but still must the man rule over them. A child is in essence part of the father and so he owns him as chattel until he is of age (*NE*, 1134b10–11). Aristotle was scathing of Spartan women, who he believed yielded too much power and influence and lived outside the discipline for which Sparta was famed – this was detrimental to the Spartan state (*Pol*, 1269b12). What justified this for Aristotle? Essentially it is because, on his reasoning, only the aristocratic men are of sufficient good character to be capable of ruling either the household or the state wisely. Again, we find Aristotle seeking to impose a rationalist order on the way of the world – the belief that the world is like this, for it can be rationally expressed as such, and that all that is to be observed and judged should also fit this vision. If it did not, or does not in modern Aristotelian eyes, then so much for other ways of doing things; as an analogy, Catholicism rejects the possibility of women priests largely on Aristotelian and ancient Judaic prejudices – that other churches accept them is a deviation from the proper nature of the world. Yet when reading Aristotle across his texts, we find a man very tolerant of debate and of the expression of theories of what the rationalist vision would normally imply, and we have to remind ourselves of the internal dissent raging in his mind between rationalist and empirical theories, between the apodictic certainties cultivated by his teacher, Plato, and the breadth of particularities his own scientific learning disclosed – and we can take note in his advice that compared to people with their individual circumstances, the law has no soul and must give way in the particular. People matter before abstract justice, and when the law fails, it is better for many citizens to deliberate over what ought to be done than a single wise man (*Pol*, 1286a10–31).

The women and children of *eleutheroi* – free men – are to be educated according to the constitutional requirements of the state in which they live: (male) children because one day they will take up citizenship and women because they make up half the population (*Pol*, 1260b15–20). Numbers count for something, then! But once again Aristotle veers away from imposing an abstract rationalist vision on all: it would be wrong for a state to educate all equally – just as an equal distribution of property could lead to people having too much and hence leading a life of too much luxury, or too low and hence living in poverty (*Pol*, 1266b24–26), so an equality of education is to be avoided as not being appropriate and reflecting the natural needs of the pupils. Equality of education may encourage all to strive for money or for honors, say, and this would cause strife, something that egalitarians are typically keen to avoid (*Pol*, 1266b34–38). Rather than equalizing property or education, it is better for the state to ensure that the powerful do not *wish* to gain more, and hence that their desires be curbed, even though Aristotle recognized that it is hard for anyone to master the intoxication of success; he submitted that the socially inferior should not be able to get their hands on more than their share (*Pol*, 1267b5–9; 1308b15).

At the apex of Aristotelian politics are the statesmen whose rule is to be just – meting out the benefits due to the people as a whole – and virtuous. The education of the ideal statesmen – aristocrats – or of the ideal king is to be the same as that which produces the ideal citizen (*Pol*, 1288b1), for, although these are not Aristotle's words, the ruler is in effect a *primus inter pares* (first among equals), not a philosopher-king in the Platonic mold, whose intelligence and rationality puts him in a superior position to all. Again, Aristotle confounds the forming expectation and retreats to a commonsensical position: democracy should be the guiding principle, not what we would now call absolutist rulers or benign despots. In a democratic constitution, liberty and justice prevail. Liberty implies both ruling and being ruled in turn, as well as the right to live as one likes. Democracy means that political power rests with the multitudes, whose majority verdicts justify political action; demographically, the best democracy is one that is agrarian based rather than urban, for rural people will not spend inordinate time in the assembly seeking to gain their hands on other people's property (*Pol*, 1318b8). In summary, the justice of democracy entails that the free citizens have the right to elect their officials, that they have an equal right of access to stand for power and that the property qualification is low, that offices are filled by lot rather than aptitude, that officials sit for only short periods and that they are paid regularly, that the citizens must sit on juries, and that the free assembly of citizens is politically sovereign (*Pol*, 1317a40–1318a3).

Within this framework, then, liberty – Hellenic style for the male elite – exists. It is not quite the liberty to do as one wishes, Aristotle demurs, for that would unleash the bad elements which reside in all of us (*Pol*, 1318b39); instead, he returns to the underlying theme of much of the *Politics*, namely the education of the citizenry. For, he asked, what is the most desirable life? (*Pol*, 1323a20). This is the question that can help us to understand what the best polity is and what the appropriate education will thus be.

The good life requires three basic ingredients: goods of the body, external goods, and goods of the soul, as Jowett translates them. That is, a man must be healthy, possess adequate means, and a capable intellect. Before considering the nature of the balance that will emerge here, Aristotle proclaimed that we could not call a man happy or blessed who, in a passage worth repeating in full, is:

> without courage or self-control or practical wisdom or a sense of justice, who is scared of flies buzzing past, who will stop at nothing to gratify his desire for eating or drinking, who will ruin his closest friends for a paltry profit, and whose mind also is as witless and deluded as a child's or lunatic's.
>
> (*Pol*, 1323a26–34)

The propositions are acknowledged as soon as they are uttered, he added, and in turn they act as reminders through the ages that, indeed, certain forms of intellect and behavior are expected to present themselves as standards, even if they are presented in contrast to the lack of such standards as in these examples.

Wealth is a necessary condition of happiness, but the possession of property is no guarantee of excellence of character; rather, the possession of good character is likely to lead to maintenance of wealth. Wealth is a tool which is used for certain purposes, but possessing too much wealth, like too many tools, is detrimental to the mind (or soul), whereas the possession of a good soul is illimitable, not in the sense that the goods of the soul are useful as possessions are useful but that external goods are deployed precisely for the good of the soul. The highest soul, God's, is content in itself and because of what it is – the presence of external goods cannot add to his supremacy in that regard. For the citizen, this means that happiness comes from excellence of character, from practical wisdom, and from the wise choices made. Material resources are needed to support the virtuous life, but they do not form the moral end in themselves; a good character needs fewer resources than someone of a poor standing, who needs all the help he can get! (*Pol*, 1332a1).

The healthy body

A necessary condition to learning well in Aristotle's educational philosophy is the possession of a healthy body. In this he reflected the Greek triumvirate of health, wealth, and good birth, but Aristotle also innovated on the nature of the body and its relationship to the natural world, which had implications for medical teaching.

The general Ionic and aesclepiad theory was that the universe possesses four elements – earth, wind, fire, and water – and the body possesses four corresponding humors – hot, cold, wet, and dry. Earlier philosophers argued whether one of the four elements was indeed primary, but Aristotle preferred to make a logical leap and assert that the beginning of everything as understood in his 'prime mover' possessed no magnitude nor movement: from immateriality everything began and so exists (*Phys*, 258b5–6; 267b18–19). Today, we can interpolate that physicists now speak of a similar origin to the universe – the Big Bang theory, and indeed much that modern science employs, such as atomic theory, has Ancient roots. But such reasoning that we find among the Ancient sources, once it left the perceptual abilities of the human body, belongs to the field of conjecturing, and we are more likely to be impressed by their insights into modern truths than we may recall their mistakes – of which there were many.

From a generally materialist outlook, Aristotle reasoned that all matter was inextricably linked, such that a person's actions and ability to learn were dependent partly on forces external to the mind. 'Man is begotten by man and by the sun as well' (*Phys*, 194b13–14). This leans toward a determinist view of actions, that they are affected by external or environmental factors, and indeed, much of Aristotle's thinking on education relates to the importance of forming a good environment for the child to be brought up. Some elements are what we would today call genetic, that is they are biologically given; other elements include the effect of the climate on lives, and diet, for the highest element in man, the soul, must feed (*An*, 416b19).

People possess the capacities of nutrition, appetite, sensation, locomotion, and thinking. This separates the human race from that of the planet's flora, which possess only nutritive abilities, and other animals that possess all the above except the power to think. There may be a race of pure thinking beings above man in the hierarchy (*An*, 414a29–b19), which is later grasped by Aristotelian theologians to explain the Great Chain of Being of God, Angels, Man, Beasts, Plants.

The body, Aristotle held, possesses an internal heat which breathing in air helps to cool down (that dying people do not combust may not have occurred to him). His thrust was to bring into harmony the Ionian four-element theory of the universe with medical thinking, but in doing so he sought to impose a rational scheme upon the body implying that any disease or failing was due to an imbalance in the workings of the four elements in the body, hence a person could be too moist, too dry, too hot, or too cold. In turn the theory of oppositional remedies or allopathy emerged (and still governs much medical thinking) in which ailments are treated with their opposites, as opposed to the theory of medicine that prefers to treat like with like (what is called homeopathy). In action, pleasures generally leaned toward the warm and pains to the cool (*MA*, 702a1).

Birth and sex

Since the child's life is going to be entwined with that of the state's, it is only right that the state should take an interest in the birth of the child, forming the best foundation for its beginnings. Since birth implies conception, the state should thus look to the union of parents: the statesman should consider what age people should marry, and who should marry, taking into account their life and reproductive expectancies to ensure that the father's procreative capacity is in tune with the mother's ability to bear children (Aristotle not believing that women played a fertilizing role in conception). Then the forecasted age of parents should be considered, for it is only right that children grow up and are able to look after their parents rather than being too young to do so; on the other hand, if the parents procreate too young, this is not helpful either as their closeness in age is conducive to argument and in the animal kingdom those who reproduce while they are still young tend to produce weak offspring – he adds that the Troezen oracle was referring to this when he said, 'do not plough a new furrow' (*Pol*, 1335a20). Young brides also tend to become wanton while young grooms become stunted, so women should marry at 18 and men at 37, giving time for their seed to mature properly. Their physiques should also be balanced between the extremes of athletic strength and flaccidity – the citizen should be capably fit and not coddled. If the parents are too old, again the children tend to be feeble mentally and physically; for the man, the latest age at which he should reproduce is 50, which is when the Greeks believed a man had reached the peak of his mental powers, but he can still continue to enjoy intercourse (*Pol*, 1335b37). Adultery – that is, in Hellenic terms, extramarital sex with other citizens' wives – should be prohibited and the parties punished.

Not only does he advise on the right age appropriate for marriage and child-rearing and that parents should get advice on child-rearing, but Aristotle also gives advice on the season to conceive: winter, customary among Hellenes supposedly, was the best time, particularly if there is a northerly wind. During pregnancy, the woman ought to look after her body, eating and exercising appropriately, and being a statist, Aristotle advises that it is the statesman's duty to require pregnant women to go walking to worship the gods of childbirth. Although the body should be fairly exercised, the woman's mind should be more relaxed, 'for the offspring derive their natures from their mothers as plants do from the earth' (*Pol*, 1335b18–19). Too much mental exertion, it seems, would, according to Aristotle's thinking, draw from the nutrients required for a healthy fetus.

Then the legislator should act to ensure that the newborn's physique is suitable. No deformed neonate should be allowed to live (*Pol*, 1335b20), and if the population begins to grow and the laws do not permit exposure of the healthy child, then couples should be limited to the number of children that they may have and abortion encouraged should the wives fall pregnant. On abortion, Aristotle believes that this is permissible up until life and sensation are evident; that is, a specific gestational limit, vague in his description and not alluded to again. However, not all aspects of the child's qualities are in its parents' or the legislator's hands, for Aristotle allows that certain character traits are present from birth – notably irascibility and madness (*Cat*, 10a1).

While children are born with the potential for higher reason, which emerges as they age, their main moral powers lie with their passion, willfulness, and desire. Thus the priority with children is to ensure that they can take care of the body and then learn to control their passions, preparing them for subservience to the higher reasoning faculty (*Pol*, 1334b24–26). Thus the early years of rearing the baby into infancy are critical especially in terms of having a great impact on bodily strength (*Pol*, 1336a4–5), although some will be destined not to rule by virtue of their more extreme physical abilities (athletes or the sickly). Not surprisingly, those of middling health are to be generally preferred (*Pol*, 1335b5–8), which presumably means that the average build is best for maintaining a control over appetites and for learning, given that elsewhere (in *Politics*) Aristotle believes that those who excel too much in ability will tend to deviate from political norms for they will not suffer obedience well.

Public health

But man is a political animal, goes the Aristotelian thesis, so it is not surprising to find the philosopher also turning his attention to what makes a population healthy. The physician should look to what is conducive to healthiness and hence form views on health and disease (*SS*, 436a18). Indeed, in the *Politics*, he advances an epidemiological theory that good health, which is necessary for the good *polis*, is best gained in cities facing the east and second best in those that are sheltered from the cold north winds. Similarly, pure water supplies should be secured, for they also impact on a city's health (*Pol*, 1330a36ff). Diet thereby plays a critical role in feeding the soul (mind); taste distinguishes the pleasant from the unpleasant, and we flee from the latter (*SS*, 436b16); digestion is produced by heat, hence the reason that the stomach is close to the heart, he argued (*OY*, 474b10–24). The diet of animals and people affect their manner of living: shepherds are lazy, for they are able to get their food without much effort (*Pol*, 1256a21–b6), but too much good living reduces the desire for sex (*GA*, 726a3). In what becomes a regular downgrading of gastronomic delights in Western culture, Aristotle proposed that the nutritive element plays no role in human excellence, for it is shared by the animals and plants and digestion has no choice in action (*NE*, 1102b11–12; 1144a10). This is a philosophical view of the relationship of food and digestion, but it also links to a degradation of any aspect of human nature that is 'shared' with the animal kingdom – accordingly, for Aristotle, who followed Plato and Socrates in this regard, and many philosophers following him, the mind or soul is the highest element of man, his body is lesser, and although the physical health of the body is necessary for good learning and good morality, philosophical attention should highlight the mind and the senses most related to it rather than the body.

Two considerations arise concerning the kind of education required for the *polis*. Are the same people to rule by virtue of their patent supremacy above all others, or are the citizens, generally equal in talent and ability, to take turns ruling? The possibility of a supreme race more capable than everyone else is remote, so the constitution and its educational aims must prepare for the sharing of power and responsibilities while acknowledging that those who will share in the ruling (the free citizens) will have to be relatively superior to the people over whom they rule. Accordingly, the education of the free citizens should at once be different from the education that takes place in the lower echelons of society and, making a logical distinction so familiar to readers of Aristotle, within the citizenry it should be different according to status – whether one is presently ruling or being ruled. Such is to some extent a matter of education, but also the distinction is akin to the difference expected between the young and old – the young being prepared to rule in their time. It is thus incumbent on the good statesmen that each is thoroughly prepared to fulfill his role at the appropriate time (*Pol*, 1332b32–1333a15) and the young need to be immersed in learning about their constitution for the laws to be respected, for the law of the *polis* is the foundation to the citizens' freedom (*Pol*, 1310a14–35).

Prior to explaining the nature of education for the citizens, Aristotle summarizes some key thoughts on the nature of man, for this provides us with an understanding of the proper aims of education. The aim of education is to cultivate reason and intelligence. Whence does education begin? With habit, or reason? Nature is given to us, but the other two are within our remit to control and use or to ignore and abuse; initially, Aristotle held that the two go hand in hand – reason can be led astray by bad habits as much as habits can deviate from what is good because of wrongful thinking. Keeping in mind the aims of education, a good birth provides the groundwork, but then training and the formation of a reasoning mind are vital: a man of good habits can learn from the wise, while a man of poor habits will learn nothing. This is because the man of good habits is rationally oriented and can fathom good starting points for his understanding and for his discussion (*NE*, 1095b9).

The citizens' children are incomplete citizens who are being formed and are developing into citizens, but anyone else below the order of citizens will not attain that level of excellence to which the children's education aims. The slave does not require much excellence of character, only enough to ensure that he or she performs tasks well, but cannot be a citizen at all; the skilled artisan must be excluded from citizenship, because of the demands that citizenship imposes upon a man – artisans do not possess the time to consider and to debate properly, so the 'best form of state will not admit them to citizenship' (*Pol*, 1278a8–9). Aristotle was critical of Athenian extension of citizenship to those of a lower social status, particularly the rowers in the navy who helped to secure Athenian access and control of its colonies – such people are of use for the state, but they should not be part of the state (*Pol*, 1328b16–19). Likewise, citizens should not engage in skilled work or manual labor or engage in commerce or farming (*Pol*, 1328b38ff): the citizen needs his leisure to pursue the higher forms of Aristotelian life. This runs contrary to some veins of Hellenic thought, which encouraged agriculture as befitting the agrarian-based societies and the requirements of soldiering, but so long as the immediate means to an end (working the soil to live and eat) do not become ends in themselves, the proper hierarchy is maintained. Children should be so educated to think about the higher ends to which they can strive and not become *banausic* or mechanical in their lives. Of the child, recall, that Aristotle thinks that he is imperfect, not yet developed, so any excellence of character that may be exhibited is not the child's as such, but his father's or his teacher's; similarly, the slave reflects the goodness of character of his master (*Pol*, 1260a32–33). The child of citizens is a hypothetical citizen – an incomplete citizen, as it were (*Pol*, 1278a4–5).

The young child's education

For the first five years, there is no need for formal education as such; instead, a solid foundation is to be provided, especially with regard to nourishment. Recalling Aristotle's biological surveys, it is not surprising to read him offering analogies with the animal kingdom – a diet rich in milk is an excellent beginning for boys who are to grow up to be strong warriors. Wine is to be avoided as it produces illnesses. Physically, they are to be exercised to strengthen their limbs and to keep them supple. He makes note of some nations even using mechanical devices to straighten children's bodies, probably not dissimilar to the braces used today to help correct scoliosis.

From an early age, the child should become inured to the cold, a useful ploy to produce soldiers capable of campaigning in all weather: the Celts put little clothing on them, while other peoples dip newborns into cold water. The newborn certainly possesses a good constituency to protect it from the cold, he reckons, but as with many comments Aristotle makes, it is not clear whether he sought to test this by observing a newborn being dipped into water after emerging from a pleasing 37.4 degrees Celsius – a contented child should squirm and gurgle rather than scream; although he does later note that permitting children to cry helps to expand their lungs, it is not obvious that he means to do so purposely. Nonetheless, such processes of adapting the child to harsher temperatures, as John Locke was to write about many centuries later, should always be gradual, accustoming the children to colder weather or to wearing less. The emphasis placed on physical exercise should not be so demanding as to diminish their strength, but enough to help them build up stamina and ability: such exercise is best found in the games and play that children engage in, so long as these games are not demeaning to their class (*Pol*, 1336a25).

Teachers (in effect, the Directors of Education) should consider well what kind of stories children should hear at this age, being mindful of the impact for later life; that is, the stories should mimic what they will later on be occupied with, just as the games, he adds, should also mimic future activity. Accordingly, the children of citizens should be kept from slaves' company, for they can be tainted by what they hear and see (*Pol*, 1336a42). Indeed, proscribing the company of slaves is extended to a general prohibition of unseemly or indecent speech, which can have such a detrimental impact on the moral upbringing of the impressionable child: such young citizens that act in a dissolute manner should be punished and whipped and older freemen degraded accordingly for acting like a slave. Similarly, the young should not be permitted to see degrading images and representations as found on stage or in the temples or hear ribald limericks (iambic meter) until of maturity. What the child first encounters should be considered – just as a famous actor of the stage would not allow any other inferior actor to speak first to avoid the audience getting used to his voice, so should the statesman (and presumably parents) be wary of the first impressions that a child receives: all things inferior and particularly of a hostile nature should be kept from the young.

Since many societies possessed a very wealthy class, a middle class, and a poor class, Aristotle briefly turned his attention to the moral and educational limits of each class. The very rich tend to bring up unruly children who are used to getting their own way and therefore do not learn the importance of obeying – implicatively that is obeying to learn and to understand what it is to follow another's direction, for if these children are destined to become rulers, they grow into violent and great rascals, while those who are too poor are too degraded to obey their superiors, and so are disposed to become petty criminals and rogues and thus need ruling as slaves. The two extreme classes become masters and slaves, which does not form a healthy polity; the middle class – again reflecting Aristotle's general thesis that the middle action is often the best – present, in contrast, a polity of equals who are not interested in plotting and coveting others' goods (*Pol*, 1295b7–34). Similarly, those who excel in beauty, strength, and breeding also find it difficult to follow rational moral principles (*Pol*, 1295b8).

Between the ages of 5 and 7, the next foundations should be set: these involve preparing the child for explicit learning; by observing those lessons they will be later engaged with but not engaging with them yet.

From seven to fourteen

Generally agreeing with the poets, who divide life into periods of seven years, the next period of education falls between 7 and puberty; these divisions, Aristotle admits, are natural and it is best to follow the natural rhythms of life, rather than sticking to the exactness implied of following the seven-year rule, say (Simpson, 1998, p. 250) – but now education's import is filling in the gaps that nature has left with arts and skills (*Pol*, 1337a1). He then asks whether schooling should be a private or a public affair, and given the prominence that the *polis* plays in his philosophy and that it is argued to encapsulate all that is highest in human life, it is unsurprising to read that he believed that state education should be a public concern.

Comparing other *poleis*, although he does not name them, the lack of public education causes the constitutional arrangements and hence the polity to suffer. When the *polis* oversees the education of youth to ensure that its character is good and virtuous, then in turn the constitution remains similarly healthy – the aim then for the education of the young is to ensure that they become virtuous, which justifies, for Aristotle, compulsory and comprehensive education: all children should be taught at the expense of the state and all children should be taught the same thing. Parents should not be allowed to teach them what they see fit (*Pol*, 1337a24); only the state is in a position to deem what is good and useful for the young of the *polis*. Moreover, no individual should see himself as belonging to himself; he belongs to the *polis*, for each person is a part of the state and the responsibility for the part logically implies a responsibility for the whole – and so, he finishes this flurry, on this account the Spartans 'are to be praised' for attending to the needs of educating the youth and all at public expense (*Pol*, 1337a32).

Standing alone, this passage (*Pol*, 1337a11–32) would make perfect sense, but in the greater context of Aristotelian thinking it leans awkwardly away from the usual emphasis placed on *sōphrosunē* or balance – the seeking of a mean between extremes. The fate of the Spartans barely needs recalling, as Aristotle was wont to remind his listeners that they lost hegemony. However, the passage can also be read as amplifying the intense connection that Aristotle sees existing between the citizens and their political body – it is a logical outcome of all that has gone before. If the soundness of the polity and the happiness of the citizens mirror one another, their fates being intimately connected, then it makes sense for the politician to meld education to the state. If the foundations are correct, a healthy citizenry will emerge and so will the state remain good and virtuous. Aristotle, like many aristocrats, feared the marketplace and the plurality that it could engender; unity and common purpose were deemed to be so critical of the Hellenic *poleis*, for without unity the *polis* would be vulnerable to defeat by threatening neighbors. Perhaps: yet the aristocratic-encouraged political goals of the Athenians, Spartans, Thebans, and Macedonians led to internecine warfare and rivalry – international affairs were far from sound, so the Aristotelian thesis, accepted throughout the ages by all statists, is questionable.

Returning to the aims of education: should it be concerned with the intellect, that which is useful or virtuous in life, or with the soul? Regarding useful things, some things are indeed useful for life, but those things must reflect the needs of an aristocratic youth of free citizens and not learning trades or crafts, in which Rousseau was to later encourage the young Émile. Any skills that are detrimental to the development of the body are to be eschewed as are any that would involve payment, for they tend to distract the mind from more important pursuits. But the purpose or end to which the activity is ordered should be kept in mind, for while some skills may be useful for the free man's child to learn, attention to too much detail should be avoided. To do or to make something for a friend is one thing, but to seek to make money out of it and to trade as lowly hireling or slave is opprobrious.

Echoing the general Hellenic curriculum for children (see Part 1), Aristotle advises that children be taught grammar (reading and writing), gymnastics, music, and perhaps drawing. Learning is not about amusing the young children, he maintained, for it should be painful in that it involves effort; it is not a form of play. The training of the body must precede the training of the mind (*Pol*, 1338b5), so the boys should be handed over to the *paidotribes* in the gymnasia. Gymnastics and physical training are good for promoting courage, health, and vigor, of conditioning the body and putting it through a range of exercises for action. The idea of a healthy body healthy mind rings down the ages through the Romans and Renaissance thinkers to the modern era, with present concerns about the indolence of youth raising Ancient issues. However, physical exercises should not go too far: although he applauded the Spartan public educational system, Aristotle returns to criticizing the extremity to which they veered in training their children to be like wild animals to cultivate courage. It is wrong to emphasize one virtue over others, he warns, adding that the Spartans also failed to secure courage anyway – probably a reference to the defeat at Leuktra – and, he adds, their victories were only secure when other *poleis* did not train their people as Sparta did: 'We should judge the [Spartans] not from what they have been, but from what they are' (*Pol*, 1338b36). It is a useful reminder for anyone indulging in nostalgia for times past and for peoples once great and powerful – as noted in Part 1, the Spartan army has attracted attention throughout history – people forget that it did fall.

Courage, though, is distinguishable from fierceness and is more fitting the civilized peoples than the warlike or the barbarians. The fierce tribes around the Black Sea (the Achaeans and Heniochi) were ferocious cannibals, but they were not courageous. When training is exaggerated, as it was in Sparta, it leaves the citizens imbalanced in their abilities, prone to behaving mechanically and obediently and not nobly, that is with courage and conviction. Such virtues can only come from a balanced education.

Pre-pubescent exercise should not be too strenuous as to exert a deleterious effect on the body, stunting its growth and sapping its strength. Aristotle observes how boy champions in the Olympics rarely come back as adult men, for they have ruined their potential by peaking too early; it remains a common observance today among young gymnasts and tennis players – the body requires time to mature and the mind of the player needs experience and learning too to improve and to maintain a high level of fitness. From experience, which comes to 'rest in the soul,' skill and understanding are developed (*APst*, 100a5–8).

Reading, writing, and drawing should be included in the daily education 'in a variety of ways,' which suggests that teachers did deploy or should employ different strategies to advance skills. Reading and writing are useful for business and for household management, for study, and other useful pursuits that depend upon a knowledge of *grammata*. Drawing is of use for it allows the citizen to judge better the works of artisans; it is also good in that it teaches the pupil to understand and observe physical beauty. The young cannot engage in rational dialogue, so intellectual enjoyment is not suitable for the young boys (*Pol*, 1339a30): they are, recall, incomplete citizens, for their rationality is only potential (albeit growing). But that does not mean that they should not be exposed to serious amusements, for these will in turn be enjoyed one day by the boys as men.

Utility is not the point of an aristocratic education; the pupil should not ask whether something is useful or not, for that is the hallmark of the artisan classes. 'When will I ever use that?' is a regular retort in modern mathematics lessons, which Aristotle would have bridled at as a question unbecoming those who are destined to become great characters. Hellenic citizens' children must have asked the question – it is a common enough occurrence today and one that deserves answering. Aristotle prefers, though, to hold such questions as too low rather than to explain why some things are learned, even if they merely add to the character of the pupil.

Music

Aristotle raises a query on the utility of music. Originally, music was learned in order to provide a leisurely activity, and recall that work is engaged in for the higher pursuit of leisure, but he notes that music was increasingly enjoyed for its own sake. Playing cannot be an end in itself, he claimed, for its purpose is to act as a remedial relief from the toil of hard work; properly, leisure is enjoyed by those who are not manual laborers or skilled artisans, for they are not civilized. Thus, for the children of the free citizens to grow up to enjoy their leisure time properly, they need 'a certain amount of learning and education' (*Pol*, trans. Sinclair, 1338a14) and this includes music. Music promotes education, amusement, and the noble or aristocratic pursuit of intellectual enjoyment (*Pol*, 1339b14): it is good for amusement's sake as a rest from work, and intellectual enjoyment of music is commensurate with happiness – the highest state attainable to rational man. For the very young, it keeps them occupied, just as a rattle diverts the attention of the baby from wrecking things around the house (*Pol*, 1340b27). Music is a sweet and pleasant thing, whether played on an instrument or sung and is good for social intercourse.

Indeed, Aristotle gave music much reflection: there are 50 questions allotted to music in his *Problems*, some concerning the physicality of sound, the nature of musical divisions and modes, and the psychological aspects of music such as 'why do men take greater pleasure in listening to those who are singing such music as they already know than music which they do not know?' (*Prob*, 918a3). All people enjoy rhythm and melody and particularly children 'rejoice in them as soon as they are born' (*Prob*, 920b29). Thus Aristotle is hinting at a natural origin to music and in his writings on music he is certainly curious as to its nature and how it acts upon people, rejecting any argument that it should be prohibited or controlled. Nonetheless, the political and rationalist justifications are not far from Aristotle's mind and they tend not to overwhelm his curiosity in the beguiling and universal pleasure enjoyed in music but to provide what he seemingly believes to be a securer analysis. For Aristotle, all things possess a purpose and for people that purpose can only, ultimately, be rational. So, it should be remembered what the original purpose of music should be – of occupying the citizens in their leisure time. Leisure is not wasting time as such but the reward for work, that for which we work. It is of a higher value than work, for work is a toil, but as time spent it should be spent well in pursuits that reflect our highest nature – and listening to music is immanently appropriate.

Yet it is not often apparent that the citizens themselves engage in playing music rather than just listening to it. However, later (*Pol*, 1339a34ff; 1340b35ff) Aristotle does explain that it is important that pupils learn how to play, not so that they can learn a career, for that would be beneath the aristocratic ethos, but so that they can engage in something harmless, pleasant, and enjoyable and amusing in company. As children they learn their instruments (or singing) to a good level, but when they are older, they ought to give up their instruments as unbefitting their growing status.

The naturalness of music's pleasure is universal, which raises the question whether it has any beneficial effects on character development: it certainly has its effects, he notes, for the compositions of the Phrygian Olympus (perhaps mythical) could effect an enthusiastic frenzy. When listening to music, it is natural to follow its mood and to be affected by it – anger, gentleness, courage, temperance, can all be portrayed in music. That they produce sounds like these feelings suggests that music can mimic reality well, and this is deemed to be valuable and analogous to enjoying a realistic portrait of someone we know. On that point, it is right for the young to enjoy the portraits of good artists rather than mediocre ones. But in music, character is present in the very tunes heard – the Mixolydian scale is mournful, while the Phrygian is conducive to excitement. The Dorian provides a balance between the two; it is steady, ethical, reflective of courage, and highly suitable to teach to youngsters. These divisions are broadly 'ethical, active, and exciting' (trans. Sinclair) or 'of character, of action, and passionate' (trans. Jowett). Interestingly, Aristotle comments that philosophers have investigated these theories and have shown that music does indeed have its effects (*Pol*, 1340b6): the thesis still circulates two millennia later, from how beneficial Mozart is for babies (my baby son tends to prefer Dvořák, for some reason) to how classical music can reduce crime in shopping malls or stimulate sales, although Anthony Burgess parodied the theory in his *Clockwork Orange*.

That music can help to form character means that it must be employed in the education of children. The children will naturally prefer pleasant music and a musical education is one that gives greater enjoyment to life (*Pol*, 1340b16): it assists education, promotes civilized relaxation, and is also cathartic (*Pol*, 1341b36ff). All the modes should be taught, deploying each according to its effects: the ethical, Dorian mode for education; the Phrygian for listening to others performing. When relief is required, a dirge should be played, for music is powerfully cathartic: 'why do those who are grieving and those who are enjoying themselves alike have the flute played to them?' he asks in the *Problems* – is it because it is cathartic in lessening the stress of the grieved and enhancing the pleasure of the latter? (*Prob*, 917b18). Evidently so, he later observes.

Incidentally, each social group has its mode of music that reflects and thus represents it – the lower classes, for instance, whose nature deviates from that which is best, are represented by unnatural modes, 'high pitch and irregular colouring' (*Pol*, trans Sinclair, 1342a24).

When learning, the child ought not to acquire such a skill that would encourage his entrance into public competitions, for that would be unbecoming a future free citizen. (It is tempting to describe the citizen at this point as a gentleman; this concept, so redolent of modern England, does capture a good part of the Aristotelian ethos, but other elements act to refract the original Hellenic vision of the goodly citizen.) The child should learn enough to appreciate finer melodies and rhythms and not just be moved by the basic effect of music on the body, which any child, slave, or animal feels (*Pol*, 1341a15). Certain instruments should not be given to children for their education – particularly the pipes, for, like profane representations and theater, they are synonymous with the orgiastic Dionysian rites; pipe playing also loses one's ability to speak, which is of importance to Aristotle for some reason. He also relates a tale of

Athena, the goddess of knowledge and skills, who invented the pipes and then threw them away, perhaps because of the facial distortions they created or that the pipes add nothing to the intellect, and that is a graver fault for Aristotle (*Pol*, 1341b4ff). After prohibiting pipes and other instruments that require a dexterity of the hand and which, implicatively, would engage the attention of the child too much relative to its moral worth (and be reminiscent of the skills cultivated in the lower classes of hirelings), we are left wondering what instruments the pupils could be allowed to play!

Education – the later years

At the age of 14, the young man should now increase his study time for a period of three years (*Pol*, 1339a5), after which he should return to vigorous exercise and physical activity. This is the age when the soldier-citizen is formed and it is a natural period to increase strength and ability. Aristotle is against trying to combine the vigor of exercise with studiousness, for the two tend to oppose one another – the labor of the body impeding the mind, and the labor of the mind impeding the body.

A man's musical education should now change: as a child he learned an instrument to a tolerable level, but now he must lay down the skill (*Pol*, 1340b37); it is sufficient that he has learned enough to be able to judge good from bad music and to appreciate in turn the effects on character that music can play. The role of the soldier and citizen must now take priority. Singing, though, does not disappear, for Aristotle notes how it is more appropriate that older men sing lower parts than younger: we must be considerate of what is possible and what is appropriate, so in more mature years, we may turn to the Lydian key, which possesses attributes of order and education. He is not yet ready to hear lectures on politics, for his purpose now is to act not to gain knowledge (*NE*, 1095a1).

Man's mind divides into a rational element and a non-rational element, the latter capable of listening to reason, though. The rational element is the superior, so the inferior, non-rational element must serve the ends of the higher aspects of the mind; similarly, with regard to reasoning itself – theoretical reason divides from practical reason, and so a man must strive to aim to fulfill the higher aspects of his mind and his nature. With regard to action, war should be waged for the higher principle of peace, work is done for the sake of leisure, and useful things generally done for the higher more noble and moral aims. These are the ends deemed proper for children's education – to aim for the highest that man is capable of and which is appropriate for him *qua* rational man.

Here Aristotle turns from the Hellenic traditions in education, which he believed had fallen short of the best that could be produced, for the educators and statesmen had fallen prey to a vulgar error of aiming for the useful virtues and abilities rather than those which are good in themselves; similarly, those who applaud the Spartans because their program led to war and conquest fail to recognize the higher elements of man (*Pol*, 1335b10ff). Spartan rule is no more, Aristotle reminds the reader – they have lost the good life. The virtue of conquest does not necessarily produce a happy state with virtuous citizens, and it also sets up a dangerous precedent that the citizens themselves may strive for control within the polity, thus creating the conditions for future instability: military states tend to fall once they are no longer at war (*Pol*, 1334a4). What will be best for the state will also be best for the free citizens and waging war and seeking mastery over equals is not conducive to peace or the good life for either – the statesmen must educate the people to prepare for the higher goal of peace.

Military training has as its immediate aim the preservation of the state and its rightful rule over those who deserve to be ruled, but, Aristotle notes, more importantly, it teaches the free man to learn how to obey and to command in turn, as well as to instill in him the moral strength not to surrender to those who would make him a slave (*Pol*, 133b37ff).

For the pursuit of leisure, the state has to ensure that material means are provided adequately, for while war gives an edge to men's abilities and teaches them to be secure, self-restrained, and courageous, leisure can be abused and make men insolent and arrogant. Thus, the successful must be taught to deploy philosophy, justice, and self-restraint in leisure as much as in war; and since the state and its free citizens are intimately linked, it too should reflect the virtues proper for peace and leisure time in remaining just and restrained.

Once through his formal training, the citizen can now engage in the great educational vision that Aristotle has for the educated citizenry – of learning to think for themselves, to cultivate a practical wisdom, and gradually as they mature to become philosophers.

Part 3

The Reception and Influence of Aristotle's Work

Chapter 5

Ancient to Modern

The roots of education are bitter but the fruit sweet.
(Aristotle, attributed by Diogenes)

The fate of Aristotle's work and philosophy is entwined with political, religious, and educational movements. Having founded a school – his most direct contribution to education – his indirect influence was bound to continue, as Berkeley comments: 'So close and immediate a connexion may custom establish betwixt the very *word* Aristotle and the motions of assent and reverence in the minds of some men' (orig. italics; Berkeley, 1972, p. 60). However, Aristotle's school's fate was intimately tied up with political events and eventually it fell prey to political machinations and later, after a revival, to Christian intolerance for pagan schools under Justinian I (AD 482–565). Ironically, Aristotle later became an integral part of Catholic Christianity, which raised him to the level of orthodoxy and which in turn caused no end of generalizations and snide remarks on how bad his philosophy was because it was tied to ecclesiastical authority. And so Aristotle was once more toppled and he became vilified in the rush to modern scientific thinking, but gradually the bits were picked up once more as philosophers could not help but recognize what a powerful and influential mind he possessed – he can still enlighten us today.

The fate of Aristotelianism initially mirrored the fate of his books, and in turn they influence the relative strength that Aristotle's educational legacy has had on thinkers. Since his educational theories have generally related to the maturing and mature mind rather than children, it is unsurprising to find that his greatest influences have been on the equivalent of high schools and universities as well as in political and ecclesiastical courses and that is where our attention will reside in this Part. Although we could chart graphically the popularity of his works, the influence on a host of writers, teachers, theologians, and politicians has been immense – at times we recognize a distinct Aristotelian voice in later philosophers, other times a more subtle influence, sometimes thoroughly supportive, other times critical. Some philosophers became thoroughly Aristotelian, holding him as the best thinker ever to have lived (which is understandable), but some then turn that to assert his quasi-divinity as an unquestionable authority on a range of topics (which is less understandable). For others, though, Aristotle provided the intellectual paving for further examination or critique and it is this departure from the orthodox that in turn helped to foment the intellectual revolutions in Europe in the seventeenth century.

But throughout, of two important aspects to Aristotle that are appropriate to us, the more relevant enduring educational legacy has been the importance of a moral education built upon forming good habits in the young. In a nutshell: the good man becomes good by doing good things, and this should be started when he is young, not when he is old. Behind this lay Aristotle's epistemology that the good is knowable and accessible – that it is reasonable, compared to Plato's theory that what is truly Good lies beyond moral men to comprehend or to religion's acceptance of revealed knowledge. The secularity of Aristotle thus attracts those who believe we ought to be concerned with life on this earth and with how we ought to live. In turn, the good was dependent on the form that the agent took – one's materiality is the shape taken by the body, but the form was the inner essence (substance or thingness) that makes the agent what he is in effect through action. Form gives purpose and through purpose potentiality becomes actuality; that is, the boy has the potential to become good, and so becomes good by doing good things. Standing above the philosophical discussion is the state: children are to be educated to be good in order to serve the state well, which, for Aristotle, is the basis for contentment in the adult.

The second impact on human thought was Aristotle's encouragement of scientific study – the collection and analysis of knowledge. Some modern thinkers have argued that Aristotle's philosophy retarded scientific development for two millennia: an unjustifiable charge when we engage with what Aristotle wrote rather than what became the Aristotelian orthodoxy controlled by authorities in the Scholastic era (twelfth to fifteenth centuries AD), which was when his works formed a central part of the curricula of the great universities and his ethical readings were mandatory discussion for students. The attachment of any thinker's works to a mandatory course and effective orthodoxy kills critical analysis and stultifies intellectual progress; it was only when the authoritarian barriers that had been formed by ecclesiastical authorities were removed that philosophers could return to discussing Aristotle unhindered and freely and thereby gain a better sense of his influence as well as the philosophical importance of his works. If we return to the general Aristotelian notion that the world is knowable, then we can ask whether it is deductively or inductively knowable (or of course a mixture of the two): adherents to his name pursued different emphases here, some claiming that armchair reasoning should be sufficient to understand the nature of the world, others that only collecting data can offer any certainty; there are problems with both positions, as well as the middle position of what Popper termed critical rationalism. Aristotle favored logical analysis but also claimed that we must always return to what the senses inform. Debate and many paths led from these epistemological positions.

In this Part, we trace the fate of Aristotle's works and relate the detectable influences on the various eras and thinkers predominantly in the Ancient World following his death and down through the Middle Ages, when his influence was at its explicit apex. Naturally, as time progresses, the influence broadens as his legacy becomes part of the great river of human intellect flowing into our present, and so our story will retreat from the details to acknowledge the enduring vestiges and the continued work that has attracted scholars since antiquity. Because his influence has been predominantly philosophical and hence within intellectual circles, I shall leave an assessment of his direct impact on education through the ages till the last Part and the discussion of his relevance today.

Chapter 6

The Ancient World

The Lyceum/Peripatos

In 323 BC, Alexander died leaving his vast fragile empire to be split among his generals, and Aristotle's relatively comfortable position in Athens was under threat; the change also stands as a symbol of the passage of his works through time, which also became vulnerable to political change and the vicissitudes of war and migration. On removing from his university to Chalcis, Aristotle took several assistants and his possessions, so his flight was unhurried; moreover, the university was not targeted by his enemies, for Macedonia was to remain politically powerful for a long while and the Lyceum had been a popular place with Athenian philosophers (Grayeff, 1974, pp. 44–50; 52). Headship went to Theophrastus, Aristotle's companion whom he had befriended in Lesbos and with whom he had worked on his researches from pupil to colleague for forty years.

The non-Athenian Theophrastus (370–279 BC) rode anti-Macedonian surges, and through a clever land deal effected by the governor of Athens, was permitted to purchase land at the Lyceum giving the world's first university legal stability. From then on, the Lyceum generally flourished as the principals were also its owners; only twice did the anti-Macedonians effectively disrupt the school in 306 BC, which closed it, and in 288 BC a riot resulted in damage to buildings and statues. Nonetheless, student numbers increased, lecture rooms were built, the curriculum expanded; Theophrastus established botany to complement Aristotle's zoology and augmented Aristotle's logic, and at the school medicine and music were taught too. It was, for a century or so, a flourishing university and accordingly scholars began to specialize. Theophrastus continued much in his master's footsteps, writing prodigiously on a variety of subjects; his headship also signaled a transition toward empiricism, continuing Aristotle's pursuit of collecting data and histories and away from the Platonic vestiges in his thinking – Eudemus, for instance, worked on physics and mathematics, while Aristoxenus studied the history of music. Theophrastus, whose leaning was more to physics than metaphysics (he was called *ho physikos*, the scientist), shifted the school's emphasis from Aristotle's 'first philosophy' to empiricism (Baltussen, 2000, p. 12); he also penned an enjoyable work, *Characters*, on the psychology of various types of people (Ironic Man, Arrogant Man, the Chatterer, the Late Learner, etc.), expanding Aristotle's themes in his ethical writings, as well as writings on the history of ideas on sensation, and wrote on botany. Critics note a subtle shift away both from Aristotle's teleological theses and especially from Aristotle's comments on the theoretical unmoved mover of the universe (Sharples, 1999, pp. 148–50). Theophrastus was succeeded by Strato (335–269 BC), who continued the scientific drive that Aristotle had begun, and under his leadership the Lyceum became the educational center of the Hellenic world. Lyco (299–225 BC), his successor, an orator rather than a philosopher, capitalized on its growing wealth to court kings; although its reputation held, its intellectual qualities were beginning to ebb (Grayeff, 1974, pp. 50–53). But the Lyceum continued to hold its own while Macedonia was strong, with important academic connections with the university at Alexandria, whose intellectuals pursued a slightly altered peripatetic methodology, compiling encyclopedias of knowledge from the Lyceum collections, and performing dissections which the peripatetics of Athens avoided (Sharples, 1999, p. 148).

Competition in the Hellenic world for students came from the continuation of Plato's Academy under various heads, which the Macedonians tolerated on their part, while in 307 BC Epicurus (341–270 BC) opened his 'garden' in Athens, and Zeno (333–264 BC) founded the Stoa in 304 BC. The Academy passed over to Arcesilaus (316–241 BC), who had been Theophrastus' *eromenos*, and with it a critical and skeptical school of thought emerged that dominated the Academy for a long while.

There was also 'the Stoa' or painted portico (*Stoa Poikile*), where Zeno taught. A former Academy pupil, he set up a curriculum of ethics, logic, and physics, personally concentrating on ethics, while the

Stoic logicians Diodorus Cronos and Philo helped to improve Aristotle's logic by setting out prepositional logic formally. Posidonius (135–51 BC) studied in Athens before removing to Rhodes, where he taught philosophy – incidentally to Cicero – and worked on collecting and observing around the Mediterranean in the spirit of Aristotle; he seemed highly interested in the causes affecting individuals and groups (Morford, 2002, p. 32; Sellars, 2006, p. 10). At the time, Stoic logic was seen to compete with that of Aristotle, but modern critics see them as developing logic in tandem, developing different areas of logic and both anticipating modern prepositional and predicate calculus (Kenny, 2004, p. 144). In another extension to Aristotelianism, the Stoics also claimed that one should 'live according to nature'; they also demanded the best from human capacity, as well as a humility and fortitude in understanding our meager position in a vast, ordered universe that is absent in Aristotle. The world according to the Stoics is material and rationally ordered, and with Aristotle, they agreed that the universe is divinely ordered by a higher intelligence. They also agreed that we learn sensibly: the truth is the correspondence of our senses with the world (cf. *An*, 431a1), although the senses are not sufficient guarantors of the truth (Hankinson, 2003, p. 60). Against Aristotle, they held that history was cyclical rather than eternally linear and they also rejected the moral hierarchy imposed apodictically upon people; nonetheless, for educational purposes, they were in general agreement that assenting to obey nature and recognizing its laws forms the foundation to becoming virtuous. Virtue is thus deontological – duty oriented – but based on education; however, they rejected Aristotle's thesis of forming the mean between extremes, for they asserted that there are either vices or virtues – nothing in between. The other Stoical twist to Aristotle's philosophy is that I need to mentally mature to know my humble role, to accept the way of things. Happiness thus comes from obedience to nature rather than the pursuit of ephemeral pleasures, and wisdom can only come from straining to apply our reason to the world (and thereby acknowledge our humble position therein). The ephemera of life possess no value whatsoever to the Stoic, hence he or she is indifferent to pain, poverty, and even death. Fortitude, benevolence, indifference, self-sufficiency characterize the Stoic; most importantly, one should live by one's philosophy – Epictetus (AD 55–135) proposed strongly that living is more important than reflecting as such.

Stoicism became the guiding ethic of Rome's greatest philosopher-emperor, Marcus Aurelius, and within it we still hear Aristotelian echoes, for by the time of the 'middle Stoics' of the first century, its philosophers began to look upon Aristotle as a great philosopher from whom much could be learned rather than the head of a competing school (Sellars, 2006, p. 11); indeed, they owed much to Aristotle.

The other competing school founded in Athens was the Garden, founded in 306 BC by Epicurus. His followers included slaves and women and like the later Christian monks, lived simply in seclusion. In many respects, Epicurus developed elements of Aristotle's philosophy along lines that Aristotle would not have condoned but which were partially embedded in his logic for development. The senses provide us with a means to knowledge and we are essentially motivated by pain and pleasure, Epicurus held, just as did Aristotle (and for which Barnes calls him the precursor of the Utilitarians [1976, 31]); however, while Aristotle sought to impose reason upon the appetite and emotions, Epicurus believed that pleasure alone could provide the best end for man rather than the rational life. But thoughts on pleasure, like those of Aristotle, were hierarchical – some pleasures are better than others, such as friendship (to which we should compare Aristotle's *NE*, Books VIII and IX). According to Diogenes Laertius, Epicurus was mainly self-taught and favored the philosophy of the atomist Democritus and penned a work *Against Aristotle*; however, of his three hundred works only three letters, a couple of sets of maxims, and others' somewhat malicious gossip have been found. From his maxims, as Aristotle held, we learn that the just and wise life was pleasant; wisdom cannot be found in the myths but must be based on scientific study; the purest pleasure is one that has no concomitant pain attached anywhere to it – so the pleasures of sex and nutrition, which involve a modicum of pain, are not as pure as the philosopher's pleasure; the wise man directs his life with reason, so chance does not impair his actions – he is thus settled rather than restless or disturbed; dreams result from experiences and sensory impressions; the life of the mind procures the complete and perfect life; the most important means to happiness is friendship; the youth cannot be happy for they are subject to too much chance, so only the mature can be wise and happy; the just and wise *polis* treats all alike and defends itself against threats so as its citizens live in peace (Epicurus, 1986, *passim*). But he detracted from Aristotle by agreeing with the atomists, rejecting the notion of a prime mover, and pursuing a thoroughly materialist vision of life, removing Aristotle's more mysterious thesis that thought is immaterial and eternal. Metaphysics is abandoned in favor of what we could almost call an existentialist vision of man thrown into the universe to rely on himself and a few good friends: 'God is nothing to be afraid of: death is nothing to worry about: good is easy to get: evil is easy to bear' (quoted in Armstrong, 1965, p. 139); and so too does he abandon Aristotle and Plato's political philosophies: 'We must free ourselves of public education and politics' (Epicurus, 1986, p. 70). In him we detect that proto-scientist vision that the Stoics also picked up from Aristotle and which anticipate much that modern science would find familiar: 'We must not resist nature but obey her' (Epicurus, 1985, p. 67); and we hear a moralist who renounced desires and wealth as illusory vehicles of happiness – despite the modern epithet of hedonism associated with the epicure.

The Academy, Lyceum (aka the Peripatos), Garden, and Stoa stand as testament to Athens' philosophical greatness; there were also the Cynics after Diogenes the Cynic, who lived at the time of Plato and who proposed a nihilistic anti-establishmentarianism, and the Pythagoreans, whose mysticism continued to have an influence. Generally speaking, Stoicism successfully transferred into the Roman mindset, while the Academy underwent a revival from the first century BC to the sixth century AD with the Neoplatonists. Epicurus, despite the failure of the majority of his texts to survive, maintained an attraction to later philosophers who were encouraged by his egalitarian ethics and empiricism. The Academy *qua* university fared somewhat better in that it was later revived in the first century BC and sustained itself until the sixth century AD. Speusippus and Xenocrates developed slightly different aspects of Plato's thought, with the former's influence forming a Neopythagorean Platonism that surfaced in the works of Plotinus (AD 204–70) (Dillon, 2005, p. v). Its last fruition was in the sixth century AD, just before the school was formally closed by the Emperor Justinian in AD 529 (Evans, 2000, p. 68), who sought to renew the Roman Empire and to impose the Nicene Christian orthodoxy on its peoples and so attacked the heterodox – fighting and murdering those who disagreed: not a conducive time for philosophy to survive. The Academy's scholars fled, ironically in some respects, to Persia and the city of Ctesiphon, which offered them sanctuary and where later pupils were to influence Islam with Hellenic science and to pass on the works of Aristotle into the Arabic world.

Aristotle's university's fortunes effectively dwindled with the collapse of Macedonian influence and the death of Lyco in 225 BC, who had willed the Lyceum to all of his colleagues rather than stipulating a single principal, thereby undermining the legal strength it had possessed. Some tried to continue the scholarly traditions but the cultural shifts were such that both the Academy and the Lyceum were diminishing. Nonetheless, the Lyceum had produced numerous graduates who went out into the Hellenistic world to advise or teach; its curriculum expanded and its academics made important additions to scholarly work, but in that itself issues arose: Grayeff hints that the Lyceum may have become stuffy relative to the other schools, for it failed to attract the young or to have a palpable influence on contemporary culture or politics (Grayeff, 1974, p. 57).

Aristotle's intellectual impact could now be seen to be spreading its wings and finding new critics and influences outside of the Lyceum's walls, merging with other thinkers, being rejected and accepted amid the flow of the great conversation that reaches our ears today. His voice is so apparent in the Hellenes that followed him, whether they were in Athens, Alexandria, Pergamon, or Rome. However, the disappearance of his works until Andronicus (c. 60 BC) formed his edition left many scholars studying Aristotelianism second hand rather than first hand with the texts, although it is conjectured by Sharples that not all of his works would have disappeared, there being plenty of copies to circulate of some of the texts, and that why Aristotle fell into lack of study was because later thinkers did not find him that interesting (Sharples, 1999, p. 152). Indeed, the early peripatetics studied more in the spirit of the master, whereas those who picked him up following Andronicus' edition now shifted the emphasis to cultivating a belief in the master's words as canonical (Sharples, 1999, p. 153), something that Aristotle would have rejected.

The rise of Rome and its Hellenization

A critical geopolitical turning point and a fortunate twist of fate for Aristotle's legacy came with the Roman annexation of Greece. Pergamon was bequeathed to Rome in 133 BC by their last king, Attalus III, who saw that his nation could not compete. The Romans had defeated the powerful Macedonian phalanxes at Cynoscephalae in 197 BC and in 168 BC at Pydna; the latter led to the formation of a Roman protectorate over Greece in 167 BC. Minor uprisings from 152 to 146 BC and internecine Hellenic fighting (Achaeans fighting Roman-protected Spartans) finally led to Macedonia becoming a Roman province and the Achaean league being dissolved, and Rome holding sway over all of Greece, proving, for our interests, a new channel for Aristotle's philosophy.

In 155 BC, the Athenians sent three philosophers to Rome to appeal against a fine. They were the peripatetic Critolaus (200–118 BC), head of the Academy Carneades (214–129 BC), and Stoic philosopher Diogenes of Babylon (230–150 BC); 'sensitive to the Roman emphasis on public service they did not include an Epicurean' (Freeman, 1999, p. 399). In many respects, the delegates' speeches were a success, both in reducing the 500-talent fine (for the sacking of Oropus) and in exciting intellectuals about Greek ideas; however, Cato the Elder (234–149 BC) thought that they were too corrupting of Roman traditions and had them sent back to Athens. But Hellenic philosophy, notably Stoicism, had begun to seep into Rome: teachers followed and Roman thinkers learned Greek as a language of the civilized. In 159 BC, Crates of Mallos introduced *grammatika* into Roman education; many grammar schools had opened up and Greeks were employed (or slaves bought) to teach Roman children (Freeman, 1999, p. 399).

However, when Cicero visited Athens in 79 BC, he found no trace of the Lyceum or the Academy – from then on, Aristotle's philosophy had to survive through his works rather than through the legacy of the Lyceum. Indeed, his extant works were also seemingly lost for a while; according to legend, they were packed off to Neleus in the Troad (western Turkey), who was, by then, one of Aristotle's last surviving students. His descendants hid them in a cellar to avoid the local

Pergamon King Eumenes stealing them for his library. In a cellar or a cave they began to decay and philological troubles began.

The master's texts were discovered (or looted) following the fall of Pergamon to the Romans by the bibliophile Apellicon, who took them to Athens and sought to copy them; they then fell into the hands of Sulla (138–78 BC), who sacked Athens and the Lyceum in 86 BC and removed them to Rome to be copied by the grammarian Tyrannio, a friend of Cicero. When Cicero ran his eyes over the manuscripts he suddenly reappraised Aristotle as a great philosopher in his own right rather than a leading Platonist. This was a fortunate act since Sulla was a renowned cruel and brutal man, who became dictator of Rome and murdered many enemies, hardly the kind of character one would suspect of appreciating philosophy. The texts were later compiled by Andronicus of Rhodes into the Aristotelian *Organon* that we now find more or less in the *Complete Works* (Sharples, 1999, pp. 151–2). Andronicus was the tenth titular head of the Peripatetic School, the descendant school of the once great Lyceum, which by then had transferred to Rome; he also penned a critical work on Aristotle and his productivity effectively encouraged an intellectual revival of studying Aristotle in the original, although dispute (naturally) arises concerning the circulation of Andronicus and the existence of other circulating copies. Snyder notes that other intellectuals did not mention Andronicus' edition, which suggests that it may have circulated privately and in limited circles (Snyder, 2000, pp. 68–9), and evidence exists that Aristotle was known prior to and independently of Sulla's horde looted in his sacking of Athens in 86 BC (Grayeff, 1974, p. 74; Morford, 2002, p. 5).

Incidentally, Strabo, geographer and Roman apologist (63 BC–AD 24), complained of the earlier peripatetics that they did not possess Aristotle's books to study. Why was this a problem? According to Snyder, unlike the Stoics or Epicureans, the peripatetic followers of Aristotle were very text oriented, lessons being taught with texts and commentaries (Snyder, 2000, p. 66), a disposition that has not left Aristotelianism! Controversy thus began over the authenticity of Aristotle's writings. Initially, the *Nicomachean Ethics* were viewed skeptically and believed to be the hand of Aristotle's son, Nicomachus, but Aspasius (AD 100–50) argued successfully that the work was indeed by the hand of the master. The *Eudemian Ethics* and the *Magna Moralia* were then considered to be posthumous representations of Aristotle's work while some maintained the latter to be genuine. Recent analyses put the three together by connecting elements from within the three books and that evidence points to the *Nicomachean Ethics* as not being consistently produced compared to the *Eudemian Ethics* (Kenny, 2004, p. 80). Similarly, philologists have always been concerned over the reproduction of texts, which were done by hand, of course, until the printing presses were invented, and copying presents an inevitable quality risk as is evident when we challenge a pupil to copy over a hundred words perfectly.

Although questions surfaced then and now over the authenticity and quality of the works, obviously Aristotle was still taught and discussed; today, non-Greek readers should compare different translations to gain their own reading of favorite passages or words. Two millennia ago, scholars faced similar problems over copyists' work: did Aristotle put a 'not' here, has this passage been accidentally added to this book, what do other copies say, what do other commentators say? and so on. And of course, different commentators and copyists had their own leanings to impose upon the texts, which in turn gave the Aristotelians a further employment beyond learning his philosophy – to sort out his works (Snyder, 2000, pp. 72–4), again a scholarly job that persists today.

Under the Roman sun, Aristotle had a mixed reception: Stoicism found the ground much more fruitful. Nonetheless, Aristotelians do emerge, some – like Philo, head of the Academy – literally fleeing Sulla's sack of Athens in 86 BC just as scholars fled the rise of Hitler in Nazi Germany in the twentieth century. Panaetius (185–110 BC), head of the Stoa in 128 BC, studied in Athens before heading to Rome, and the company of the famous General Scipio Africanus (who had defeated Hannibal) enjoyed Aristotle and supported his theory that the physical world was eternal and that the soul was mortal. Cicero appreciated both Aristotle and Plato for their moderation and for the intellectual source of Stoicism, so popular with the Roman thinking elite; his own views on Aristotle represent the changing fortunes of Aristotle's works – initially upholding him as a Platonist, gradually realizing that the two masters differed philosophically, extolling him, and then, as he engages the texts more deeply, not sure whether they hold contradictions or not (Grayeff, 1974, p. 76), a troubling journey which sent scholars back to the original texts.

The peripatetics gradually became more attractive to scholars and those who opposed the Stoics could find something in Aristotle's works to justify their positions. Nonetheless, Antiochus (130–68 BC), who also taught Cicero, sought to amalgamate Aristotle's thought with that of the Stoics back into the Platonic fold, while Plutarch, who was mainly a Platonist, who opposed the Stoics politically, found much in Aristotle to help attack the Stoics, whose members included Brutus (assassin of Julius Caesar) and Cato the Younger. His critique of the Stoics and Epicureans ushered in their philosophical decline (Kenny, 2004, p. 112). Philo (20 BC–AD 50), Cicero's teacher at the Academy, also acted as an important bridge between the Hellenic and Judaic worlds and in turn forged intellectual paths into Christianity, which becomes a vital river for Aristotelian thinking and for his works in the Middle Ages.

For a brief time, Aristotle's Lyceum resurfaced in the Pax Romana of Marcus Aurelius (AD 121–80), who reinstated four chairs of philosophy in Athens, one for each of the famous schools. So for a while (nobody is sure how long) the Lyceum was back in business! Peripatetics revived the school. And this is where Aspasius fits in (see above), who is also known for writing the oldest extant commentary on Aristotle's *Nicomachean Ethics* and who in turn was read by Plotinus (AD 204–70) and Boethius (AD 480–524/5). There was also Alexander of Aphrodisias, head of the peripatetics (fl. second century AD), who criticized the Stoics from Aristotle's philosophical view; he was known as *ho exogetēs*, the expositor, on Aristotle. Indeed, Stoics and Academicians also discussed Aristotle's theories during this Indian summer for philosophy, particularly his logic – Simplicius of the Academy (AD 490–560) wrote a commentary on the *Categories*.

The Lyceum continued as the Peripatetic School possibly until AD 267, when Germanic Heruli tribes sacked the city, but most certainly when the *coup de grace* of the Christian Emperor Justinian I abolished all pagan schools in AD 529. In Rome, the rise of Neoplatonists began to undermine the Aristotelian legacy (and that of others) of scientific and logical pursuits. The Roman Neoplatonists sought to merge

Aristotle, Plato, and Stoicism, with Eastern mysticism under the Egyptian Plotinus (AD 204–70), who founded a school in Rome. For Plotinus, merging the strands of Hellenic thought, Aristotle's notion of the prime mover was particularly handy. His pupil Porphyry (AD 233–309) worked on logic and sought to meld Aristotle's logic with Neoplatonism. Boethius translated Porphyry into Latin (*Isagoge*), which provided a textbook on logic used down into the Middle Ages; similarly, it entered the Islamic world through Ibn Al-Muqaffa.

However, as time went on, philosophers had only a few manuscripts of Plato and Aristotle to peruse, otherwise relying on traditions passed down through the peripatetics and Neoplatonists such as Cicero, the Church Fathers, and Islamic and Jewish intellects (Artz, 1954, pp. 181–2); until the fifteenth century, philosophers had to rely on Plato's *Timaeus* and Aristotle's works on logic translated by Boethius.

As befitting an era of increased uncertainties, philosophy responded by retreating into more mystical forms and away from the scientific tendencies fostered by Aristotle and the peripatetics. Platonism (through the *Timaeus*) offered a philosophical approach to mysticism that hailed the power of eternal forms or of the One (an earlier Parmenidean notion); such moves by thinkers such as Plotinus also drew upon the more intriguing and perhaps Platonic passages of Aristotle of the unmoved mover and the hierarchical nature of the universe with the presumption of beings higher than man above us. Plotinus' school in turn shifted from Rome to Athens following his death, where it flourished until Justinian I closed the universities. But ideas cannot be constrained by buildings and the Neoplatonism of Plotinus and others found a convivial home in Christian thinking, particularly that of St. Augustine of Hippo (AD 354–430).

Augustine was primarily a Christian but one who merged it with Platonism, rejecting the implication of polytheism that he insisted it logically implied. From a philosophical perspective, he was the most influential Christian theologian until Thomas Aquinas. He mentions Aristotle in passing and hints that he had read some of his work: 'a man of commanding genius, [but] no match for Plato in his literary style, but still far above the general run' (Augustine, 1984, VIII.12). So by Augustine's time in the Roman West, Aristotle's influence had become small relative to the Platonists', although critics note echoes of

Aristotle's theories of the good, of politics, and of the hierarchical nature of the universe in Augustine's *The City of God* (e.g. Heyking, 2001; O'Connell, 1986). Although as an intellectual Augustine drew deeply from Plato and indirectly Aristotle, he fumed against them in his sermons: who were they compared to Christ? Proud and arrogant nothings (van de Meer, 1961, p. 580).

Augustine was finishing his famous work as Rome fell to barbarian invaders. Rome continued often as an ideal but also as a pale political entity over the next century or so, so Boethius (AD 480–524) penned at the end of the Roman era in the West, prior to his execution on the orders of King Theodoric of the Ostrogoths and king of Italy, his Stoical *Consolation of Philosophy* written while awaiting execution for falling foul of politics. Boethius desired to translate Aristotle's works into Latin and to merge them with Plato's philosophy; it was through his translations that Aristotle was passed down to the schoolmen of the 'Dark Ages' – he was known to Alfred the Great, for instance, who had the *Consolation* translated into English.

But by now we are grasping for tenuous connections as scholarly institutions have their doors closed and the intelligently minded turn their attention to the other world of heaven and God's nature. Boethius' life was a last flicker of philosophy in western Europe until the gradual revival of Hellenism and particularly Aristotle from the eleventh century (see below). Gregory the so-called Great (AD 540–604) represented the disappearance of the Hellenic traditions: he did not speak Greek, nor did he feel he had to, Roberts remarks (1996, p. 89). West and east were dividing.

The broader Hellenic world

In the closing of the Athenian schools, the remnants of Plato's Academy fled to Persia for sanctuary, but Greek influence had already been planted in the East, not just by the usual and subtle, perhaps sub-historical flows and exchanges of ideas, but also by Alexander's Empire. In some respects, while the bias in the declining Roman Empire was toward Platonism, in the East Aristotelianism fared much better, and since the peripatetic descendants were more concerned with the actual world and what we now term scientific studies than Platonists, it is not surprising that science flourished more in the East for many centuries.

Aristotle's pupil had taken Hellenism eastward as far as the Indus Valley and in turn, Alexander had encouraged a mass migration of Hellenes eastward, and they brought with them their genes and memes. Upon his death, Alexander's Empire broke up into factions: the Ptolemies ran Egypt, the Seleucids the Middle East to India; Bactria was ruled by Greek soldiers, and the Hellenic Kingdom of Pergamon arose in modern day Turkey, often the historical gateway for 'East' and 'West.' Accordingly, Greek became the main language of the Near East and in many of the cities of the post-Alexandrian Empire. While their rulers took on the trappings of Easter despotism, intellectually they and those they influenced looked back to Greece for knowledge and culture (Roberts, 1996, pp. 42–3).

A copy of one of Aristotle's works has been found in Ai-Khanoum, Afghanistan, for instance, its ink miraculously imprinted on the clay bricks in what appears to be a missing Aristotelian dialogue called *The Sophist*. Aristotle's student Clearchos seems to have worked at the Hellenic outpost. Also, the Lyceum had strong intellectual contacts with Egypt and the professors of Alexandria, having been established by Demetrius of Pharleron, one of Theophrastus' students and an adviser to the first Ptolemy, Alexander's general who took over Egypt (Kenny, 2004, p. 93). A library at Pergamon was also created by the Hellenes; it housed over 200,000 manuscripts, many written on parchment which took its name from the city (*charta Pergamon*), and which is one of those unintended products of state intervention: when the Egyptians curtailed papyrus exports, the Pergamon king (or entrepreneurial innovators) sought an alternative for writing – the breaking of the papyrus monopoly helped to encourage the flow of writings across the Mediterranean just as the printing press opened up freedom to publish and share ideas in fifteenth-century Europe. Augmenting the copying of texts was the gradual emergence of private libraries and the book trade, which also helped the spread of ideas (Kenyon, 1932, p. 24), as well as the formation of the great libraries of Alexandria, Pergamon, Antioch, and Rhodes.

Aristotle had possessed an excellent circulating library, which was symptomatic of the greater ease by which books could be procured, and in turn the peripatetics' writings were stored in the great libraries for further dissemination, mainly at Pergamon (Grayeff, 1974, p. 72). Pergamon produced excellent scholars including Galen (AD 129–200), whose writings on medicine influenced medical thinking for over a millennium. However, the Pergamon library was handed over by Mark Antony to Cleopatra as a birthday present: such ignorant audacity left the Ancient World bereft of an important source of knowledge and counterbalance to the forces of ignorance and barbarity.

The Alexandrian library began with the collection of Demetrius of Phalerum, a student of Theophrastus who probably, and possibly with Aristotle, had a hand in its planning; he was encouraged by Ptolemy I in his policy of Hellenizing Egypt. In the third century AD, the Egyptian Ammonius Saccas, who taught Plotinus and Origen and who is credited with founding Neoplatonism, supposedly sought to reconcile Aristotle and Plato; controversy reigns as to whether he was also a Christian, but the rise of intolerant Christians reduced Alexandrian academia despite its founding in the spirit of Hellenism by Aristotle's pupil. Hypatia (AD 350–415), one of the last mathematicians and intellects of the end of the Roman era, was brutally torn to shreds by Coptic monks and her passing may be regarded as one of the significant landmarks in the decline of Western civilization. The fate of the peripatetic Alexandrian library in turn is infamous: the greatest library of the Ancient World was according to legend burned to the ground during Julius Caesar's campaign against Ptolemy XII; however, historians disagree on whether it was completely destroyed or not, for later references note a sizeable library. Its importance dwindled by the seventh century, cutting the last important tie to the Hellenic world in Egypt, for Alexandria and the Lyceum had always enjoyed strong intellectual ties, and although the fate of the library is still subject to historical inquiry, the school that surrounded it survived. Alexandria was a flourishing city and the crossroads for trade between the Mediterranean, the Middle East, and India. Intellectually, Jewish and Hellenic theologians mixed and hence other conduits from Greece outward remained in place despite the decline or destruction of the library. Fortunately, receptive schools further afield were in a favored position to disseminate Aristotle's thought – notably in the city of Baghdad.

Aristotle became available to the Islamic world through Arabic translations in the eighth and ninth centuries, and they too, like so many until the paradigmatic shifts in science particularly in the seventeenth century, tried to remain loyal to his words and system (Artz, 1954, p. 163) or reconciled him with their religious views. From the eighth to the twelfth centuries, Aristotle's philosophy was influential in both Jewish and Islamic science and thought – Al-Farabi, Avicenna, and Moses Maimonides – as was Neoplatonism, which makes sense with any theologically oriented philosophers. Indeed, up until the modern era and the scientific revolution, Plato's legacy proved attractive to the theologically oriented and Aristotle's to the worldly oriented, with great minds seeking a reconciliation between the two and their own religion.

Abu Nasr, also known as Al-Farabi or properly Abū Nasr Muhammad ibn al-Farakh al-Fārābi (AD 878–950), hailed from Turkestan, spent forty years learning and writing in Baghdad, and died in Damascus. Similar to Aristotle he was a polymath of prodigious talent – a scientist, musician, inventor, logician, and philosopher. He claimed that there was no difference between Aristotle and Plato, accepting Aristotle's logic and categories as a good starting point but then extending it in non-Aristotelian lines; he had access to most of Aristotle's works and wrote commentaries on Aristotle's logic and ethics, and though he agreed with Plato's utopianism he tempered it with Aristotle's recognition of the importance of private property and good monarchical rule (Hammond, 1947, *passim*). He became known as the 'second master' of philosophy, Aristotle being the first, and is generally accepted as being a peripatetic who sought to revive the ancient philosophies that were once so powerful across the Hellenized world, although Fakhry calls him a Neoplatonist for his metaphysical leanings (Fakhry, 2004, p. 20). His impact on Islamic philosophy in turn was enormous thereby securing another vein for Aristotelianism to plunge into.

Avicenna or Abu 'Ali al-Husayn ibn Sina (AD 980–1037), born near Bukhara (in modern day Uzbekistan) on the famous Silk Road and possessing an excellent library, in turn produced a highly influential work, the Canon (*al-Qanun fi'l-Tibb*), which became a textbook for Islamic and European scholars down to the early modern era (sixteenth century) and a critical influence on Thomas Aquinas (see below). His works quickly spread across the Islamic world, and via the Moors in Spain were translated into Latin and hence gained a European audience. A physician highly influenced by Galen, and a philosopher, he wrote on a wide range of topics in peripatetic tradition rejecting the Neoplatonism in favor of a more Aristotelian approach and then progressing beyond the old master. As a young man (18), Avicenna read Aristotle's *Metaphysics* forty times and was still unsure of its meanings until he fortuitously came across Al-Farabi's *On the Object of Metaphysics* (Goodman, 1992, pp. 14–15), but his investment paid off for he became one of the world's greatest philosophers – a lesson we should all follow, perhaps!

Maimonides (AD 1135–1204), evidently from his references, had access to a range of texts – including the *Metaphysics*, *Physics*, and *Nicomachean Ethics*. While disagreeing with some elements, he agreed with Aristotle's physics believing only a fool would challenge it (Seeskin, 2001, p. 119). He accepted the theory of the spheres of the world, the theory of the prime mover, and so sought to reconcile Aristotle with Jewish theology, claiming that Aristotle's philosophy is in concordance with that of the prophets and theological scholars, just as Thomas Aquinas was to attempt for Christianity: for him, Aristotle was 'chief of the philosophers' (Maimonides, 1956, pp. 18; 159; 210). Maimonides also accepts the Aristotelian hierarchy of the senses and 'disgracefulness' of touch compared to sight (Maimonides, 1956, pp. 226; 234).

The Jewish and Islamic philosophers acted as a bridge between the Ancient World and the Renaissance that was to unfurl in the West (Artz, 1954, p. 163) – Avicenna's works in particular play a vital role in stimulating a resurgence in Aristotelianism in Europe, notably through the writings of Aquinas (see below).

Byzantines and the East

Meanwhile, in what remained of the Greek-speaking eastern half of the Roman Empire, the Byzantines attempted to maintain Roman juristic ideals and Greek philosophy to some extent. Many historians have claimed that the Byzantine Empire, centered on Constantinople, did not produce anything original except an influential theory of the nature of the emperor that acted as a conduit from the ancient Hellenic world to the Middle Ages. The great minds of Byzantium were content to be disciples and copyists of the great minds of antiquity:

> Classically educated, they succumbed to a tendency which, even in our own days, a classical education often tends to promote – the tendency to think that the whole of wisdom is to be found in the past, and that the duty of the present is to recapitulate and restate 'the wisdom of the ancients'.
>
> (Barker, 1957, p. 2)

Instead, from the second century AD onward, the Byzantines emphasized rhetoric and form over matter and argument, which, like their paltry modern day soundbite cousin, stifled originality and extended thought – subtlety came from manipulation of words rather than the meaning and consequences of argument, which in turn was a hangover from the sophists of classical Greece, whom Cato had wanted to send packing from Rome as being of great danger to Roman values, as they had initially been considered in Greece by traditionalists (Freeman, 1999, p. 263). The sophistic birds found their nest at Constantinople and indeed thought suffered; in turn, their language suffered and lost its moorings with everyday language (Barker, 1957, p. 3), which was far removed from Aristotle's policy to think with everyday language, stretching it to its limits in trying to understand philosophical issues, but certainly not putting it beyond the norm. Such an extremity, he may have observed, would have been bad both for philosophy and for philosophers: language constrains our thought as Wittgenstein noted, and so pedantic, flowery language in turn reduces what we are capable of expressing.

Before its ossification, Byzantine scholars were part of the great Greco-Roman nexus in which ideas and scholars migrated and found influence. For instance, Themistius (AD 317–87) sojourned in Rome but spent most of his life in Constantinople; he wrote *Paraphrases* of Aristotle's works – the *Physics*, *On the Soul*, and the *Posterior Analytics*.

These were translated into Latin and came to the attention of Boethius (see above). Leontius, a Nestorian monk (AD 485–543), is also considered as the first of the peripatetics to have introduced Aristotelian concepts into religion. Indeed, in Constantinople, study of Aristotle was favored over that of Plato until the eleventh century (Barker, 1957, p. 14).

But by the sixth century, the intellectual freeze had begun: Constantinople's university disappeared leaving scholars to work independently, which has some merits, as Barker notes, of avoiding over-specialization, but the downside of a lack of institutional continuity (Barker, 1957, p. 50). A revival began in the ninth century with the founding of a general university; this gradually grew and in AD 1045 interestingly had chairs of faculties set up for a Platonist (Psellus, who revived Platonic studies in Byzantium) and an Aristotelian (Xiphilinus). The university had to move in 1204 following a conquest by Crusaders on their Fourth Crusade but returned after the Greeks retook the city, and so the university survived until the fall of Constantinople to the Turks in 1453 (Barker, 1957, p. 51). Incidentally, the Crusaders pillaged the Library of Constantinople, the kind of event, as we have seen, which seriously disrupts the flow of knowledge from one era to another. Looting may have caused an indiscriminate and serendipitous scattering of texts but the violence and destruction also laid waste to unknown quantities of antiques. The library had been one of the great depositories of Ancient texts and commentaries, whose preservation had been supported by several patriarchs of the city. Crusaders also massacred and raped thousands over three days: 'Never in Europe was a work of pillage more systematically and shamelessly carried out' (Pears, 1987, p. 345).

Before its final fall in 1453, Byzantine scholars had also been moving westward once more taking books and encouraging scholarly interest in the legacy that they had saved, and thus helped the revival of Hellenic studies that eventually developed into what we know as the Renaissance. The works of Aristotle entered the Italian and northern universities via Venice but also into Spain via the Moors.

Chapter 7

The Middle Ages

Christianity and Aristotle

Following the demise of the Roman Empire, the philosophical lights shut down across most of the tattered empire and so in Europe, Aristotle's legacy merely drabbled through the Dark Ages, while his works continued to be read intelligently and commented upon in Byzantium and in the Islamic world. In the West Neoplatonism was favored as its mysticism connected better with theology.

The little of Aristotle that was studied following the dissolution of Rome down to the twelfth century was confined to his logic and categories: Boethius' translations of the *Categories* and *De Interpretatione* and fragments of the *Topics*, at first were the only texts known to be in circulation, until other translations of his surfaced in AD 1120 completing the logical *Organon*. Notker (AD 950–1022), incidentally, translated the logical works into German as early as the tenth century (Inwood, 1999, p. 8). Then there was a rush to travel to Byzantium: one James of Venice traveled in 1136; then there was Gerard of Cremona, Lombardy (1114–87); the Catanian Henry Aristippus (c. twelfth century), who went in 1158, and a John of Sicily (all of them worked on translating Aristotle into Latin, augmented by influential translations in the thirteenth century by the Bishop of Lincoln, Robert Grosseteste, who furthered scientific inquiry by his challenging of some of Aristotle's logic – on what constitutes a necessary condition); Nicholas of Sicily; Bartholomew of Messina; Durandas of Alvernia (Auvergne); and William of Moerbeke. Translations were also made from the Arabic (notably by Gerard) but those from the Greek into Latin were preferred. Grosseteste's work, including his own translation of the *Nicomachean Ethics* and commentaries, circulated well (Copenhaver and Schmitt, 1992, p. 6; Lines, 2002, pp. 45–9).

Critically for our purposes, the *Nicomachean Ethics* proved to be very popular, possibly first translated by Michael Scot around AD 1215–20, although philologists also point to one Burgundione of Pisa with a possible translation in 1150. Certainly, though, Grosseteste's work (1260–70) became the standard text for lectures for the next three centuries or so, gradually being supplanted by other translations (Leonardo Bruni's and John Argyropoulos's) in the fifteenth and sixteenth centuries; Grosseteste's translation of the Greek commentators on Aristotle's ethics also lasted until 1541 and the publication of a new translation by Feliciano. The *Magna Moralia* was translated around 1258–66, the *Politics* by 1260 with Moerbeke's coming out in 1265, and the pseudo-Aristotelian manuscript on *Economics* around 1295 (Lines, 2002, pp.46–8).

Lines has catalogued the number of surviving manuscripts from this early period and argues that it shows that the *Nicomachean Ethics* was much more popular than the *Politics* and *Economics* – a ratio of 388 to 100 to 105; the number of commentaries underlines his thesis of its popularity. The three works become the essential triad of school education in the Middle Ages, with the *Nicomachean Ethics* the dominating text (Lines, 2002, p. 49).

But for Aristotelians to get their master accepted into the Christian West, they had to play their philosophical cards right to remain within the Christian Catholic orthodoxy. The primary problem faced by Aristotelians was the philosopher's twofold belief that (a) the earth existed for ever, which was contrary to the Christian theology of the Creation, and (b) the universe was created by the Unmoved Mover. Second, the emphasis on reason, as all theological philosophers quickly realize, can encourage the rejection of biblical stories and assumptions as well as encourage the mind to atheism or at least to heterodox views. Finding a coherent argument to reconcile faith and reason was Thomas Aquinas' great contribution, while the eternity of the world was typically rejected outright. On the other hand, his theory of the soul was particularly attractive: he had rejected materialism in his analysis of earlier thinkers in favor of the argument that the soul provides living matter their form – an ingenious argument that would alone have secured his name on the philosophical roll of honor.

One synthesis of Aristotle with Christianity forged by Albert the

Great (Albertus Magnus) and Thomas Aquinas sought to justify the
role that reason can play in understanding the world while remaining
loyal to the Christian vision of the Creation and the epistemology of
revelation. Albert the Great (c. AD 1193–1280) wrote commentaries
on the *Ethics* but was also the first to do one for the *Politics*; his own
thinking was tinged by the Neoplatonist elements of spurious
Aristotelian works, despite warnings concerning their authenticity
from his pupil Aquinas (Kenny, 2005, p. 60). Yet he was Aristotelian
enough to seek his curiosity's satisfaction in exploring the natural
world, writing notably on vegetables, plants, and animals; he was
particularly keen to keep magic, so prevalent in early experiments, out
of his work, accepting Aristotle's earthbound physics (Crombie, 1952,
pp. 36; 41). Aquinas was a truly broad-ranging and influential
philosopher and theologian, whose writings altered the mainstream
thinking of the Catholic Church supplanting those of the (in terms of
his Hellenic bent) Platonist-oriented Augustine, who merged Platonic
philosophy with Christianity with its emphasis on the duality of
worlds (the City of God and the City of the World). Aquinas'
innovation was to supplement traditional Augustinian Christianity
with an Aristotelian logic and conceptual framework that Augustine
lacked. It had, as seen, been the goal of several brilliant minds to bring
Aristotle into their religion (Maimonides, Avicenna) and Aquinas was
particularly taken by the work of Avicenna, whose works had come to
Europe via Moorish Spain.

Various Christian thinkers had been studying the earthly realm, and
the Church offered by no means a unified vision of theology and
philosophy, but Aquinas presented a way forward for what we now call
science in a manner that eventually became the acceptable orthodoxy,
and which, incidentally, promoted Aristotle to an unassailable
philosophical position that warranted execution should a monk veer
away from the doctrine! He drew heavily upon Aristotle's teleological,
metaphysical, economical, and political theories, but most importantly
emphasized the role of reason over intuition or mysticism when
dealing with earthly affairs – the mind thus could learn about the
world and thereby organize itself better in both thought and action
(political or ethical). Action ought to be end oriented, and the highest
end that man can achieve is happiness, and whereas Aristotle

proclaimed the philosophical life of contemplation to be the supreme state of happiness for man, Aquinas shifted the goal slightly and called it contemplation of God – beatitude (Aquinas, 1998, pp. 329–31).

It was Aquinas' influence that gradually led to the teaching of Aristotle in the growing schools across Europe in the Middle Ages – he befriended the translator William of Moerbeke and sought to secure the Aristotelian legacy for the Church against those who would assert Aristotle's philosophy along more heterodox lines such as the Parisian Siger of Brabant (AD 1235–82). Siger preferred the Arabian readings of Aristotle, which promoted controversy at the Parisian university causing the ecclesiastical authorities to prescribe philosophical statements (Kenny, 2005, p. 79). However, Aquinas' own works and his commentaries on Aristotle suffered from the later Reformation in the Church, which, since he had been canonized by the Catholic Church (1323), tarred him as a Catholic philosopher rather than a philosopher, which is like saying that Aristotle was Macedonian and therefore should not be consulted by non-Macedonians. Nonetheless, even modern philosophers can be so fickle in their judgment (cf. Russell, 1947, p. 484), so, ironically, Aquinas' work was to suffer a similar fate to Aristotle's – to be taken up by the bureaucracy of the Church and presented as orthodox in the form of textbook renditions. Only recently have secular philosophers turned attention to Aquinas *qua* philosopher and found not just insight but also Platonic notions, so 'Aquinas himself, in fact, was an Aristotelian on earth, but a Platonist in heaven' (Kenny, 2005, p. 78).

Thus by the twelfth century Greek works of Aristotle were translated *en masse* reviving Hellenic studies across the fledgling universities. But what is also important to note for this time period is that the emerging flexibility of language (the use of Latin, vernacular, and neologisms) planted the intellectual seeds for the eventual growth of thought beyond Aristotle; the lack of alternative languages and hence of translations was something else that may have retarded Byzantine development but which gave the European universities greater flexibility (Barker, 1957, p. 17).

Aristotle in the universities

The outcome of the exciting rediscoveries of Aristotle was a reorganization of the European schools' curricula. This was the era in which Aristotle's works became the orthodoxy, a step one always feels that he would have not accepted, for he would have recognized that just as he had learned from the past masters, so too should his intellectual heirs continue to do so and not stop at his works.

Until the flurry of translations, the school curriculum was based on teaching the seven liberal arts: the trivium of grammar, logic, and rhetoric; followed by the quadrivium of arithmetic, geometry, music, and astronomy (Joseph, 2002, pp. 3–4) – it emerged from the Stoic school of philosophy, but was thoroughly influenced by Aristotle's work on logic and rhetoric, and literary studies (Wagner, 1983, p. 11). The university scholars debated on the proper divisions between the subjects but then Aristotle's works hit them: they did not fall into the seven arts well so eventually a new curriculum emerged to teach the introductory subjects of grammar and rhetoric followed by philosophy with studies in metaphysics, mathematics, natural philosophy, and moral philosophy (practical). While the course of grammar was dominated by Priscian (sixth century AD), philosophy was dominated by Aristotle.

In Paris, Aristotle's *Ethics* were introduced into the curriculum in AD 1215 and following Grossteste's translations (1246–7) they were studied even more intensely with a range of commentaries emerging (Lines, 2002, p. 68). At Oxford, where Grosseteste taught, evidence is that it was part of the reading for undergraduates from 1278 at least. The ethics course was mandatory and seemingly taught daily, a pattern that was repeated more or less with the new universities opening after 1350, such as Heidelberg, Erfurt, and Vienna. The pedagogical pattern also followed strict guidelines on how the ethics courses were to be taught: lectures were to be followed by debate on problems arising from the text, but these too soon froze leading to Lefèvre d'Étaples' (1455–1536) outburst in his own introduction to the *Nicomachean Ethics* that such procedures did not lead to learning at all and thereby, for his supporters, rekindled philosophy in France – and a return to Aristotle in the original rather than through translators and commentators who had bent his words to their own interests (Tilley, 1918, pp. 233–4). It has been a common problem with Aristotle, similar to that which befell his works under the Byzantines.

Duns Scotus (1266–1308) or 'John the Scotsman' is hailed as one of the great philosophers of the Scholastic period; upon Aristotle's edifices, commentaries of which he wrote and lectured, that were becoming the orthodoxy of the universities, he produced a critical challenge which avoided falling into Platonic philosophy of the Forms – particularly, he argued that the abstracts 'humanity' or 'animal' do exist as such but that they exist in a 'lesser form' than the particular entities that we perceive. It is an intriguing middle position that, along with other aspects of his philosophy, has gained and continues to gain many supporters – for our purposes, though, it remains a philosophical twist on Aristotle that sets up new directions of thought.

William of Ockham (c. 1287–c. 1347) took Aristotelian Scholasticism in new directions, rejecting elements of Thomism in favor of a more empiricist approach. He is famous for being attributed 'Ockham's Razor,' which declares that 'entities are not to be multiplied beyond necessity' – in other words, keep things (ontologically speaking) simple, a jibe at flowery metaphysics one can imagine Aristotle smiling at. However, in cutting the unnecessaries from philosophy, he reduced Aristotle's ten categories to two: substances and qualities. He also proposed a particularist reading of entities in contrast to Scotus': there are no things such as universals at all – they are mental creations; only particular individual entities exist as such.

And so the Middle Ages wore on – highly charged and at times dangerous debates (William, for instance, fled from the papacy to the imperial court of Ludwig of Bavaria), with Aristotle's philosophy becoming the proverbial ball to be kicked and passed according to the flows of power, interest, and, thankfully, thought. Different great minds pulled different elements from him (they had usually written commentaries on his work for their lectures), stretching Aristotelianism but leaving the canon of his writings to be passed down through students' studies and wider publication following the invention of the printing press.

Aristotelianism in both Thomist and Averroist forms flourished in Renaissance Italy alongside a revival of Platonism, but gradually the humanist and scientific visions – so dependent on the Hellenic legacy – thrust down independent roots to produce the modern mind of which we are its heirs. In time, the humanists and scientists rejected Aristotelianism for being stifling and arid. Erasmus (AD 1466–1536) sniped at the Aristotelians in his *Praise of Folly*; a historian wrote of Peter Ramus (AD 1515–72) that 'his efforts helped to free men from bondage to medieval authority and the hold of Aristotle over the human mind, and to encourage the pursuit of the truth' (Lawrence, 1972, p. 70). Montaigne (AD 1533–92) reflected that, 'the god of Scholastick knowledge is Aristotle: 'tis irreligion to question any of his decrees, as it was of those of Lycurgus of Sparta: his doctrine is a magisterial law, which peradventure is as false as another' (Montaigne, 1891, p. 454). Francis Bacon (AD 1561–1626) wryly observed that 'For as water will not ascend higher than the level of the first springhead from whence it descendeth, so knowledge derived from Aristotle, and exempted from liberty of examination, will not rise again higher than the knowledge of Aristotle' (Bacon, 1930, p. 30).

Their rejection was not fully authentic for the great philosophers of the modern era still read him, but they sought to distance themselves from Scholasticism that had been so intimately tied up with ecclesiastical authorities and thus become politicized philosophy. Indeed, the great Jurists of Vittoria (AD 1492/3–1546), Suarez (AD 1548–1617), and Grotius (AD 1583–1645) prefaced their political works with a very Aristotelian rendition of the emergence of family, village, city state, and nation, as did John Locke, who lifted much of his *Some Thoughts Concerning Education* from Aristotle's writings. Hegel keenly noted how much more insightful his ethical theories were on knowledge and willing than his contemporaries' deployment of feeling and inspiration as principles of ethical conduct (Hegel, 1996, §140n) and arguably presented a new variation of Aristotle's teleology in his *Phenomenology of Spirit* (1977, §22). Nonetheless, Bacon, among others, castigated the Aristotelians and Scholastics sufficiently to tar the Aristotelian legacy:

> This kind of degenerate learning did chiefly reign amongst the Schoolmen: who having sharp and strong wits, and abundance of leisure, and small variety of reading, but their wits shut up in the

cells of a few authors (chiefly Aristotle their dictator) as their persons were shut up in the cells of monasteries, and knowing little history, either of nature or time, did out no great quantity of matter and infinite agitation of wit spin out unto those laborious webs of learning which are extant in their books.

(Bacon, 1930, p. 26)

The famous anti-Aristotelian Peter Ramus, mentioned above for being seen as rejecting Aristotle, rather claimed that we should 'ignore all these Aristotelians and return to Aristotle, the author of such a noble discipline [i.e., philosophy], and to Cicero, who tries to emulate Aristotle's teaching and to imitate him' (quoted in Sellberg, 2006). Hobbes followed suit seeing the mixing of the Greeks with Christianity as one of the source of 'Darknesse' (Hobbes, 1996, p. 418); Hume has similar remarks: 'the PERIPATETIC philosophy was alone admitted into all the schools, to the utter deprivation of every kind of learning' (Hume, 1987, p. 121). It was a damning indictment and out with the bath water went the baby, while quoting appraisingly where warranted throughout his own works. In his popular work, although he certainly recognized Aristotle's prodigious talent and what befell his philosophy in the hands of authorities, Bertrand Russell also repeated the anti-Scholastic tirade: 'his authority had become almost as unquestioned as that of the Church, and in science, as well as in philosophy, had become a serious obstacle to progress' (Russell, 1947, p. 182), which then gets repeated and distorted by writers: '... [Aristotle] whose teachings held up the progress of science for close to 2,000 years' (Beckmann, 1971, p. 40); 'the dead hand of Aristotle lay heavy on physics' (Jeans, 1948, p. 52); or 'for 2000 years logic remained as much as Aristotle left it' (Hull, 1959, p. 63).

Others have been less censuring: Tarnas reasonably writes that 'Aristotle's philosophical temperament [came] to define the dominant orientation of the Western mind' (Tarnas, 1996, p. 68). And although Aristotle's authority in biology, much of which has stood the test of modern investigations, transferred to an undeserving authority in physics and mathematics, for which he was less able than many contemporaries (Schwartz and Bishop, 1958, p. 6), biologists still recognize his importance and stature in a fairer light, rejecting elements of his teleological theories while admiring his observations. Nonetheless, so many in other disciplines denounce Aristotle as hindering intellectual or scientific progress 'for 2,000 years.' (Indeed, it would be entertaining to do a survey of the comment.) Of course, similar statements are also leveled at Euclid, Pythagoras, and other Hellenes, for their errors. Lloyd, incidentally, provides a more balanced assessment of Aristotle's scientific thinking and researches (Lloyd, 1970, pp. 99–124). Educationalists, on the other hand, tend to overlook the politicization of his works or the failure of (some) later thinkers to pursue the paths to improved knowledge by reminding us of Aristotle's great curiosity:

> Working without microscope or telescope, ignorant of atomic or nuclear physics and concepts of heredity and biological evolution, Aristotle stood barehanded before an awesome cosmos and asked himself the simple question: What do I see?
>
> (Morris, 1961, p. 54)

We are brought back to the opening of the *Metaphysics* and the premise that man is a curious animal. Emphatically, it was less Aristotle's than the fault of later political machinations to secure his apotheosis for theological or political gain: the philosophy still lay there to be read, as Locke was to grasp when encouraged to read Aristotle in the original Greek. But the damage by the anti-Scholastics had been done: Aristotle was put away until the twentieth century when scholars once more began debating the *Organon* and revised assessments of the chronology of his work (notably, the pioneering work of Jaeger), and in turn others were attracted to his philosophy. By the twentieth century, more critical appraisals were attracting luminaries – particularly, the analytical philosophers centered in Oxford had much in common with elements of Aristotle's thinking, while moralists rediscovered the depths of the *Nicomachean Ethics*, and liberals and communitarians found the *Politics* a good reminder of why the citizen is very much an integrated part of his nation.

Part 4

The Relevance of Aristotle's Work Today

Chapter 8

Education, Philosophy, and Modern State

Part 3 sketched the fate of Aristotle's works and how his influence fluctuated over the centuries, from the decline of the Lyceum to a general revival in the Christian era, while his works continued to attract scholarly attention across the geography of Alexander's brief empire: thereby his philosophy entered into mainstream Christian, Islamic, and Judaic thinking. While the advantage of his works being sustained and furthered by influential minds in their own regions of influence is readily understandable, the disadvantage of being tied to any religion has, in more recent and secularly oriented times, acted to tarnish his reputation – but surely only among those who barely read him or whose prejudices cloud their philosophical judgment. In education, the contrived apotheosis of Aristotle by the Scholastics of Europe's early universities has also acted to promote a view of him as arid and cerebral, the archetypal armchair philosopher pontificating about the nature of the world rather than of a thinker, scientist, and close observer of the reality around which his writings exude. In turn, his *Organon* became, in the generalized histories of philosophy and science passed down to the present, an uncontested tradition that stultified thought, innovation, and thereby progress.

Conversely, his thesis that the education of the children of the *polis* should inherently be the jurisdiction of the state arguably gained greater credence as his scientific conjectures were being traduced through the age of Enlightenment and his doctrine of the final cause being rejected as unscientific (Berlin, 2000, 42), notably but not exclusively by Protestants, who associated Aristotelianism with Catholicism, for whom he is still 'the greatest of the heathen philosophers' (Turner, 1907). In the rejection of Scholastic and even religious authority in Europe a greater emphasis was placed on the importance of the state in securing the child's education and so in turn forming the civilian foundation. In forging state-directed education either indirectly through legislative directives or directly through state-run schools, reformers were naturally attracted to the Platonic or Aristotelian advice on forming citizens; others who read his *Politics* and *Nicomachean Ethics* also drew on the specific advice adumbrated on bringing up children or the more general advice on the importance of securing good moral foundations. And so his relevance today stems from these more robust and commonsensical theories on moral and civil formation.

Political philosophers of the statist persuasion have often been attracted to Aristotle's justification of state policy to pursue that which is the best for the people – 'the good of society' – and his muted appeal to a broader democracy has similarly gained recognition, balanced by his obvious limitation on what constitutes the citizenry. Within that framework educationalists have recognized the importance of his thought as an essential instrument of state policy but also, and not necessarily attached to the state at all, the importance of a moral education. The latter has appealed to a variety of educationalists in academia, business education, and, because of Aristotle's theory of *aretē*, in the military as well. Despite the analysis of the intricacies of metaphysical and epistemological issues that underlie the Aristotelian program, his educational philosophy is intensely practical: it deals with man (and child) as Aristotle sees him and proceeds to secure a working set of policies to gain the best from the potentiality that breeding and social position present. In that respect, as the controversies persisted over translations and the authenticity or order of various works, a constant Aristotelian voice has certainly endured – one that emphasizes the practical nature of securing the ethical life.

In this final Part, we review Aristotle's present relevance. That he has any relevance implies either that his intellectual adventure to uncover the constants in human nature and ethics did in fact succeed, or that his contemporary vision remains so edifying to educationalists, historians, and philosophers that his place in the great conversation is secure as a wise Ionian, even though we may reject aspects of his educational policies or ethical arguments. Arguably, elements of his intellectual adventure have survived the challenges of intellectual criticism and cultural, political, and religious shifts – there is something in Aristotle that we can still learn from, while we may recognize and adjust our thinking to the contemporary differences that stand out. We'll look first at the role of the modern state in education and how that may link to the Aristotelian project, and second at the resurgence of Aristotelian thinking in scientific education, notably in biology and the use of eugenics, as well as how his theories are used in business teaching, home schooling, and in the military.

The modern state and Aristotelian education

Education is a part of the practical wisdom of seeking the right means and the right ends for action. For Aristotle, following Hellenic traditions, it was essential for the future of the *polis* to engage with the generations that would flow through so that they may be trained first to defend the *polis* and second to mature into understanding why it should be defended and secured – in other words to become honorable, loyal, and capable citizens, who would also understand the proper purposes of the state as he outlined in the *Politics*: to secure the good for its citizens.

That principle predominates much modern political philosophy and hence educational policies, notably as the bulk of educational services are provided by governments in the democratic West. The modern state was formed over a period of a couple of centuries in the sixteenth and seventeenth centuries; it was not the equivalent of the Hellenic *polis* except in as much as it was an institution designed for political ends, for it also developed a permanent bureaucracy and legislative tentacles that gradually stretched out into most walks of life, much further than the Hellenic civilian and even Aristotle would have countenanced. As it grew, the franchise of citizenship also grew, again beyond the expectations of most of the Greek writers, to include women and the poorer men of society and much to the chagrin of latter-day Hellenists who would have preferred a 'natural elite' of well-educated men to maintain rule and power.

Today, though, universal enfranchisement is typically heralded as an improvement and the standard by which nations' political maturity is judged. The growth of the franchise also saw the advance of government-funded projects to secure the interests of broader sections of the population, and the state – one could say inevitably – took on the role as educator, inevitably in the sense that to secure its growing bureaucratic interests statist proponents and apologists foresaw the need to gain the acceptance of future generations. That may seem a controversial argument, yet we accept that the Hellenic elites were doing the same thing training the next generation, who would secure their interests in perpetuity, as we would so describe their emulators through the ages (cf. Thut, 1957, pp. 16–17). The Greeks (but not the Byzantines) lacked the bureaucratic power that the modern state has at its disposal: the Ministries and Departments of Various Affairs that act (in principle) to smooth the daily running of government; it is, as Parkinson humorously explained, moreover, a trait of bureaucracies to encourage their own maintenance and growth (Parkinson, 1981). Accordingly, the secularly minded politicians of the modern state also sought (and perhaps we should say continue to seek) to remove independent educational programs because of perceived potentialities for perniciousness as the Church ('Faith' in today's parlance) and so schools were and remain targets for political attacks. Consider a diametrically opposed position to Aristotle's:

> The record of the development of compulsory education is a record of State usurpation of parental control over children on behalf of its own; an imposition of uniformity and equality to repress individual growth; and the development of techniques to hinder the growth of reasoning power and independent thought among the children.
>
> (Rothbard, 1999, p. 19)

For libertarians the assumption that the state has any role in educating a family's child is unjustifiable. Some in the libertarian tradition do begin from the Aristotelian historical thesis that families *naturally* emerge in society and so education of the young would be natural rather than a political process, while others prefer to assert the absolutism of individual rights and debate whether a child is said to possess a right to education as such or whether it remains in the hands of the family to choose – either way, the argument is rejected that children are somehow wards of the state to be brought up to accept and defend the *polis* or nation state.

Elements of independentist traditions have been retained in private schools or in home education in the West, but generally the state has formed a monopoly on the education of the nations' youth and accordingly also acted to pull private or faith schools within its remit using various political claims often to 'ensure quality standards,' which assumes that parents are incapable of discerning the quality of education that their children get, a thoroughly Aristotelian premise (*Pol*, 1337a24–32). And so the need to define educational agendas and promote visions of what education should entail and/or produce became and indubitably remains the order of the day: and so Aristotle reenters educational debate not just historically but also in the theoretical discussions.

Recall that for Aristotle, perfect happiness is found in the life of contemplation, for contemplation is the best activity for man *qua* man: if we are to recognize the Aristotelian bent of modern education, we must search for hints that all education and all moral activity should thus aim for the highest that our nature can offer – the life of *theoria*. On the one hand, we are stricken with the utility of many modern courses found in the equivalent of the Lyceum – the modern universities. Our general impression of Aristotle may have him bristling at the commercial bias of most courses – of degrees in Business Studies, or Leisure and Tourism. But on the other hand, we must be mindful of such immediate reactions: why should an Aristotelian reject such degrees, when the courses act to compile information and to explore their relevant fields in such a manner as to enable the student to work better or to help promote a higher understanding of the discipline and perhaps then to attain a more philosophical view. The economic and scientific requirements of a less advanced society are necessarily lower than those of the intricate modern economy and so the educational threshold lower – the vast breadth of global economies require, one imagines, a stretching of education into a higher age. Yet the typical undergraduate finishes the degree at around the same age as Hellenic youths were completing their military service and preparing to engage more fully in the civic life – has that much changed, then? Fewer numbers continue onto the more philosophical realms of the postgraduate courses (and these do not have to be philosophical as such), which again may be said by an

Aristotelian to reflect natural social divisions of those capable of reaching the higher echelons of *theoria* and those not. 'Natural' is of course an awkward term, for it implies that some will necessarily be or are strongly disposed to become philosophical in their dotage, which of course are different things. A sustained desire is needed as is the possession of the time and resources to fund such a life of thinking for the sake of thinking, of philosophizing for the sake of philosophy rather than for the sake of a publication and hence job security. So the Aristotelian may reply that the life of contemplation should thus be subsidized by society for its own good, an argument that is implied in the *Politics*, acknowledging the caveat, though, that the purpose of Aristotelian education is not to produce a monastic, meditative man isolated from friends and family. Man is by his very nature a political/ social animal, which means that an integral part of Aristotle's thinking is that education raises a publicly minded citizen, whose being and purposes in turn reflect and support those of his *polis*, his state which he in turn serves either directly as a youth in its military or indirectly later as an adviser (and, emphatically, one among many). The philosophical body rises to provide advice to the young and to the political; it was not, in Aristotle's prudential mind, designed to impose its will upon the *polis* as his master Plato would have preferred – therein lies *theoria*'s corruption, we may add. The philosopher's job, when not engaged in discussing or contemplating first principles (metaphysics), would be to remind the politically active that the purpose of the state is to procure the best form of life for its citizens – peaceable, prosperous, and healthy.

Yet in securing the best for the *polis*, Aristotle may have been disturbed at the modern development of bureaucratic management of political projects, for his vision of the best kind of *polis* was one run by and for a large population of middle-class citizens, not for the masses nor for the powerful family elites. And the presence of a self-seeking bureaucracy would also have seemed to him an intrusion into the purest form of democratic management, for it takes power out of the hands of the people (i.e. Aristotle's citizenry of educated males) and places it in the hands of an extended court disposed, in the eyes of many critics from economists to libertarian philosophers, to machina-tion and myopic policies (Gottfried, 1999; Mises, 1983). Hence, the best, his philosophy implies, could not be gained in an institution such as the modern state – just as he would have rejected the usurpation of politics and education by prelates in the Middle Ages, who used his philosophy to impose intellectual restraints on those who would question.

It is unfortunate that Aristotle's more conservative prejudices as we now term them have at times been employed directly or indirectly to justify far-reaching interventions in societies, often in the name of securing the best for the nation or people. Consider the Hellenic acceptance of infanticide; although Christians categorically have rejected the practice, at various times in the past century, intellectuals have rekindled the ancient morality in the name of eugenics programs designed to strengthen and/or improve the population. Even the highly Aristotelian Catholic Church, which prohibits abortion and involuntary sterilizations, accepts a weaker form of eugenics through chastity and the higher purpose of moral purity (Gerrard, 1914). Whether they would have directly referred to Aristotle in other ecclesiastical circles is debatable, but that they would have read him is less uncertain, since the *Politics* has remained on university reading lists for centuries. In reviewing the history of the modern eugenicist movement, we do hear the philosopher's voice: 'Let there be a law that no deformed child shall live' (*Pol*, 1335a20); a similar position is found in Plato's *Republic* in which he also highlights the need for 'the best of either sex should be united with the best as often, and the inferior with the inferior as seldom, as possible' (*Rep*, 459d–e), an argument that may belong to a more rudimentary society needing to keep its numbers healthy, but one that provokes our conscience today in a manner that the Greeks (the male writers at least) would have found strange.

Aristotle's ethical and educational theories develop from his political philosophy but also from his observation of human nature, which, like the goals we strive for, he saw as hierarchically ordered in the sense that humans are higher than animals which are higher than plants: some people are born to rule over others and men are superior to women, which was justified, in his thinking, on the physical and reasoning differences between men and women. Likewise, he also argued for what we call a physiognomic approach to human behavior; that is, physical traits affect a person's abilities and dispositions, which in turn are linked to the natural laws of the universe and the operation of the four elements through the four humors of the body. Moreover, and what becomes critical for our understanding of his educational thought, his thinking often draws upon the divisions that humanity seemingly naturally divides into – stations of moral and intellectual capability reflecting individuals' innate dispositions as well as the habits that they cultivate, although all in their turn must seek to fulfill the best of their abilities according to their social station. Accordingly, his prescriptions on child-rearing and early education are formed by the philosophical groundwork laid out across his vast oeuvre: hence today we have echoes of Aristotle in the various pro-choice movements, the eugenicist proponents, and physiognomists, who have not truly departed academic departments despite the putative ludicrousness of Victorian phrenology of measuring head sizes and determining criminality.

The writer who coined 'eugenics,' Francis Galton (1822–1911), was certainly aware of the Greek etymology and philosophy (Llobera, 2003, p. 81), and was no doubt aware of Aristotle's philosophy. Consider this highly neo-Aristotelian observation by Galton, taking up the determinist thesis often evident in Aristotle:

> I have no patience with the hypothesis occasionally expressed, and often implied, especially in tales written to teach children to be good, that babies are born pretty much alike, and that the sole agencies in creating differences between boy and boy, and man and man, are steady application and moral effort. It is in the most unqualified manner that I object to pretensions of natural equality. The experiences of the nursery, the school, the University, and of professional careers, are a chain of proofs to the contrary.
>
> (Galton, 1892, p. 14)

Eugenics became a political fashion for the interwar years of 1919–39 with the formation of Eugenics Societies in the United States and Britain, but dropped precipitously from decent conversation following the defeat of eugenicist Nazi Germany in 1945; nevertheless, it has not wholly disappeared as the Eugenics Society principles resurface, in the eyes of critics, in various correlations between race, gender, and intelligence (the British Eugenics Education Society became the Galton Institute), with academics striving to secure a fair debate on hereditary issues and intelligence rather than emotional polemics against implied racism or sexism: Aristotle remains implicit in such 'biosocial' and 'psychometric' studies and the educational conclusions drawn.

If breeding is said to count and thereby will have an impact on education, then Aristotle is vindicated; to those holding a more optimistic view, such genetically limiting elements can be overwhelmed by a counteracting and progressively supportive education and so Aristotle's emphasis on breeding and class are to be reviled as antiquated nonsense or a mild limitation on potentiality.

Truth, as the philosopher himself would no doubt have recognized, is more complicated than the simplistic nature versus nurture debate.

The eugenicist elements – in part derived from the influential Hellene philosophers – may have diminished in the post-WWII atmosphere that rejected the abhorrent application of genocide as state policy (although that has not stopped this ancient practice emerging since then in the former Yugoslavia or Rwanda), but the desire to improve the population through education has not diminished: hardly a day goes by in England, for instance, without some plan for improving the population's skills, health, fitness, diet, or appreciation of some value or other (art, other cultures, religion, history, geography, climate). However, the state's purposes are rarely as singular as Aristotle would have desired: they become, by virtue of the extent of the modern educational system, multifarious and inevitably the various ideals presented may at times be inconsistent or contradictory; that is not to say that we can no longer discern the influence of Aristotle's political-educational blueprint, either because of its continued influence in the humanities and philosophy circles from which educationalists emerge or because of its simple and enduring message that attracts statists of all political persuasions. We hear it particularly in any classes that are designed to teach civil virtues as apart from particular subject matter – 'citizenship classes,' for instance – and we recognize the stately Aristotelian beat in broad plans to secure a better future through the public education of the citizenship.

Aristotle's influence is not the only philosopher's voice in modern education, of course, but standing at the fountainhead – with Plato – it is difficult not to acknowledge vestiges of his moral program for citizens, never mind the more patent influence that he has had on scientific investigation and the collection of data to satiate our curiosity. The next section reviews the Aristotelian legacy in scientific education.

Reductionism and materialism

As the humanist revolution in education and philosophy got under-way, its greatest thinkers turned from criticizing the perceived traditionalism of the Scholastics to reviewing the works of Aristotle in particular in their original state; while broad elements of Aristotle's conjectures on physics and the nature of the universe were replaced with the work of Copernicus, Galileo, and Newton, the objectivist thesis that sustains most of Aristotle's metaphysics continued to gather support in the writings of various scientific thinkers and educators, even if they rejected the 'Scholastic Aristotle.' This was particularly true of John Locke, whose writings on education are particularly Aristotelian and who also developed a significant theory of knowledge that certainly possesses Aristotelian principles.

Moreover, in the field of causality, Aristotle still had much to teach later philosophers. Consider Aristotle's logic that an event may be due to either human or non-human causes: the distinction and its implications for education are profound. In grasping reality, we encounter regularities which provoke our curiosity; man is after all a curious animal, Aristotle commented, but is there a strict duality between the two causes or are there overlapping elements, such as when children watch a video and physiological, neurological, and psychological effects can be monitored – and how does it affect their character? Broadly speaking, science, as it is generally held today, deals with mechanistic causality, effecting a change using a physical force, for example falling barometric pressure and rain; Aristotle referred to such events as happening from necessity, but today science's remit is generally reductionist in seeking to reduce or to eliminate non-physical causes from events. Much that he described in human behavior and illness he also sought to connect to the physical world, positing physical man within the universe, although he permitted his mind to be causal of action in its own right.

In the modern period, the reductionist thesis – of seeking material and causal connections in human behavior – has also been extended to actions and education: behaviorism, outlined by J. B. Watson in *Behaviourism* in 1925 and expanded by B. F. Skinner, sought to apply an inductive, data-based educational program mimicking the laboratorial successes of physics and chemistry. Accordingly, mental intentions were held to be unverifiable and thus useless for understanding action. This, termed metaphysical behaviorism, asserts that psychological concepts can be analyzed purely in behavioral terms, and such terms are verifiable in that they are observable, public events. Nonetheless, the category of human-initiated acts did not disappear philosophically with the advent of behaviorism, for there are patently events (actions) brought about by human intent with which Aristotle would certainly counter: I intend to learn a piano piece, the intention is self-activated; what I do to learn may become mainly public, although I can rehearse bars in my head without that becoming public knowledge.

Nevertheless, to explain actions and events reductionistically has been very popular; for instance, determinists argue that our human actions are in reality only part of the great physical-mechanical nexus and notions of our free will or purposeful action are in effect illusory. For determinists, there is no such thing as choice, for every action is caused by prior events that in turn determine our next move. But to assume that all actions are in effect mechanistic events is to claim that everything human is reducible to physical processes and that the stuff of literature, psychology, art, etc. makes no sense at all – and so education is merely what happens because it must happen and whatever 'changes' that do occur are not the result of purposeful design but the automated functioning of the world's systems both animate and inanimate, there being really no difference between the two. Yet the human world is patently replete with intentions, dreams, and ambitions which cannot be readily reduced to purely physical determinants; and the disciplines of biology, psychiatry, neuroscience, sociology, anthropology, and artificial intelligence to name a few would be much the poorer if human intention were eliminated (Perlman, 2004, p. 3). Two worlds of causation thus face us: the mechanistic world of physical forces and the human world of values, and the twain shall never meet (Mises, 1949, p. 25).

Aristotle was indubitably aware of this broadly described dichotomy and the nuances between the two positions, and he sought to explain the nature of how man fits into the world of elements and natural laws, effectively in this context by referring to the purposes that we produce. In proceeding, arguably his medical and biological studies influenced his overall philosophy on causation; it is indeed difficult to abstract teleology from biology for living creatures possess purposes – they aim for ends and either fail or achieve them, but to a great extent he extended biological teleology into the material realm as well, which modern science generally dismisses as a categorical mistake. The problems that immediately arise for the modern reader then are how consciously deliberative intention affects choice, the possibility of undetermined choice, and the possibility of a transcendent intelligence guiding the universe and people.

Each in turn relates to educational thinking once the educationalist recognizes the importance of historical analysis of the perennial questions that pervade the philosophy education: does the student possess innate will, are there predispositions to learning certain kinds of knowledge, to what extent does climate or town planning affect education? Should we hear that 'Mozart is good for babies' or 'Futurist houses are not conducive to human happiness,' we can be assured that Aristotle would have perked his ears up and entered the debate, as should any philosopher, of course, but there is a constant curiosity in his works to see how the world around us affects our behavior: color therapy, art therapy, music therapy, nutritional advice – all would have entertained him.

But to return to his ethical theories, we become aware that one of Aristotle's greatest contributions to philosophy remains highly attractive to educationalists across a variety of disciplines, and next we shall review two less orthodox areas of research, namely education in the military and in business studies.

Given that Aristotle held an aristocratic aloofness towards the *banausic* traditions of commerce it is a little ironic to find that his ideals flourish in one of the most influential 'success' books of recent times: Covey's *The 7 Effective Habits of Successful People*. Like Aristotle's focus, the subject matter is the adult world of choices – especially of responses to others' choices and reactions. Covey holds that we are absolutely responsible for our thinking and choices but that the effects of our choices are soon out of our hands, although we do not lose responsibility for their initiation (Covey, 1999, p. 90). So as to live and work more effectively, we ought to be aware of the thoroughly Aristotelian teleological thesis that in a choice there is implied the end as well as the beginning; that is, in choosing a course of action, there is an operative final cause as well as an efficient cause. " 'Begin with the end in mind" is based on the principle that *all things are created twice.* There's a mental or first creation, and a physical or second creation to all things' (orig. italics; Covey, 1999, p. 99). The psychological world of Covey's advice is thoroughly Aristotelian – he proclaims the importance of forming habits of excellence: 'our character, basically, is a composite of our habits' (Covey, 1999, p. 46). Behind the values that we produce, Covey stresses that we must seek the principles that underpin authentic moral behavior and which then foster the ethical habits of fairness, integrity, honesty, dignity, and excellence (Covey, 1999, p. 34); indeed, the subtitle of his work, which has sold over ten million copies and thereby gives credence to the continuation of the Aristotelian ethic, is 'restoring the character ethic' to our life rather than quick-fix or 'personality ethic' solutions that do not alter embedded habits, and this refers back to the changeless self that acts within a world of change (Covey, 1999, p. 108).

Home educators are also keen to emphasize the importance of Aristotle's ethos; Bauer, for instance, relates how critical the classical educational curriculum is in order to help produce adults of integrity and excellence: 'virtuous men (or women) can force themselves to do what they know is right, even when it runs against their inclinations' (Bauer, 1999, p. 47). The classical education, which she derives from the trivium of the Scholastics (Bauer, 1999, p. 43; 2003, p. 18), is to provide the general education that Aristotle underlined (*NE*, 1094b28) that enables the student to learn, master, and evaluate topics. The trivium, incidentally, relies much on Aristotle's logic and categories (cf. Joseph, 2002, *passim*) and, with the quadrivium, remains the origin of the liberal arts of today.

Arguably, Bauer provides a deft ironic twist to the Aristotelian premise that man is a social animal to proclaim that home education rather than public education is better for children: socialization is the process by which people acquire the habits, beliefs, and the accumulated knowledge of their society, and as such it does not just happen in a school institution. It involves family, peer groups, clubs, travel, neighborhood, etc., which are contrasted positively with the socialization that may occur in many schools where:

> the child learns how to function in a specific environment, one where he's surrounded by thirty children of his own age. This is a very specific type of socialization, one that may or may not prove particularly useful. When, during the course of his life, will he find himself in this kind of context? Not in work or in family or in his hobbies ... the socialization that best prepares a child for the real world ... happens when the child is living with people who vary widely in age, personality background, and circumstance.
>
> (Bauer, 1999, p. 590)

While Aristotle believed that social habits are best taken over by the state (for the state), Bauer relates the work of various critics who emphasize the destructive nature of such selective socialization: Bronfenbrenner in his *Two Worlds of Childhood* drew attention to the 'alienation, indifference, antagonism, and violence on the part of the younger generation' (quoted in Bauer, 1999, p. 590). The failure of schools to socialize youth properly by drilling age cohorts into homogeneous curricula may in turn reflect the failure of planned or centrally controlled education in economies which have much broader needs and potential paths than the city states of two and half millennia ago. The Greeks, however, sought to maintain peer dependency for, in their thinking, it would play a critical role in solidifying military and political cohesion as each new cohort took over the responsibilities of the previous. Consider Spartan festivals and the three choirs of old, young men, and boys:

> The choir of old men (*gerontes*) would chant first: 'We were once bold youths (*neaniai*).' Then the young men at their physical peak

(*akmazontes*) would respond: 'We are so now, if you wish look and see.' Finally the third choir, that composed of boys (*paides*) sang: 'We will be mightier men (*andres*) by far.'

(orig. italics; Garland, 1990, p. 5)

Appropriately then, in the military academies, the Aristotelian ethic of civic service naturally complements the forces' priority of forming good habits to produce soldiers of excellence.

From the author's personal experience, at conferences Aristotle's name and theory of *aretē* is often noted: education and the moral ethos are practically oriented, as are military and political skills, so it is unsurprising to find military lecturers using Aristotle explicitly in the forces' academies. Wilson, for instance, writes that the United States Military Academy 'is decisively Aristotelian in its four-year developmental process of ethics training and education, emphasizing balance and equanimity ...' (Wilson, 2008, p. 36); Cook comments on ethics teaching in the military that 'it is rather obvious that Aristotle is the intellectual father of the enterprise' (Cook, 2008, p. 58); while in the Netherlands, Olsthoorn notes that Aristotle's *Nicomachean Ethics* 'is still pivotal in many texts on military ethics ... and it has been argued that Aristotelian virtue ethics, with its emphasis on character building, provides a better basis for military ethics than rule-based, deontological ethics or utilitarian ethics' (Olsthoorn, 2008, p. 124). Yet is it the Spartan model of obedient soldiers that the military seek to emulate or do they sincerely wish to encourage Aristotelian curiosity, an issue the author and Cook have raised – for *phronēsis* implies not just success in practical activities but also reflection upon those actions (Cook, 2008, p. 58; Moseley, 2008). The virtuous man is one who is reflective and seeks to do the right thing in terms of both his means and his ends (*NE*, 1144a26), but politically he is also one who acknowledges that the state (or at least the Hellenic-style *polis*) is the best form of government, which he should defend. But to what extent? To be taught to be reflective and wise suggests that allegiance is conditional; after all, Plato's contemporary Alcibiades (450–404 BC) was renowned for changing his allegiance as he saw fit – from Athens to Sparta to Persia to Athens and then death. Here was a brilliant military commander who divided contemporaries between those who saw his actions as damaging to their own *polis* when he was not serving it and those who saw his actions as exceptionally excellent when he was serving them – modern commentators divide accordingly too: some follow the Hegelian notion that great men must be allowed to redefine the rules; more objective assessments hold him as precocious but fickle, while Aristotle calls him proud (*APst*, 97b16). In a sense, Alcibiades' acts reflect the capriciousness of the Hellenic gods, and Aristophanes asked 'what should be done about Alcibiades? Athens is in a very tricky situation ... They love him. But then they hate him. And then again, they want him back' (Aristophanes, 1974, p. 208). Such 'great souled men' (*NE*, 1123a34), Aristotle warned, should be allowed to exit from weaker states – they are too powerful to be of continued good to a city: they are either gods or beasts (*Pol*, 1253a29). The good of the average city cannot come from those who would take its fortunes to the extremes, defeating its enemies but also turning to defeat the city in turn. And so in turn, Aristotle draws us back to the virtue of pursuing the mean between the extremes and of asserting the benefits of the *demos* against the tyrants or those predisposed that way. Yet the great *polis* should have the courage to let nature take its course (*Pol*, 1284b28–34). Gribble believes that such great men act as theoretical boundaries for Aristotle's political philosophy, just as the categories of women, barbarians, and slaves do – they help to focus our minds on what a *polis* ought to do (Gribble, 1999, p. 20); Aristotle, like contemporaries, thus presents an ambiguous reading of loyalty: it would be presumed for the common run of humanity, but in exceptional circumstances it could be waived. We today reflect upon such dilemmas as what if Erwin Rommel (1891–1944) had defected to the Allies in World War II – should he have been allowed to offer his genius to the effort? An intriguing issue that no doubt will divide us. Therein lies a problem for the Aristotelian man of virtue: is there such a thing as allegiance and if so what defines its boundaries – does the ordinary soldier owe unconditional 'unlimited liability' to his or her government, or is such an ethic reprehensibly slavish? From the pedagogical perspective, of course, such a character would be unteachable.

Apart from military and business studies, whose general remit is practical and whose academics readily turn to Aristotle, we naturally find him regularly discussed in philosophy circles and from there he seeps back into the more philosophically minded disciplines across campuses – notably political science, but what about formal education texts?

The need to help form good habits attracts many educational philosophers; Aristotle, they recognize, offered a justification for the importance of laying good moral foundations (Peterson, 1986, pp. 108; 112). Carr, who enjoys the contextual nature of Aristotelian ethics, notes that 'it has been the need to make sense of such more vocational reflection and deliberation that has encouraged recent educational philosophers to return to Aristotle's pioneering analysis of practical wisdom' (Carr, 2003, p. 65). Aristotle appears in practically every educational book, either in discussion of his theory of virtue ethics and the concept of practical wisdom, or sometimes in noting his political philosophy of state-run education, but generally a nod in his direction is made by most.

If we extract ourselves from the complexities that riddle his ethical work, we may nevertheless produce an updated Aristotle for the modern world, excising the elements that we would now find objectionable yet retaining a coherent theory.

Politically, Aristotle's utopia (cf. Jackson's defense of Aristotelian utopianism, 2001), would be of a well-educated, propertied middle class who live off the returns their lands provide. Male, certainly for Aristotle, but today we may adjust his vision to include women, although their lives, for the orthodox Aristotelian, may still fall into traditionalist visions of home and household economy; while slaves and freemen would have worked the Hellenic fields, we can again adjust the vision to remove slavery. The propertied class' aim is to live without having to work manually or deal with daily routines – the husband and wife thus may delegate the running of their estate to managers while keeping an eye on the overall profitability of their realm. Their purpose, and hence the ultimate purpose of their children's education, is to raise their minds to philosophy, to pure contemplation, socially though, not monastically, sharing enjoyment in intellectual and physical skills but aiming beyond the mere materiality and commerciality that pervades others' lives. However, the leisure that such a life brings the propertied is not without responsibilities –

the men (and today the women too) must train for war as well as political duties; it is assuredly not a life of idleness. Idleness leads to the corruption of the community (*Pol*, 1334a15–27).

Foremost, a child's education would not begin until the age of 7, a radical move in some Western countries, which encourage or mandate children into school earlier. This partly reflected the Hellenic belief of dividing man's life into a series of stages – seven years being particularly appropriate for most thinkers as it reflected the number of known planets (Garland, 1990, p. 3). The child would be the offspring of eugenically procured parentage and would have passed certain requirements to be acceptable to the state, for the legislator 'must consider first the union of their parents' (*Pol*, 1334b29, trans. Sinclair), who preferably would marry at 37 and 18 for groom and bride respectively.

Once in school, the child would then begin to learn the skills and knowledge appropriate for his upbringing and gradual accession to politics: to learn at first to be ruled before ruling, and to accept the decisions of the Hellenic citizenry before being a part of that decision-making process.

Initially, the child is without reason, but grows to become increasingly reasonable, so education must cultivate rational habits through beginning with that which is within our ability to effect – the promotion of good bodily habits. He (or she) should be trained to endure physical work but not so much as to damage them. For the first two years he (or she) should be brought up on a healthy diet (milk and little wine), gradually inuring them to the cold to strengthen their bodies' abilities to their environment; between 2 and 5 they must not be taught intellectually, although they can enjoy stories, but must be given free rein to enjoy physical exercise. The company of servants should be avoided, for they are apt to deprave the young child: today, as I wrote in the Locke volume, the equivalent would be curtailing access to popular television, websites, or computer games that immerse the child in immoral themes. The child's cultural upbringing ought thus to be censored appropriately: only when they are older may the youth be allowed access to the more licentious comedies and spectacles (films, theater, music, cartoons), for if their education has worked, they become immune to its effects: in the *Politics*, Aristotle relates how the actor Theodorus would not let anyone else appear on stage before him, 'because the spectators grew fond of voices which they heard first. And the same principle applies universally to association with things as well as with people, for "we always like the best whatever comes first"' (*Pol*, 1336b33), underscoring the psychological effect of cultural exposures: if only he had adjusted his writings to include more on child psychology!

From 5 to 7, the children may be allowed to observe lessons that they will later learn, for their formal education begins at 7. They are to learn how to appreciate the trades while not immersing themselves into them so they lose their path of becoming virtuous citizens, otherwise they learn how to read and write; play and enjoy music, which can help with education, play, and virtuous behavior; physical training; and art, so they may appreciate beauty. The subjects are thus more academic than vocational, for always the purpose is to secure capable but virtuous citizens rather than producers, men (and women) who are elevated above the mundane and commercial worlds.

Education begins with physical training, then a gradual immersion into the world of learning, but for Aristotle, the importance is on the growth of the adult's mind, for, as his citizenry are free of toiling for their livelihood, they are free to pursue the contemplative life of the philosopher as they mature in years. In many respects, the caricature life led by the English aristocracy in the eighteenth century captures a modern incarnation of Aristotle's political vision: the children were to go to public schools and their destiny lay with managing the affairs of the state, the great commercial concerns (suitably monopolies to ensure little competition), or preaching to the souls of the land through the proprietary Anglican Church. Educated in the liberal arts, they received a strong dose of Aristotle's politics and ethics and Hellenic history; they thus cultivated a strong desire to do well by their country. Perhaps the eighteenth century was the closest a modern nation got to replicating the Hellenic world: even its architecture and art reflected the classical styles and themes. But of course it was also a time of dissent and non-conformism, of religious and scientific upheaval and economic growth, which tends to undermine protected interests through sheer weight of economic wealth. Since then the explicit aristocratic Aristotelian philosophy has been overwhelmed by the scientific and vocational courses that now flourish in today's universities, and elements of his psychological analyses have been adapted – not quite beyond recognition, for there remains his interest in the relationship between the physical and mental worlds and the study of habits and conditioned behavior.

The philosophical legacy today

The greatest influence on Aristotle's successors right down to the present – and any philosopher who has picked up his works must surely agree – can only be the philosophical attitude that he took to all subjects: the open-ended curiosity and logical methods to analyze the subjects at hand and thereby to encourage our further education. Following that were his empiricist bent and enthusiasm for collecting specimens and books, his emphasis on the importance of logical analysis, and his teleology and vision of how man fits into a grand scheme of things, the latter two particularly entering Christian thought. The skeptics provided a powerful alternative to the empirical methods of the Lyceum, while the Stoics and Epicureans offered different philosophical visions that attracted new followers, but Aristotle's thoughts were not rejected as such but assimilated. When reading later philosophers, we can still hear his philosophy or pedagogy and quite clearly at times, notably in those philosophers who sought the middle ground between nihilistic skepticism or strict empiricism and the metaphysical flightiness of Neoplatonists or theologians.

Aristotle offered, and still offers us, sense with an element of spirituality, science with a strong dash of morality, and politics with a prudential eye on human nature: he was the first *doctor*, properly speaking, the spring of much of our learning since. But to learn well requires a good education which leads to practical and then contemplative wisdom, which form the necessary conditions of the pursuit of happiness – the ultimate to which education aims.

References

Ackrill, J. L. (1981), *Aristotle the Philosopher*. Oxford: Oxford University Press.

Acton, (Lord) J. E. E. Dalberg- (1948), *Essays on Freedom and Power*. Glencoe, IL: Free Press.

Aquinas, St Thomas (1998), *Selected Philosophical Writings*. Oxford: Oxford University Press.

Aristophanes (1974), 'The frogs,' in *The Wasps, the Poet and the Women, the Frogs*, trans. D. Barrett. Harmondsworth: Penguin.

Aristophanes (2000), *Clouds*, trans. P. Meineck. Indianapolis, IN: Hackett.

Armstrong, J. H. (1965), 'The Greeks and their philosophy,' in H. Lloyd-Jones (ed.), *The Greek World*. Harmondsworth: Penguin, pp. 130–41.

Artz, F. B. (1954), *The Mind of the Middle Ages, A.D. 200–1500: An Historical Survey*. 2nd edn. New York: Alfred A. Knopf.

Augustine (1984), *The City of God*. London: Penguin.

Bacon, F. (1930), *Of the Advancement of Learning*. London: J. M. Dent & Sons.

Baltussen, H. (2000), *Theophrastus against the Presocratics and Plato: Peripatetic Dialectic in the de Sensibus*. Boston, MA: Brill.

Barker, E. (1957), *Social and Political Thought in Byzantium, from Justinian I to the Last Palaeologus: Passages from Byzantine Writers and Documents*. Oxford: Clarendon Press.

Barnes, J. (1976), 'Introduction,' in H. Tredennick (ed.), *The Ethics of Aristotle*. Harmondsworth: Penguin, pp. 9–43.

Barnes, J. (1987), *Early Greek Philosophy*. Harmondsworth: Penguin.

Barnes, J. (1989), *The Presocratic Philosophers*. London: Routledge.

Barnes, J. (2000), *Aristotle: A Very Short Introduction*. Oxford: Oxford University Press.

Barrow, R. (2001), *Greek and Roman Education*. London: Bristol Classical Press.

Bauer, S. W. (1999), *The Well Trained Mind: A Guide to Classical Education at Home*. London: W. W. Norton & Company.

Bauer, S. W. (2003), *The Well Educated Mind*. London: W. W. Norton & Company.

Beckmann, P. (1971), *A History of Pi*. New York: St Martin's Press.

Berkeley, G. (1972), *The Principles of Human Knowledge*. London: Collins.

Berlin, I. (2000), *The Power of Ideas*. Princeton, NJ: Princeton University Press.

Blondell, R., Gamel, M.-K., Sorkin Rabinowitz, N., and Zweig, B. (eds) (1999), *Women on the Edge: Four Plays by Euripides*. New York: Routledge.

Brunt, P. A. (1997), *Studies in Greek History and Thought*. Oxford: Clarendon Press.

Burckhardt, J. (1999), *The Greeks and Greek Civilization*, trans. S. Stern. London: HarperCollins.

Burnet, J. (1903), *Aristotle on Education*. Cambridge: Cambridge University Press.

Cameron, R. (2004), 'How to be a realist about *sui generis* teleology yet feel at home in the 21st century,' *The Monist*, 87 (1), 72–95.

Carr, D. (2003), *Making Sense of Education: An Introduction to the Philosophy and Theory of Education and Teaching*. London: Routledge-Falmer.

Cartledge, P. (1993), *The Greeks: A Portrait of Self and Others*. Oxford: Oxford University Press.

Cook, M. L. (2008), 'Ethics education, ethics training, and character development: who "owns" ethics in the US Air Force Academy?,' in P. Robinson, N. de Lee, and D. Carrick (eds), *Ethics Education in the Military*. Aldershot: Ashgate, pp. 57–66.

Copenhaver, B. P. and Schmitt, C. B. (1992), *Renaissance Philosophy*. Oxford: Oxford University Press.

Copleston, F. (1985), *A History of Philosophy: Volume 1: Greece and Rome*. Toronto: Doubleday.

Cornford, F. MacDonald (1957), 'Introduction,' in *Plato's Theory of Knowledge: The Theatatus and the Sophist of Plato*.

Coulter, H. (1994), *Divided Legacy: A History of the Schism in Medical Thought: Volume I.* Washington, DC: Center for Empirical Medicine.

Covey, S. R. (1999), *The 7 Habits of Highly Effective People: Restoring the Character Ethic.* London: Simon & Schuster.

Crombie, A. C. (1952), *Augustine to Galileo: The History of Science, A.D. 400–1650.* Melbourne, VIC: William Heinemann.

Curlew, S. (2005), 'Joint structure and function,' in P. K. Levangie and C. C. Norkin (eds), *Joint Structure and Function: A Comprehensive Analysis.* Philadelphia, PA: F. A. Davies Company.

Dante (1995), *The Divine Comedy.* London: Penguin.

Davidson, D. (1980), *Essays on Actions and Events.* Oxford: Clarendon.

Dawkins, R. (1989), *The Selfish Gene.* Oxford: Oxford University Press.

Dillon, J. (2005), *The Heirs of Plato: A Study of the Old Academy, 347–274 B.C.* Oxford: Clarendon.

Dobson, J. F. (1932), *Ancient Education and its Meaning to Us.* New York: Longmans Green.

Dupuy, R. E. and Dupuy, T. N. (1995), *The Collins Encyclopedia of Military History.* 4th edn. London: BCA.

Edmonds, D. and Eidenow, J. (2001), *Wittgenstein's Poker.* London: Faber and Faber.

Ellwood, C. A. (1938), *A History of Social Philosophy.* New York: Prentice Hall.

Epicurus (1985), *Letters, Principal Doctrines, and Vatican Sayings*, trans. R. M. Geer. London: Collier Macmillan.

Euripides (1999), 'Helen,' in R. Blondell, M.-K. Gamel, N. Sorkin Rabinowitz, and B. Zweig (eds), *Women on the Edge: Four Plays by Euripides*, trans. B. Zweig. New York: Routledge, pp. 217–301.

Evans, J. A. S. (2000), *The Age of Justinian: The Circumstances of Imperial Power.* London: Routledge.

Fakhry, M. (2004), *A History of Islamic Philosophy.* New York: Columbia University Press.

Freeman, C. (1999), *The Greek Achievement: The Foundation of the Western World.* London: Allen Lane Penguin Press.

Galton, F. (1892), *Hereditary Genius.* London: MacMillan.

Garland, R. (1990), *The Greek Way of Life: From Conception to Old Age.* London: Duckworth.

Gerrard, T. (1914), 'The Church and eugenics,' in *The Catholic Encyclopedia*. New Advent. www.newadvent.org/cathen/16038b.htm.

Golden, M. (2003), *Children and Childhood in Classical Athens*. Baltimore, MD: Johns Hopkins University Press.

Golder, H. (1999), 'Introduction,' in Sophocles, *Aias: Ajax*, trans. H. Golder and R. Pevear. Oxford: Oxford University Press, pp. 3–22.

Goodman, L. E. (1992), *Avicenna*. New York: Routledge.

Gottfried, P. E. (1999), *After Liberalism: Mass Democracy in the Managerial State*. Princeton, NJ: Princeton University Press.

Graham, D. W. (2006), *Heraclitus*. www.utm.edu/research/iep/h/heraclit.htm.

Grayeff, F. (1974), *Aristotle and his School*. London: Duckworth.

Gribble, D. (1999), *Alcibiades and Athens: A Study in Literary Presentation*. Oxford: Clarendon Press.

Hammond, Rev. R. (1947), *The Philosophy of Alfarbi*. New York: Hobson Book Press.

Hankinson, R. J. (2003), 'Stoic Epistemology,' in B. Inwood (ed.), *The Cambridge Companion to the Stoics*. Cambridge: Cambridge University Press, pp. 59–84.

Hayek, F. A. (1963), *The Constitution of Liberty*. London: Routledge & Kegan Paul.

Hegel, G. W. F. (1977), *Phenomenology of Spirit*, trans. A. V. Miller. Oxford: Oxford University Press.

Hegel, G. W. F. (1996), *Philosophy of Right*, trans. S. W. Doyle. Amherst, NY: Prometheus Books.

Herodotus (1998), *The Histories*, trans. R. Waterfield. Oxford: Oxford University Press.

Heyking, J. Von (2001), *Augustine and Politics as Longing in the World*. Columbia, MO: University of Missouri Press.

Hobbes, T. (1996), *Leviathan*. Cambridge: Cambridge University Press.

Howatson, M. C. (ed.) (1989), *The Oxford Companion to Classical Literature*. Oxford: Oxford University Press.

Hull, L. W. H. (1959), *History and Philosophy of Science: An Introduction*. London: Longmans Green.

Hume, D. (1983), *An Enquiry Concerning the Principles of Morals*. Indianapolis, IN: Hackett Publishing.

Hume, D. (1987), *Essays, Moral, Political, and Literary*. Indianapolis, IN: Liberty Classics.

Inwood, M. (1999), 'Hegel and his language,' in M. Inwood (ed.), *A Hegel Dictionary*. Blackwell: Oxford, pp. 5–17.

Jackson, M. (2001), 'Designed by theorists: Aristotle on utopia,' *Utopian Studies*, 12 (2), 1–12.

Jeans, J. (1948), *The Growth of Physical Science*. Cambridge: Cambridge University Press.

Jensen, A. R. (1998), *The G Factor: The Science of Mental Ability*. Westport, CT: Praeger Publishers.

Joseph, Sister M. (2002), *The Trivium: The Liberal Arts of Logic, Grammar, and Rhetoric*. Philadelphia, PA: Paul Dry Books.

Kant, I. (1977), *Prolegomena to any Future Metaphysics*. Cambridge: Hackett Publishing.

Kenny, A. (2004), *A New History of Western Philosophy: Volume 1: Ancient Philosophy*. Oxford: Clarendon Press.

Kenny, A. (2005), *A New History of Western Philosophy: Volume II: Medieval Philosophy*. Oxford: Clarendon Press.

Kenyon, F. G. (1932), *Books and Readers in Ancient Greece and Rome*. Oxford: The Clarendon Press.

Kirk, G. S. (1965), 'Greek Science,' in H. Lloyd-Jones (ed.), *The Greek World*. Harmondsworth: Penguin, pp. 117–29.

Korsmeyer, C. (1999), *Making Sense of Taste: Food & Philosophy*. Ithaca, NY: Cornell University Press.

Laertius, D. (1853), 'The Life of Aristotle,' in *The Lives and Opinions of Eminent Philosophers*, trans. C. D. Yonge. London: Henry G. Bohn, pp. 181–93.

Laistner, M. L. W. (1947), *A History of the Greek World from 479 to 323 B.C.* London: Methuen.

Larmarck, J.-B. (1914), *Philosophie zoologique ou exposition des considerations relatives à l'histoire naturelle des animaux*, trans. H. Elliot. London: Macmillan.

Lawrence, E. (1972), *The Origins and Growth of Modern Education*. Harmondsworth: Penguin.

Lines, D. A. (ed.) (2002), *Aristotle's Ethics in the Italian Renaissance (ca. 1300–1650): The Universities and the Problem of Moral Education*. Leiden, Netherlands: Brill.

Llobera, J. R. (2003), *The Making of Totalitarian Thought*. New York: Berg.

Lloyd, G. E. R. (1970), *Ancient Culture and Society: Early Greek Science: Thales to Aristotle*. London: Chatto & Windus.

Longrigg, J. (1993), *Greek Rational Medicine: Philosophy and Medicine from Alcmaeon to the Alexandrians*. New York: Routledge.

MacIntyre, A. (1998), *A Short History of Ethics*. London: Routledge.

Magill, F. N. (ed.) (1998), *Dictionary of World Biography: The Ancient World. Vol. 1*. Chicago: Fitzroy Dearborn.

Maimonides, M. (1956), *The Guide for the Perplexed*, trans. M. Friedländer. New York: Dover Publications.

Mill, J. S. (1884), *A System of Logic*. London: Longmans, Green, and Co.

Mises, L. (1949), *Human Action*. London: William Hodge & Co.

Mises, L. (1983), *Bureaucracy*. Cedar Falls, IA: Center for Futures Education.

Montaigne, S. de (1891), *Montaigne's Essays*. London: Ward, Lock, Bowden & Co.

Morford, M. (2002), *The Roman Philosophers: From the Time of Cato the Censor to the Death of Marcus Aurelius*. London: Routledge.

Morris, V. C. (1961), *Philosophy and the American School: An Introduction to the Philosophy of Education*. Boston, MA: Houghton Mifflin.

Moseley, A. (2008), 'The ethical warrior: a classical liberal approach,' in P. Robinson, N. de Lee, and D. Carrick (eds), *Ethics Education in the Military*. Aldershot: Ashgate, pp. 175–86.

Neils, J. and Oakley, J. H. (2003), *Coming of Age in Ancient Greece: Images of Childhood from the Classical Past*. New York: Yale University Press.

O'Brien, J. M. (1994), *Alexander the Great: The Invisible Enemy: A Biography*. London: Routledge.

O'Connell, R. J. S. J. (1986), *Imagination and Metaphysics in St. Augustine*. Milwaukee, WI: Marquette University Press.

Olsthoorn, P. (2008), 'The ethics curriculum at the Netherlands Defence Academy, and some problems with its theoretical under-pinnings,' in P. Robinson, N. de Lee, and D. Carrick (eds), *Ethics Education in the Military*. Aldershot: Ashgate, pp. 119–32.

Parkinson, C. Northcote (1981), *The Law*. Harmondsworth: Penguin.

Pears, E. (1987), *The Fall of Constantinople Being the Story of the Fourth Crusade*. London: Darf Publishers.

Perlman, M. (2004), 'The modern philosophical resurrection of teleology,' *The Monist*, 87 (1), 3–51.

Peterson, M. L. (1986), *Philosophy of Education: Issues and Options*. Downers Grove, IL: InterVarsity Press.

Plutarch (1878), *Plutarch's Lives of Illustrious Men*, trans. J. Langhorne and W. Langhorne. London: Chatto and Windus.

Pomeroy, S. B., Burstein, S. M., Donlan, W., and Roberts, J. T. (1999), *Ancient Greece: A Political, Social, and Cultural History*. New York: Oxford University Press.

Popper, K. (1986), *The Open Society and its Enemies: Volume 2*. London: Routledge.

Posner, R. A. (1992), *Sex and Reason*. Cambridge, MA: Harvard University Press.

Randall, J. H. (1960), *Aristotle*. New York: Columbia University Press.

Roberts, J. M. (1996), *A History of Europe*. Oxford: Helicon.

Roberts, V. M. (1962), *On Stage: A History of Theatre*. New York: Harper & Row.

Robinson, T. A. (1995), *Aristotle in Outline*. Indianapolis, IN: Hackett Publishing.

Roll, E. (1987), *A History of Economic Thought*. Rev. edn. London: Faber and Faber Ltd.

Ross, Sir D. (1977), *Aristotle*. London: Methuen & Co. Ltd.

Rothbard, M. (1999), *Education: Free & Compulsory*. Auburn, AL: Ludwig von Mises Institute.

Russell, B. (1947), *A History of Western Philosophy*. London: George Allen & Unwin.

Ryle, G. (1970), *The Concept of Mind*. New York: Barnes & Noble.

Sachs, J. (2006), *Aristotle: Metaphysics*. www.iep.utm.edu/a/aris-met.htm.

Schwartz, G. and Bishop, P. W. (eds) (1958), *Moments of Discovery: Vol. 1*. New York: Basic Books.

Seeskin, K. (2001), *Autonomy in Jewish Philosophy*. Cambridge: Cambridge University Press.

Sellars, J. (2006), *Stoicism*. Chesham, Bucks: Acumen.

Sellberg, E. (2006), *Petrus Ramus. Standford Encyclopedia of Philosophy.* plato.stanford.edu/entries/ramus.

Sharples, R. W. (1999), 'The peripatetic school,' in D. J. Furley (ed.), *From Aristotle to Augustine.* London: Routledge, pp. 147–87.

Simpson, P. L. P. (1998), *A Philosophical Commentary on the Politics of Aristotle.* Chapel Hill, NC: University of North Carolina Press.

Singer, C. (1959), *A History of Biology to about the Year 1900: A General Introduction to the Study of Living Things.* London: Abelard Schuman.

Smith, A. (1982), *The Theory of Moral Sentiments.* Indianapolis, IN: Liberty Classics.

Snyder, H. G. (2000), *Teachers and Texts in the Ancient World: Philosophers, Jews, and Christians.* London: Routledge.

Sophocles (1999), *Aias: Ajax,* trans. H. Golder and R. Pevear. New York: Oxford University Press.

Taplin, O. (1995), 'Greek theatre,' in J. R. Brown (ed.), *The Oxford Illustrated History of Theatre.* Oxford: Oxford University Press, pp. 13–48.

Tarnas, R. (1996), *The Passion of the Western Mind.* London: Pimlico.

Thucydides (1998), *History of the Peloponnesian War,* trans. R. Crawley. London: Everyman.

Thut, I. N. (1957), *The Story of Education.* New York: McGraw Hill.

Tilley, A. A. (1918), *The Dawn of the French Renaissance.* Cambridge: The University Press.

Turner, W. (1907), 'Aristotle,' in *The Catholic Encyclopedia.* New Advent. http://www.newadvent.org/cathen/01713a.htm.

van der Meer, F. (1961), *Augustine the Bishop: The Life and Work of a Father of the Church,* trans. B. Battershaw and G. R. Lamb. London: Sheed & Ward.

Verbeke, G. (1990), *Moral Education in Aristotle.* Washington, DC: The Catholic University of America Press.

Wagner, D. L. (ed.) (1983), *The Seven Liberal Arts in the Middle Ages.* Bloomington, IN: Indiana University Press.

Walden, J. W. H. (1909), *The Universities of Ancient Greece.* New York: C. Scribner's Sons.

Williams, R. J. (1998), *Biochemical Individuality.* New Canaan, CT: Keats Publishing.

Wilson, J. (2008), 'An ethics curriculum for an evolving army,' in P. Robinson, N. de Lee, and D. Carrick (eds), *Ethics Education in the Military*. Aldershot: Ashgate, pp. 31–41.

Winch, C. and Gingell, J. (1999), *Key Concepts in the Philosophy of Education*. London: Routledge.

Xenophon (2006), *The Shorter Socratic Writings*, trans. R. C. Bartlett *et al*. The Agora Editions. Ithaca, NY: Cornell University Press.

Index

artists 31, 41, 65, 69, 77, 109–11, 126, 153,
 art therapy 204
 fine art 109–10
 sculpturee 47, 80, 110
Artaneus 45–6
Artaxerxes III 46
artificial intelligence 70
Aspasia 28
Aspasius 170, 172
Assos 45–6, 49
atavism 13, 16, 33
Athens
 7, 9, 12, 17–22, 25, 28, 36, 37–53, 126, 163–173, 207–208
 art 4
 citizens 28, 105, 146
 democracy 19
 economy 17
 individualism 23
 polis 12
 schools 174
 women 27
Athenians 6, 8, 18, 19, 31, 42, 47, 49, 50. 53, 133, 149, 169
athletes 12, 18–9, 142–3
Attalus 50
Attalus III 169
Augustine 173–4, 183
Avicenna 176–8, 183

Baghdad 176–7
balance 17, 18, 118, 133–4, 139, 142, 151, 153, 207
 see also imbalance
banausia 15, 115, 146, 204
Barnes, J. 5, 33, 166
Bauer, S.W. 205–6
beauty 18, 19, 27, 66, 88, 110, 134, 148, 151, 211
behaviorism 203
Bentham, J. 84

Berkeley, G. 82, 160
Big Bang 80
biology 6, 10, 45, 46, 51, 57, 76, 77, 85, 188, 195, 203, 204
birth 14, 25, 28, 63, 119, 140, 142–143, 145
 exposure at 25, 27, 143, 199
 see also infanticide
blind 85, 88–9

Boethius 172–4, 181–2
books 38, 160, 180, 184, 188, 204, 209, 212
 Aristotle's 11, 170–180
bouleusis 111
boys 14, 18, 24–6, 63, 77, 150–1, 161, 200, 206–7
 diet 146,
 education 22, 26, 28, 66, 71, 146, 150,
breeding 8, 17, 58, 93–4, 95, 135, 148, 194, 201
British Empire 53
Bronfenbrenner, U. 206
Burckhardt, J 9
Burgess, A. 154
Bithynia 49
Byzantine 4, 178–80, 184, 186, 196

Callisthenes, 7, 52, 53
Carneades 169
Carr, D. 209
Categories 59, 172, 181
Categories, Aristotle's 59–60, 90, 93–5, 177, 181, 186, 205, 208
Catholic Church 4, 183, 184, 199
Cato the Elder 169
cause 46, 60–4, 69, 72, 75, 78–80, 99, 102, 104, 109, 193, 205
 efficient 61, 69, 77, 80, 205
 final 46, 61, 64, 72, 78, 80, 193, 205
Celts 118, 146
Chalcidice 5, 8
Chaeronea 49
character 11–2, 17, 20, 73, 75, 88, 99, 107, 110, 112, 114–5, 119–20, 126–8, 134, 137, 140, 143, 145–6, 149–50, 151, 153, 202, 205, 207–8,
 music and character 154–5
Characters 164
chauvinism 23, *see* sexism
childhood 11, 24–26
children x, 6, 10–15, 19–22, 24–6, 28, 40, 57–9, 63, 67, 71, 74, 77, 83, 90–4, 97, 106, 110, 123, 125, 130, 132, 134, 137, 138–9, 141–8, 160, 193–4, 196–7, 200, 202, 206, 206–111
 deformed 27
 education for young 146–8
 education seven to fourteen 148–152
 education over fourteen 155–7
 Roman 169